THE
BODY SHOP

Also by Paul Solotaroff

Group: Six People in Search of a Life

House of Purple Hearts: Stories of Vietnam Vets
Who Find Their Way Back

THE BODY SHOP

PARTIES, PILLS, AND PUMPING IRON —
OR, MY LIFE IN THE AGE OF MUSCLE

Paul Solotaroff

Little, Brown and Company

NEW YORK   BOSTON   LONDON

Little, Brown and Company
Hachette Book Group
237 Park Avenue, New York, NY 10017
www.hachettebookgroup.com

First Edition: July 2010

Little, Brown and Company is a division of Hachette Book Group, Inc. The Little, Brown name and logo are trademarks of Hachette Book Group, Inc.

Except for family members, the names and some identifying details of individuals portrayed in this book have been changed.

Library of Congress Cataloging-in-Publication Data
Solotaroff, Paul.
    The body shop : parties, pills, and pumping iron—or, my life in the age of muscle / Paul Solotaroff.—1st ed.
        p. cm.
    ISBN 978-0-316-01101-3
1. Weight lifting—Social aspects. 2. Bodybuilding—Social aspects. 3. Masculinity.
4. Solotaroff, Paul. 5. Weight lifters. I. Title.
    GV546.3.S65 2010
    796.41—dc22   2009051191

10 9 8 7 6 5 4 3 2 1

RRD-IN

Printed in the United States of America

For my father, who knew and knew

THE
BODY SHOP

One

Go Down and Out, Moses

August 1976

THE NOONER FROM PENN STATION pulled in twenty minutes late, which was steady as she goes for the Long Island Rail Road. I clomped down the steps into a lot void of cabs, squinting against the yellow glare. Two hours removed from the bed of a woman whose name I never quite caught, I was sporting the same splint-tight Nik Nik shirt I'd worn to work her daughter's sweet sixteen. Its seams chafed the flesh of my upper lats.

The _____ _____ Temple was a steel and stucco eyesore eight long blocks from the station. By the time I'd walked them all, I was sheathed in sweat and incensed at my race for staging bar mitzvahs in the high, holy heat of August. The feeling proved mutual when I stepped in the door and my employers for the day, Barbara and Martin Weiskopf, got their first gander at me.

"What in God's name... He's a showgirl with muscles," Martin said to his harried wife. "Of all the things to contend with now! How could you do this to our son?"

"Don't look at *me*," she flared. "Talk to your friend Raffy. He swore they only send Jews to work these functions."

"Does he *look* Jewish to you, with the shirt open to there and—and sweating like the greaseball who does our lawn?" He shot me a hasty, fearful glance. "No offense to your people, of course."

"None taken," I said. "I'm as Jewish as you are."

We were huddled in a room off the center stairs, after they'd whisked me away from the buzzing adults and the kids who giggled and stared: the erratically balding Martin; his pretty, stoop-shouldered wife; and her parents, who gaped in horror. "Pffuh!" said her father, as if gulping a bug. "They don't make Jews like you and never will!"

"Dad, please, let us deal," said Barbara. "Take Mom and go wait in the hall."

"But for God's sake, Barbara—*Moses*?" he said. "Who has these ideas, and where do they come from?"

"Where do you think?" snapped his son-in-law. "From Suzie 'Big-Shot' Mellman and the rest of that Great Neck crowd. They think it adds 'zest,' or some such nonsense. What was the word she used? *Sizzle*."

"Sizzle!" Her father stumbled, and his eyes rolled skyward. For a moment I thought he was seizing. Then a door opened, and the rabbi entered, quick-walking toward us holding his shawl. A small, handsome man, no older than forty, with a beautifully kept, kohl black beard, he gathered reconnaissance as he came, casting his eyes adroitly from face to face. At a glance he sized me from head to toe, as if I was merely the latest strumpet to mistake his temple for the boom-boom room at Billy's Topless. "How can I help things along here?"

"Ah, Rabbi, what a mess," said Barbara, breathless. "So we hired this—this fellow on the say-so of the Mellmans to play the part of Moses at the reception. Not a *speaking* part, mind you. Just to stand there holding the tablets while they passed out hors d'oeuvres and brought drinks—"

"I'm familiar," said the rabbi. "The Frandsens last week, though they, of course, went with Samson. But go on."

"Well, so Martin was opposed, he called it crass, but I thought it brought—"

4

"Not crass," said Martin, "just not serious. Our David is a boy who views life deeply."

"And I object to the whole business!" roared Barbara's father. "Today is a day we put away the dreck and focus on the contents of the soul: a boy's pact with God and the men who came before him, not some *shtarker* from a—a Times Square peep show!"

"A Jewish *shtarker*," I slipped in edgewise. "Let's not lose sight of that."

The rabbi gave a wincing frown. It encompassed the suffering of millions. "If I might," he said. "In the interests of time."

He laced his fingers at his lips, turning a thought around. "This family, the Weiskopfs, whom I've known for years, you surely see their side of it, no? They've struggled, inched forward, overcome losses—in short, the whole human story. Whatever you think of their moral traditions, let me assure you they're earned and felt."

"Well, fine," I said, "but it's ninety degrees out, and they jumped down my throat for not wearing a tux."

"Please," he said calmly, "take a breath out. Would you like something cold, perhaps a soda?"

His voice, an instrument of gentle candor, knocked me down a peg. It was his eyes that shamed me, though, held up a mirror in which I inspected myself: a big-armed preener with a rock-star shag and a dreadful sense of timing and decorum. Who'd raised me like this, to mock and strut, a butch burlesque of male pride? And who, more important, would knock it out of me before the sneer turned to concrete on my face?

"You're right," I conceded. "I should've worn a blazer. It's just, I sweat like a horse in this heat."

"And that's your excuse?" scoffed Barbara's mother. "This is sacred property you entered, which you'd know if you were any kind of Jew."

"But I am," I whinnied. "I'm honors English at Stony Brook, and my father happens to be a famous editor."

This was wild embellishment on at least one count, and my father, while esteemed, was no household name, at least in the Weiskopf household. Invoking him now only deepened my gloom, conjured up his acid disappointment. *Oh, Paul,* I could hear him tut in horror, *can't you leave me out of your dopey stunts?*

"Yeah? Who's he edit?" she challenged.

Pinned to the spot, five pairs of eyes upon me, my mind went dust-bowl blank. "Well, lots of big writers," I stalled.

"Yeah? So name one."

I frowned, I groped, I searched dead air: nothing; just snow in my head. It was all the more dismal because I'd told the truth, but the truth was no friend in those days. I was much more adept at telling lies and found them easier to deploy than the facts. "Wait." It suddenly came to me. "Harold Brodkey, for starters, and—and Ed Doctorow and Tom Robbins..."

"Who? Never heard of them," she said. "*Harold* Robbins I'm famil-iar, but this other fellow, no. Who is he, the cousin?"

I continued to blank on the books my father midwifed and racked my head for the most recent roster of *American Review,* the definitive literary quarterly he put out. "Aha," I said, laying my trump card down. "And, of course, Philip Roth."

"Philip Roth!"

His name hung the air like mustard gas, poisoning the Weiskopf clan. "That bastard!" said Barbara's father. "That lying fraud! He's no more a writer than my shoe."

"He should rot in hell for a million years and have to sit next to Himmler in the lunchroom!" said her mother.

"Wha-at?" I sputtered. "Have you *read* a page of *Portnoy?* Do you know what a comic tour de force it—"

"Wouldn't soil my hands," she said. "A pack of lies is what it is, about a boy who has sex with his mother's pot roast."

"All right, *enough,*" said the rabbi. "How is this constructive? What his father does is neither here nor there. He's apologized for not coming better dressed, and you went to the expense of getting a robe made for him. If he washes himself up and maybe ties back his hair, is there a way that we can reach some accommodation?"

Martin and Barbara consulted in baleful looks. "But no talking to the guests, especially the children," he said. "I shudder, what comes out of his mouth."

"That's fair," said the rabbi. "Can we agree on that? You'll just stand with quiet purpose and embody strength?"

"Not a problem," I said. "I'm a professional."

His eyebrows went up, forming a circumflex. "For that, first you'll need a profession."

THE WEISKOPFS, DECRIERS OF zest and sizzle, seemed to have made their terms with it for the day. At the mammoth reception, which could have filled a Macy's and sent its overflow celebrants down to Stern's, there were roving trios of folksong singers, a pinball arcade for the preteen set, and waiters dressed as great Jews in sports, resulting in some odd inclusions. Sandy Koufax? Naturally. Hank Greenberg? Doubtless. But Ron Blomberg, the Yankees' part-time DH? It struck me as a stretch, and pass the knishes. Needless to say, the event was short-staffed, though they'd wisely doubled up on the Sid Luckmans.

As for me, I was no second coming of Moses. The costume, an off-the-shoulder, flowing robe, made me look like the ring card girl at a Friday night smoker in Newark. It flattered my chest and oiled-up delts but was sheerer than the hostess might have liked and allowed my string bikini to shade through. What I knew about Judaism you could put on a cracker and still have room for smoked salmon, but Moses in high-cut, leopard-print briefs? Render unto Caligula, sayeth the Lord.

Also no picnic was the long gray beard they had me plaster on. It was made of some fabric that itched like wool, though derived from goats, not sheep. Each time I tugged at its board-stiff backing, it connived to pinch me in a different place, digging at my day-old stubble. The wig was no better, a musty number that smelled like the pace horse at Belmont. As I stood there, gripping the tablets in one hand and a tall shepherd's crook in the other, I couldn't help wonder who had worn it before me and what karmic crime they'd committed. It beat trying to pin down my own offenses, which violated most of the Ten Commandments, several of them many times over.

For the first hour I posed by a wing of the partition that divided the room when closed. Guests milled past, giving awkward smiles or eyeing me over highball glasses. Standing there, wearing a freeze-dried look of what I hoped was holy rigor, I felt like a lobster at one of those seafood joints that lets you pick your dinner from the tank. It didn't help that all I'd eaten that day was a sleeve of Hostess Sno Balls and that the buffet table, heaped with finger foods, was a five-step jog away. Some of those who stopped to pile their plates ventured a remark in my direction. "I'll bet they didn't have all this delicatessen when you were up on Mount Zion," chirped a woman. She grinned, baring a mouthful of lobster salad; a mustache of Hellmann's topped her lip. Her spouse, a gargantuan chap of sixty, gurgled like a backyard fountain. "And it was cold up there, for forty days and nights. I hope you dressed warmer than that!"

"Hey, watch it," said a bystander, joining the fun, "or he'll turn that rod to an asp."

The big crowd kept building, as late-coming arrivals clotted the narrow foyer—the men in their wide-peaked blazers and suits, the women with bone-deep, melanomic tans and cheekily short, mid-thigh skirts. Everywhere I looked glowed the nimbus of money: the gold that shimmered off wrists and necks; the silver orthodontia in the mouths of kids; and the high-buff polish of ambitious poise in the bearing of the oldest sons. It was like a one-day version of those weeklong retreats in which the rich huddle together to swap ideas on how to wring more wealth from Third World labor. Or, to say the same thing self-indictingly, it was a convocation of the things I never was and stood little chance of becoming: contented, connected, en route to somewhere stable—a member, to quote my father, of the hive.

"You part Negro?" said a boy with a knowing grin, hovering with two of his friends. "You must be, because white guys don't get that big. You gotta have some *schvartze* in you somewhere."

He couldn't have been more than twelve years old, but with a crown of thick hair and dazzling teeth, he had the panache of a high school senior. His pals hung back, either in awe of him or in sensible terror of me.

"Move it along. I'm working here."

"No, really. Make a muscle with your arm."

I glared at the kid but hinged a biceps, making it pop and jitter.

"Cool!" He traded pounds with the kid behind him. "Show's over," I said. "Go bother Dolph Schayes."

Instead he drew closer, leaning in from the waist. "Actually, we came to see if you had some weed."

I laughed out loud, drawing a flurry of looks from the people in the buffet line.

"Just a joint," he begged. "We're bored off our asses. I had some killer sess, but I left it home."

"Well, that's drugs for you. You get high and forget your stash."

"Ah, pleeease. We're dying here."

I looked him over closely, then checked around again. "What made you think I was holding?"

He snickered.

"Oh, right. I'm the nigger by default."

On behalf of blacks everywhere, and Jews like me who struggled to keep year-round tans, I should've sent the three of them on their way. But I was dizzy with hunger, more than a little hungover, and in a sourly subversive mood. I gave them my terms, which were nonnegotiable, and said I'd meet them in the first-floor men's room during the changeover to luncheon service. "And if you twerps say anything to your little friends..."

"Don't worry," said Jake, flashing a gleamy smile whose cost could have built a treatment plant in Ghana. "We're all, like, totally down."

I SAT IN THE STALL with my gym bag open, mulling whether to fire up the amp of Deca-Durabolin while I waited for the kids to join me. It was past one p.m., and I was seriously late for the shot that started my day. Generally, it galled me to miss a morning, but my buttocks were a motley of blue-gray bruises in various stages of healing. Most of the welts had come courtesy of test cypionate, the oil-based bastard form of human testosterone that was much in favor with my crew. It grew big, freaky muscle in a short period of time, made you mean as a hornet by the end of week two, and raised some nasty blisters where you shot it. One way around those was to take a month off and use something like Deca that went in smoother. Alternatively, you could act like the junkie you were and start fishing around for other sites — the webbing between your toes, say, which didn't show much, or the meat of the inner thigh. Or you could do what I did — stack Deca *and* test cyp — and hope that no one noticed the shiners peering out of your French-cut Speedo bikini.

I gauged myself for signs of withdrawal — arrhythmia, faintness, a flaccid prick — but wasn't sure exactly what to look for. I'd heard Angel and the others use nebulous terms like "washed-out" and "naked" to describe it, but I didn't feel much more exposed than usual, even in my Red Sea getup. All I detected was a coil of irritation pinging away under the skin. I had never, by all measures, been a cheerful sort and had set up sarcasm as my default mode since the end of my parents' marriage when I was ten. The past several weeks, though, I'd been hell on wheels, an open chord of grievance with New York. In the summer of my life — or, more precisely, my *new* life, the one that had started only seven months prior, when I'd discovered the campus weight room and its alchemies — I was making cash money hand over fist; filling out my closet with hand-stitched shirts from that men's store of the gods, Charivari; and having aerobic, if unskilled, sex more or less at will. Nonetheless, I felt ambushed, under barrage, the target of seemingly fluid and random events whose connection only I could see. The rainstorm that ruined my new Bottega boots; the hair dryer that shorted out before a hot date — they were all part of a loose (and anthropomorphic) conspiracy to keep me in my place. Putting fifty pounds of muscle on a skeletal frame and emerging from the molehill of adolescence, I had broken some cardinal law of physics, and someone, or something, was angry. You are what you are, said my fatalist mother, but I, for better or worse, had begged to differ.

The door banged open. I stashed the syringe, peeking out over the stall.

"You bring it?" Jake asked.

"Yeah. You?"

"Yup, but let's see yours first."

I fished the skinny joint from my pack of Winstons. "It's shake, but it'll get you high."

He snatched it from my hand and flicked a lighter.

"No! Not here, dope. It's a temple."

"Right," he said. "Let's go out back."

"Hey!"

The fat one came forward and held it out. "The caterer counts his plates, so bring it back."

I lifted the cloth napkin on my contraband: a thick but sloppily built corned beef sandwich with the fat kid's palm print on the bread. "Whoa. Where's my coleslaw and latkes?"

He shrugged at Jake. "I didn't hear him say that."

"Hey, don't look at me—you're the food guy."

"But can't I bring it later? They want us up there."

"No, you can't bring it later. Your word is your bond," I said. "That's the whole point of this day."

Jake sniggered. "Where's it talk about dope deals in the Ketuvim?"

"Don't be a smart-ass," I scolded. "I'm not the one who made all the waiters dress like Norm Van Brocklin."

"Yeah? So?"

"So today at least *pretend* that you've read the Torah, instead of using it for one big score. And you can't start fucking people over in business till you're an adult and selling hi-fis at Crazy Eddie's."

They looked at each other in mystification, then made a sudden dash for the door. I started after them but was slow off the line and tripped on my shepherd's crook. It glanced off the sink with an angry clatter; the straight end cracked where I'd tromped it. "*Fuuuuck!*" I screamed, not at the sacrilege but at the corned beef sandwich that had gone flying. It struck the unclean lip of the sink, then, like a drunk holding on to the arm of his stool, slid off sideways and went plop.

Now, we Jews, with exceptions, are a cleanly race, and many is the mother who's been moved to boast that you could eat off her bathroom floor. This floor, however, no mother would claim, rife as it was with black heel marks and the film from a dirty mop. But panicked—I pictured Yiddish cops descending, their tin shields embossed with six-point stars—I went to my knees and salvaged lunch, shoving what meat wasn't touching the tiles into my greedy gob. Mustard splotched the porcelain base, but that I sponged with hunks of rye and stuffed them into my mouth. I'd gotten most of the mess down in three or four bites when, as dusk follows dawn, I started to gag.

Alas, choking, I'm pained to say, was no novelty act. For months I'd been eating like a trash compactor, forcing all manner of half-chewed *treif* down in a death-march drive to gain weight, and once a week, minimum, a Frito or heel of pizza would catch in my throat and lodge. Usually, I managed to move things along with a lot of red-faced huffing and hacking, but this time nothing budged when I inserted a finger. I could breathe, with some effort, pulling in from the gut, and seemed in no imminent danger of dying, but I was terrified to think what would happen next if the opening in my trachea narrowed. I pawed at my tonsils, using two and three fingers, and turned on the hot water till it blasted, thinking the patchy steam would *melt* the meat. But the clump just sat there, wedged in solid like a punchball in a Cyclone fence.

Panicked now, I searched for something to push it down. There was, of course, the crook, with its loop at the top, but the curve was too broad to clear my molars. Ditto the handle of a toilet plunger, the taste of which brought me to stinging tears. That left my bag, and in it one option: the steel syringe and inch-long needle. I trembled at the thought of poking my pharynx with something sharp enough to split wood but opened my jaws as wide as they went and threaded the barrel in. It barely passed my tonsils when reverse peristalsis stopped it in its tracks. The clump, however, shifted the slightest bit. I fed the needle through again and pushed the plunger: the clammy, oil-based hormone greased my throat. I refilled the chamber with water and shot; the clump began to slide. I held my breath while gravity nudged it toward the cliff drop of my esophagus.

For several minutes I sagged against the stall, letting it prop me up till my heart stopped pounding. I listened vaguely to the *thrush* of plumbing and, through the wafer of drop-tile ceiling, a klezmer band. Slick with perspiration, I began to shiver, crouching under the downdraft of a vent. When I was able again to stand, I stumbled to the sink and gaped in the mirror, shamefaced. "What are you doing?" I said. "Are you *trying* to die, gorging like Mama Cass at a double wedding? This can't go on. It's eating your brain—the drugs, the stripping. It's over."

Good and worked up, I grabbed the syringe and stuffed it into the trash. That felt cleansing, so I went for my bag and tossed its contents out—the sluttish T-shirt and shorts so tight as to get me collared for exposure. Relief suffused me, a sense of pride reclaimed, of being back in the embrace of my tribe. I couldn't say exactly what tribe that was, but such things would keep until later. For now it was enough to repudiate muscle and the deeply strange path it had led me. I had a nimble mind, according to my mother, who saw in me a future poverty lawyer. It bears noting, of course, that she thought the moon landing a fake, that Bobby Kennedy had paid to have his brother rubbed out, and that there was a fortune to be made selling big-butt mannequins to dress shops in Spanish Harlem. On that last, at least, she was a woman before her time.

Feeling ten percent smarter for having tossed my works, along with the man-whore togs, I blotted myself with paper towels and straightened the shaft of the crook as best I could. But pausing for one last

13

glance in the mirror, I felt a ripple of panic go through me. Either I was crazy or my biceps had softened, the belly of the muscles a quarter of an inch smaller than when I'd measured that morning. I took a step back and shot a pose, holding it till my forearms shook. It was true, goddamnit, I was shrinking already, the Pump in reverse, but double speed. Was my body so graspingly steroid dependent that a half day off had me wilting faster than the flowers in a Broadway bodega?

I hit the pose again, checked and rechecked it, then launched myself headlong at the trash can. The short shorts could stay there, but where *was* that fucking needle, buried beneath paper and crusts of rye? Finally, I found it at — where else? — the bottom, the sharp in a wad of Dubble Bubble. Prying the gum off, I ran the syringe under water, cranking the tap high to mute my curses.

Two

The Unbearableness of Being Light

Nine months earlier

IN THE FALL OF 1975, I was having such a rough go of it that even my hair was depressed. Styled on David Bowie of *Aladdin Sane* vintage, it was long in back and purportedly spiked on top, but drooped like Three Dog Night in a two-day downpour. Though I piled on half a can of White Rain Extra and did everything but toast it in a waffle iron, thirty minutes later the mop would crowd my face, mocking my glam-rock affectations. I stood six foot one, weighed 140 pounds, and hadn't been laid since Nixon's reelection, making me, like George McGovern, a landslide loser.

Absurdly, though, I seemed to have ascribed my failure to not being tall and spindly enough and fire-walked Manhattan in Nunn Bush platforms with patent-leather, five-inch heels. To better strike terror into the hearts of pigeons, I topped off the urban-scarecrow ensemble with tourniquet-tight jeans, glitter-spangled T-shirts, and a trousseau of abominable jackets. Once, tottering home in sky-high sandals and a foul-smelling fake-mink coat, I ran into my father in the lobby. He sized me up in pity and horror and punched the elevator button. When the lone car platformed, he swept me inside and backed off, kneading his skull. "You go ahead," he said to my footwear. "I'll catch the next one up."

At the ripe age of twenty, I had a mad crush on Ginger, the D-cupped dingbat on *Gilligan's Island,* and organized my day around the four p.m. reruns, staying tuned for *The Munsters* and *The Addams Family.* I had plenty of time to watch, having dropped out of college and been fired from a series of flathead jobs, including two for which I'd actually volunteered. In the worst economy since the peak Depression—a jobless rate topping nine percent; a city near failure on its Class A bonds—the wonder wasn't that I got canned so often but that anyone would hire me next. The last firm so feckless was a Wall Street bank that trusted me to cut its float checks. An important-sounding task, it was actually performable by lesser primates, double- and triple-checking long rows of numbers, then putting their sums through an embosser. Alas, no lemurs were available to work, and every third day or so the company opened for business several million dollars overdrawn.

Unemployed, friendless, and freshly evicted from the cot in my brother's sublet, I'd come to rest finally in a furnished room over a newsstand on Amsterdam Avenue. Two doors down was a bagel place that fired up its ovens at five a.m., doing battle for olfactory dominance with a pizza joint three doors north. By noon I'd have a splitting migraine and the makings of a yeast infection. But the Ukrainian widow whose room I rented insisted on open windows, citing fresh air as her secret to health, even in mid-December. Pacing the hall in reindeer boots and a watch cap pulled down low, she knocked on my door at two-hour intervals to thrust her cooking upon me. "*Look* you, you skeleton," she clucked, seizing my wrist. "Need bratwurst and big plate of kasha. Also need turn off idiot TV and get job laying tile with my godson Ilya."

And so, down to my last twenty dollars and the flop-sweat realization that my next stop was likely the street, I swallowed what threadbare pride I still had and called my father for help. He asked that I drop by after ten p.m., when his third wife, a woman who richly despised me, would be packed off to bed and none the wiser. (I'd been banned from her house for a heinous act, the details of which do no one honor.) As a token of contrition, I wore my one blazer, a glen plaid horror that I'd plucked from the racks of a men's store/slash/bodega called Fowad. (Socks in aisle three, cervezas in aisle four, and ask about our Easter layaway!) I showed up promptly at the stroke of ten and pumped Dad's hand with the echt enthusiasm of the door-to-door salesman I'd briefly been, hawking Kirby vacuums to single mothers in the tombstone projects of the Bronx. He looked me over with an expression of sadness and, in spite of himself, invited me in.

"Can I give you a beer? How about a sandwich?" he asked in an alarmed half whisper.

"I'm fine," I said, feeling anything but. I'd had Frosted Flakes for breakfast, lunch, and dinner.

"You sure?" he said. "My God, you're thin. There's pot roast. I can make you a plate."

"No, really, I-I'm good. I just had a burger. I had that two-week flu, but I'm getting better."

He patted my rib cage, as if checking for weapons. "Why haven't you been eating? Your asthma bad?"

I was touched and offended in equal measure; I hadn't had asthma in years. Still, the mere mention of it brought me back to a period of intense connection. From the age of two, when my asthma flared, to ten, when my parents split, my father and I had spent thousands of hours in a misty, wet-tiled bathroom. Each night, around one, I'd wake up choking, fumbling for the inhaler by the bed. Then I'd start screaming, further squeezing the hole through which I labored for air. Hunched over an essay at the dining room table that doubled as his knock-kneed study, my father would drop his pencil, shut his eyes a moment, then walk the short hallway to my room. "C'mon," he'd whisper—my brother slept in the next bed—and walk or carry me, sobbing, to the john.

Closing the door behind us, he'd turn on the shower with an exhausted flick of the knob. Between his long days at *Commentary* and the moonlighting he did writing reviews to keep us afloat, he slept, in a good week, five hours a night, not counting the evenings he watched Knick games with us and dozed off at the half. He'd station me at the sink, knead my ribs to loosen the phlegm, and tell me, in his worn but even-keeled voice, that we'd get through this one, too. Soon I'd stop moaning, the steam would enclose us, and the "junk," as he called it, would come up thickly. It was long, slow work, and I'd take breaks from it and sit down on the sweat-slick lid of the toilet. He'd park on the tub wall, pull his robe close, and ask about the one thing sure to deflect me from the unlovely business at hand. "How'd Mantle do today? Did he hit his way out of it, or is he still in his funk left-handed?"

Haltingly, I'd tell him, recounting at-bats and adding bits of improvised hokum. *Mickey went hitless but had a shot to left-center that was caught at the wall by Jackie Brandt, and a smash down the line that Brooks Robinson gloved and got him on a throw from his knees.* Like most of my lies, these were meant to regale, to deflect him from the business at hand. I felt shitty about being yet another weight on his overburdened shoulders, a constant drag on what energy he had left after dealing with the debacle that was my mother. With her endlessly variable moods and plaints, she had first dibs when he came through the door, and after her there wasn't much left to go around. My younger brother's resentment and increasingly florid misconduct (Ivan was running away every Friday afternoon to the house of his second-grade teacher, Mrs. Swift, and had founded, with a couple of other pissed-off seven-year-olds, the New York chapter of the Stealing Club of America, whose crowning ambition was the theft, in broad daylight, of the bubble-gum machine outside Woolworth's); my frequent, weeklong absences from school, brought on by chest infections; and the parlous state of our family finances, which even in the best months seemed to hang from a cliff—these and other hassles had to wait their turn for his very limited attention.

And so that hour or so in the steam each night came to feel like golden time, my one chance to have him to myself, set free from household tumult. He, too, had grown up fighting to breathe, afflicted in boyhood with double pneumonia that permanently scarred his lungs, and now slept or worked with one ear cocked for the wheeze that woke me up. No matter how embattled he was with an essay or beset by my mother's caprices, it all washed out in that foggy john, where his best and gentlest self took the floor. He'd read to me on nights I was too winded to talk, pulling from my shelf of sports biographies the story of Jackie Jensen, the great but star-crossed Red Sox center fielder who quit because of a fear of flying, or open to Robert Creamer's life of Lou Gehrig and start in anywhere. As Mantle was my god and battered king, so was Gehrig to my father's boyhood, the mensch of tape-measure power. Both, like us, were damaged goods, young men haunted by old men's worries and the specter of early death. Both were deepened by that mortal knowledge and the weight of their own greatness, and bore them with the kind of terse aplomb that teetered on the allegoric. And both, wildly famous, seemed to travel alone, enisled by tragedy. You couldn't ask for more as a sentient Jew or his seriously inward son, and to us those two were a race apart, Samsons in pin-striped *agonistes*.

"Really, I'm fine, Dad," I said now in a croak, alarmed by the catch in my throat. Perhaps he heard it, too, because he backed off the subject and took my sport coat from me. It was the first, and most stringent, of our unspoken rules: No crying, *ever*. So help us.

His study was the maid's room in the classic-six apartment that he shared with his spouse and youngest son. (There were four of us boys, from three different wives. It made for baffling custody nights.) The small space, appended by its own half bath, was wall-to-wall with books by Dad's Famous Friends. Roth, Mailer, Kazin, Rahv — the Jewish literary minyan was here in session. There was a manuscript on his desk, its pages marked in blue and the puffy brown blot of his coffee mug. He'd hidden the ashtray, but I smelled the stale haze of the Tareytons he snuck at night, and could almost hear the drumbeat of his anxious heels when up against another hard deadline. To sit there, in his heady, lamplit hull of posterity and years'-old dust, was, for me at least, like breaking into Cooperstown and camping out beneath the bats and balls. I'd no idea who or what I was, but there, on his overrun shelves and desk, was the son he had clearly *hoped* I'd become, the serious, circumspect pre-intellectual who weighed life out to the ounce.

"So, yeah," I said. "The reason I called you here."

He cocked an eyebrow, not getting the joke. To be fair, I didn't get it either.

"Well, as you probably figured, I'm not doing so great. It's been quite a year and a half."

I laughed, another of my lame red herrings. He looked at me, unblinking. I wanted to bolt.

"Just say it," he said, arms crossed at his chest. "It can't be any worse than what I've heard."

My father, a handsome, square-faced man with an ex-jock's smashed-nose vigor, had eyes that bored through my skull. I hid from them now, examining my shoes and wincing at their stacked wood heels. "Actually, well...yeah, it can."

"What'd you do now? Knock someone up?"

"No, nothing like that, no. I wish it was. At least I'd have gotten laid along the..."

I cringed: another joke, another fuckup. You didn't talk sex around my father—it reeked of desperation and male preening. Indeed, the things that irked him outnumbered the things that didn't, at least where I was concerned. In terms of safe subjects, it was sports and books, which meant we hadn't budged in fifteen years.

"Look, you call up here after five and a half months. I've already guessed you need money," he said. "So what else *besides* that do I have to deal with, and what's it going to cost this time?"

"What? When have you bailed me out of anything?"

"When!" he spluttered. "When have I *not* bailed you out? What do you call that stunt of yours in the Bronx, which set me back two thousand bucks?"

"Which? What're you saying—it was *me* that broke the lease. Why would they come after you?"

"Because I cosigned the lease, or did you forget? And the bank loan you signed for, my name was on that, too, and you hadn't made a payment in months. Did you think that if you just ignored them, they'd write it off? No, that's what a guarantor is. *I'm* the one they call when they can't reach you."

I was stunned into silence. If anything defined the deaf-dumb-and-blindness of my year-and-a-half exile from college, the stretch I spent on 174th Street easily took the cake. Forget trying to sell a top-dollar vacuum to unemployed mothers with three kids; the corker was coming home at the end of each day and stepping over chicken bones and stubbed-out Kools and the viscous squish of used condoms. Children ran those stairwells, some as young as five, and I wondered what they made of such squalid totems and their ode to viciousness. The noise, the heat, the hell's-bells stench that had me breathing out through grit teeth—it was all a come-hither to the very bottom, a jeering declaration of who cares. Join us, it said; there's no use fighting. This, or something worse, is what you get.

"I—I...I'm sorry. I didn't know."

"No, *of course* you didn't know. You hid at your brother's and left me to pick up the tab. And what was it all for, this urban safari—so you could finally figure out you aren't black?"

I winced, holding my tongue. He was owed a free shot, though my black phase, like my asthma, was well behind me.

"I mean, not to pile on, but what goes *on* with you, Paul, under that big pile of hair? Do you ever stop to think how your mistakes affect others? For that matter, do you think of others, *period*?"

This seemed a valid question to ask, though an equally valid question to lob back. His three wives in six years and litany of spurned sons; the alimony payments and child-support checks that required him to spend his weekends writing reviews instead of tossing a ball to his kids—clearly, he could stand some reflection himself on the law of unwitting effects. But per usual with my father, I said none of that, wilting under the heat of his gaze. "I—I didn't call because you hate when I'm in trouble."

"Well, if you didn't call then, we'd never speak, would we? Really, these last years, it's just been one thing after another. The bungled nose job that you *had* to have and which *I* paid for, *not* insurance; that suspension for smoking dope in the bathroom at Music and Art and the threat to hold you back until *I* wrote your senior thesis—it's like you suddenly woke up and decided to become your mother. I'm just flummoxed at the way you've fallen apart."

"Well?" I said, near tears. "And why do you suppose that is?"

"No idea," he said coldly. "But don't look at me. I've backed you to the hilt. For all *that* got me."

I sprang to my feet and turned to leave. It was that or fall down and go mad. From that miserable night in 1964, when my mother shook a spoon at him across the table and ordered him out of the house, and he, to his surprise and eventual vast relief, took her up on it, Dad and I had seldom spoken longer than motorists trading directions. In the year after their split, I was the principal culprit, reducing our post-divorce, Wednesday dinners to a recap of the Yankees' latest charades. For a while Dad endeavored to crack my sulk, taking me to twilight doubleheaders and teaching me his loping, topspin forehand at the tennis courts in Central Park. But my hurt and shock were so febrile then that a deep store of patience was needed, and my father, a man of many parts, lacked the temperance to wait me out. Soon he began to close down himself, and a fraught near silence set up around us, as thick as the steam in that john.

"Wait a minute, we're not done," he fumed.

"Well, I am." I fumbled blindly for the knob.

Slow to follow me into the hall, he reached for an arm that I snatched away. "You don't cut and run; that's your mom's way of dealing. You stay and talk this out. That's what *men* do."

"*Pardon* me?" I turned on him. "Since when did *you* stay? You're the first one off the ship!"

He went blank a moment, his jaw unsteady. "Oh, *that's* it, then? That's why I'm still paying? Because ten years ago I left your mother?"

"No, ten years ago you left *me and Ivan,* and it's all you've been doing ever since!"

"*Shut* it," he warned me. "Keep your voice down. There's a young child sleeping in this house."

"The house I'm not *allowed in* anymore."

The lid off my rage, I wanted to wake that child, rouse my five-year-old half brother Isaac and tell him not to rest easy, that the day was surely coming when a fight over dinner would crack his boyhood open. Maybe it wouldn't matter as much to him as it had to Ivan and me. Isaac had a mother who was fully functional and loved him to near distraction. He was, besides, a beauty, with heavy lids and the complexion of a Titian prince, and would always know, way down in his bones, that the world had marked him out for women's favors. But if the history of our family was any guide, he would one day have to answer the bill of indictment that a father's departure levies.

Dad looked like a man cracked open himself, cheeks bruised and palms turned upward. "Is this how you come here asking for help, laying on the king of all guilt trips? Yes, I moved out, after thirteen years; it was the most bitterly painful thing I ever did. I wish to God I could've hung in longer, but she would've done us *all* in if I'd stayed."

"Well, glad I could take that bullet for you, Dad."

His eyes goggled. "I didn't mean that, and you know it."

And there, in the crosshatched gloom of the hall, we gaped at each other like dead-armed boxers. Something seemed to flit in the dark behind him, or not flit but pulse and hover: the barometric drone of dammed-up air, or the diaspora of startled atoms. The silence that built was all sharp edges. It made my eardrums swell as if to burst.

I angled past him; he stepped aside; the door closed behind me with a thunk. I stood there a moment, dizzy and blood-dimmed, till I heard the dull report of the dead-bolt slide.

I WALKED AND WALKED, letting the wind up Broadway push me where it liked. It was, as one remembers these things, warm for November, the benches in the medians manned by drunks and the logorrheic crones who fed the squirrels. In those bad old days of SROs and plein air heroin marts, you were never alone as you traipsed the street, the strip alive with dark-world vigor and smacked-out ghosts sliding by. To venture past 86th Street was to roll the dice, at least at a certain hour, and only the derelict would cross 96th to the demilitarized zone of the barrio. I was staying on 83rd Street, but couldn't handle the horror of my overheated bedsit, and so I wandered the West Side gauntlet for hours, scarcely knowing where I was.

At some point I landed on Central Park West, the thin band of boobwah aspirations that was bounded to the east by the murderous park and to the west by the shuttered storefronts and mad-dog projects of Columbus Avenue. Compared with Broadway, it was dune-grass quiet, the wind mussing the crowns of the leafless trees and snapping the awnings of the prewar hulks that housed the area's nervous middle class. From the brown depths of shadow, I stopped at a light and was stunned to find myself at Park West Village, the tall brick eyesore I'd grown up in.

In 1961, a year removed from the Midwest, where my parents had been raising two small boys on grad-school stipends in Chicago, we had installed ourselves in this newish complex that took up four blocks abutting the park. Built on a site razed by Robert Moses in a particularly vicious act of slum clearance, these twenty-story towers were a shot over the bow from arriving gentrifiers. The developers filled the complex with cops, teachers, and, in a transit of well-earned guilt, prosperous blacks. Two floors down from us lived the great Floyd Patterson, as gracious at the mailbox as in the ring. Above us was Olatunji, the African drummer, whose children taught my brother to dance but deemed me past all help. In the next building over was the bachelor Ray Charles, and it occurred to me to wonder what a star of his luster was doing around the likes of us. It wasn't till high school, and my enrollment in fad socialism, that the pathos of the word *redline* came across to me in all its thudding bluntness.

Still, there'd been perks at Park West Village: an enormous and well-kept nexus of playgrounds in the commons between the buildings;

machines in the basement that sold cans of Pepsi for the fair price of a nickel; and a vast supply of kids our age to play smashmouth two-hand touch with. The first couple of years there were a useful tonic for the marital strife at home — the backyards full of restless boys, even on winter days. Ivan and I ran with different crowds, he with kids in awe of his thieving, I with comic-book geeks. At nine I'd nicked the bug from Brian Correa, a smallish kid with glue-like hands who caught every pass I threw in his direction. He had, besides the kid-size uni of the New York Jets, a sealed-in-plastic copy of *The Amazing Spider-Man #1,* which even then was a trophy find. Barely a year after his tepid debut on newsstands, Spidey had become a zeitgeist star, the watercooler buzz of the fourth grade. We begged, borrowed, or stole to buy his back issues, though #1 was already beyond our means, trading among collectors for sixty bucks. I still remember the pitch I gave my mother, telling her that such a purchase would be an investment in my future, a blue-chip steal that would explode in value and someday pay my way through college. But she was in a mood and said that if I kept reading drivel, I'd never make it through high school, let alone college.

Eleven years later, I stood on that corner, gazing at a third-floor window. It was the wrong one, of course (we'd lived in the back), but was lit with the kind of lugubrious pallor that kick-starts memory. I recalled now, in detail, the night that Dad left, Ivan and I hopping up into his lap and begging him to stay. I was a painfully proud nine-year-old but bawled like a baby, croaking, "Who'll take care of me when I'm choking?" He said that he'd be close, only a cab ride away if an attack got out of hand, and that Mom stood ready to fill in for him, having watched over his shoulder for a year. Moreover, he added, I'd come to an age when I could comfort myself, get up on my own, and talk my way through it, hearing his voice in my head. Even Ivan saw that for the bunkum it was and took to crying himself. A tough-egg eight-year-old, he'd had it with all of us. It was the last time I ever saw him weep.

The next morning, the pain was an anvil. How do I describe an ache so deep it hurt to lie perfectly still, and a sense of doom that trailed me to school and followed me up the stairs? I sat there in class, the teacher a blur, while the noise in my head drowned everything out, a babble of blocking static. In a couple of days the volume dropped, and I could hear the world again. But weeks or months later, lying awake in the dark, I heard a voice in my ears. It was angry and ruthless and said vile things in a low, malevolent hush: *You're skinny. You're stupid. No one likes you. You better watch out there, fuckface.*

Those were dark days in our dingy two-bedroom. I'd come home after school, scan the shelves of our fridge, and take up position on the bathroom floor, sitting with my comics spread before me. It didn't much matter that I wasn't wheezing; once the steam started, I had title to that john and wasn't coming out for hours. Ivan was off running with his larcenous crew, presumably being chased up Amsterdam Avenue by portly store detectives. My friends stopped coming by to roust me for ball games, spooked by my deep despond. My father was gone and not coming back, having landed a cheap apartment in the Village. But I'd made new friends of Batman and Robin, and I studied each panel of *Detective Comics* as if it contained the cure for asthma.

And in a sense, of course, it did, beaming me and my tight lungs into the oxygenated world of Bruce Wayne. As het up as I'd been about Spider-Man's conversion from lab geek to antihero, there was in Batman's lack of superpowers something to hang my hat on. Anyone could become his city's savior if blessed with cosmic strength, but Batman had earned his massive chest in the gym he had built in his basement. Sure, he'd inherited a stately mansion that accommodated a Big Ten field house, but the point for me was his *possibility:* with enough brute work and directed mania, I could be Batman, too.

What sealed the deal, though, was Batman's boyhood. His parents had been, famously, shot and killed during a stickup gone bad in an alley, reducing young Bruce to both an instant orphan and a front-row witness to it. An eight-year-old cringing on a bloody curb, his wide eyes flush with terror. All that leapt off the page to a kid trying to come to terms with hard loss. Like me, Bruce was handed the Gothic task of raising himself alone, and in a house as relentlessly grim as mine, he turned his back on the outside world and got to it in that dungeon of a gym. What matter that he had an English butler and a chauffeured Rolls in the drive? Like me, he was trying to figure it all out by the seat of his size-small pants, and the guesses he made looked shrewd to me. Even, you might say, a plan.

Come spring, I inveigled some starter weights out of Mom: a long bar and a pair of five-pounders. Listening to games on my pocket transistor, I stood against the wall and curled for hours, lifting in an autonomic fugue. But the load was insufficient, push-ups bored me shitless, and the enterprise proved an empty drill, another fine plan gone poof. That left me a nuclear, Pop-pulp hope: that I'd get bitten by a spider bathed in gamma rays and morph into Spider-Man. I'm pained to admit now that I lay awake nights wondering how to infiltrate the reactor at Three Mile Island with a box of black widows (and, for backup, crickets). I also stood in windows during thunderstorms, hoping halfheartedly to get struck by lightning like my other DC icon, The Flash. As drawn by the Tiepolo of sixties illustrators, Carmine Infantino, The Flash was built like a young Steve Reeves and could run the world backward at warp speed. That parlay, if duplicated, would give me free access to some head-spinning possibilities. I could single-handedly turn around the Yankees' fortunes with my tape-measure homers and steals of second; bring down Nixon and his fascist cronies by strong-arming White House tapes; and spend as much time as I liked in girls' locker rooms, because The Flash, at full tilt, was invisible.

But I won't dawdle in this vein, which has been expertly worked over by the drills of Messrs. Chabon and Lethem. All I'll add is that as I got older, I was more, not less, hooked on comics. And when even the feyest villains sported East German biceps, it was easy to come away with both a sense of my own smallness and an incipient lust for sinew. Long before anyone started paying attention to them, comic books antici-pated the muscle culture, envisioning a nation of slab-chested sprinters and shortstops built like centurions. As scrawny as I was, and as much as I loathed myself for it, cursing cruel genetics, I persisted in the hope that a change was coming, that somewhere in the world—Los Alamos? Chernobyl?—there was a million-to-one accident waiting to happen and a radioactive spider with my name on it.

Three

Pumping Myron

AND SO, IN EARLY JANUARY 1976, I did what any other middle-class white kid did when life got bored beating him senseless: I ran, hat in hand, back to college. If I wasn't exactly aflame with zeal for higher ed, Stony Brook had, likewise, managed without *me,* as the woman in Housing made clear. "At this late date," she said, "I could triple you in a room and hope that someone drops out. Or you could take your chances and try looking off campus. Assuming, of course, we're driving?"

I assured her that *we* had no such luck and would be lucky to raise bus fare for registration.

"Then hold for the number of Financial Aid," she yawned. "You got a pencil and something to write this down on?"

Though Stony Brook billed itself the "Berkeley of the East," it was fairer, I think, to call it the McNeese State of the North, a school whose students were mostly interested in cars and picking up overtime at Sears. A huge gray truss of bricks and blocks slapped down on northern Long Island, the campus's squat buildings and treeless quads let the wind off the Sound blow you sideways in winter as you tramped the half-mile to class. Such was its soulless, monochrome sprawl that I felt, stepping off the train that first morning, like I'd turned myself in for a year in lockup and would be lucky to get a job in the prison laundry. Construction was ongoing around the clock, the sound of tax dollars digging fresh morasses as backhoes went by me at dusk. In lieu of a mascot, there was a symbol of state waste: the notorious Bridge to Nowhere. It was meant to connect the student union to the campus library but was pitched so badly as to miss it cleanly if it hadn't stopped halfway there. I couldn't walk past it, on my way to lunch, without hearing its drumroll to indifference, a life of so-what torpor.

The threat to triple me, doubtless issued in earnest, turned out to be hollow. I was roomed instead with a churlish kid who snored as if his larynx had teeth. After a couple of sleepless nights, I prevailed on my R.A., and wound up moving in down the hall with a sixteen-year-old freshman. Nathan, when lucid, was a brilliant kid with an interest in Trotsky and Neil Young. Alas, he was stoned from pretty much the minute classes ended till he dropped off an hour or two after dinner and had so far overslept his nine a.m. classes three mornings out of five. As he hailed from New York, though, we had common cause against the Nassau County boys who thronged the hall. We deplored their accents, the botched *r*'s and gerunds that made them sound like rookie cops recruited to pose as students. We mocked their meat-and-potatoes aspirations in *compyootuhs* and *lore enforcement* and grit our teeth at their cornpone rock, which badgered us through the walls of our room. To walk the length of that darkened hall was to know the joys of a fierce contact high and the canon of Gregg and Duane Allman. It was impossible to go more than twenty paces without hearing the organ fill on "Whipping Post" or the bourbon-inflected mourning of the surviving brother on "Melissa" and "Midnight Rider." I'd stop by someone's room, catch two boys with Smithtown triphthongs arguing who had the better steel pedal player—between the Outlaws and Marshall Tucker—and think, *How am I going to make it till May?*

If you lived in Benedict dorm and happened to be one of those odd birds who liked to hear yourself think, you were essentially reduced to two options. The first was to head off to the library and find a carrel in the stacks, preferably one whose prior tenant had bathed since winter break. The other was to ditch your morning classes and hunker down in your room, the hall being blissfully free of noise till its residents came back around five. From that point on, all bets were off, as doors were thrown open, book bags flung down, and stereo speakers tested to their upper limits. As a kid long used to the quirks of his own company, I never fully grasped how the experience of reading Dickens was enhanced by playing "Free Bird" at jet-plane volume, or how a nap before dinner was much facilitated by the clangor of Molly Hatchet. As near as I could figure, the purpose of such behavior was to prevent *anyone else* from doing his work, such that all grades would suffer and flatten the curve, raising a C-minus paper to a C plus. My second thought was that this was a mating call, signaling to the girls on the floor above that the boys on 1A were back from class and ready, on short notice, for sex.

With the exception of ours, the one door on the hall kept closed belonged to a tall blond kid with big muscles. Actually, *big* doesn't begin to give the sense of a guy who was the most stunning male specimen I'd cast eyes on. The first time I saw Mark, I was leaving the john, bundled against the vagrant, new-year draft in a robe and hiking boots. He, on the other hand, wore a towel so small it gaped at the hip and thigh. I noticed, absurdly, that he was tanned in winter, bronzed to a shade of browned butter. What registered next was the *whole* of him, and in that stop-time moment, my worldview died and a new one stretched its lungs.

He had shoulder-length hair in ash-blond curls that danced when he ambled by. His face, or at least his profile, which I caught in passing, was like something you'd see on a quarter, a bulwark of jaw and brow. He was an inch or two taller than me at six foot three and had cannonball shoulders that looked carved from brass—burnished arcs at the tops of his arms that flowed into half-moon biceps. His chest was a slab of T-squared boxes, beneath which knelt columns of raised abdominals that bunched and torqued as he moved. Nor had he left off sculpting his legs, sporting carved quads and horseshoe calves, splendor from head to toe. I turned around, slack-jawed, and watched him go. It took all my self-control not to applaud.

"Have you seen that big blond guy on the hall?" I asked Nathan after we returned from dinner.

He passed the joint over and settled back, plopping his feet on the bed. "I'm sorry, man. What'd you say?"

"You know who I'm talking about? The pumped-up chest—goes around the hall half-naked?"

Nathan squinted, trying to pierce the fog. "I haven't seen a chick like that."

"No, not a *chick*. The guy with muscles."

He stared at the traverse rod, drawing a blank. "Sorry, I'm fried. I need more z's."

"*More?*" I spluttered. "All you *do* is sleep. What you need is a couple of days *sober*."

"Really?" he said, sitting up straighter. "You think I smoke too much?"

This was uttered not in protest but in contemplation, a good kid brought up short. The respectful son of aging parents, he gave due weight to what his elders told him, even those marginally his senior. Though he'd purposely chosen a state school so he could smoke a lot of dope and still command grades that marked him for law school, he was willing, even stoned, to reconsider. It was hard not to like him for it.

"I'm just saying, you could pick your spots. Maybe start the week sober and make it to Wednesday, then see how it goes from there."

"Himphh," he grunted. "*Not* wasted for Bio—has anyone tried that yet?"

"Couldn't tell you," I said. "But I'll bet it's been done. Anyhow, give it a shot."

He lapsed into deep-sea contemplation. "Oh, wait a while now, I know who you mean. The Gigantor three doors down."

"Yeah, that's him. Do you know his story?"

"Just that his name's Mark and he's on the football team. The one girl I've met here—Ursula? Christina?—says they talk about him nonstop."

"Really," I said. "Well, no surprise there, seeing all the white lipstick they wear."

"Yeah, I know." He added his cackle to mine. "Wait, *no,* actually, I don't. What do you mean?"

Here was a trait I was less charmed by, his dogged curiosity in social nuance, about which, he freely admitted, he knew nothing. I, by coincidence, *also* knew nothing, but that didn't stop me from making pronouncements on a wide range of human behaviors. Indeed, the less contact I had with a subject, the shriller my views on it tended to be, a trick I'd learned from my mother. Since her divorce from my father, she'd been a virtual recluse, shutting herself up for years at a stretch to translate Tolstoy's letters. Remarkably, this didn't constrain her penchant for passing sentence on modern life. She was definitive on everything from hip-hugger jeans ("Haven't the gays got it good enough in New York City without you wearing those in solidarity?") to the undocumented impact of manned space flight on our delicate ecosphere. (Once, when a moon launch was followed by three days of rain, she ran to our balcony, shook her fist at the sky, and yelled, "Get back here this instant, you fucking astronauts!")

"Haven't you noticed, especially coming from Brooklyn," I said, "that there's a certain kind of girl that likes big bruisers and wears a lot of cheap mascara?"

Nathan thought a moment before a light came on. "Oh, you mean *Italians*? But they go to St. John's."

"No, not *them,*" I said. "White trash in general. In the fifties they called that type hitter chicks, because they liked, um, being hit by men. Then they got married and moved to Long Island and had daughters that say *hay-uh* for *hair.*"

"Oh," said Nathan, mulling this over. "And do their daughters like to get hit, too?"

"Not the *point* here," I fumed, though the thing I was driving at had long since slipped my grasp. The fact of the matter was, I got high a lot, too, and could have gained as much from a week's abstention as my stoner roommate. On the bright side, of course, I'd packed on a couple of pounds from the vending machine runs at one a.m.

We lay there a while, he on his bed, me on mine, listening to the sonic shootout next door, a joust between ZZ Top and early Zep. I was thinking how easy it would be to float like this through the next three years, unhindered. Get baked and fall in with the shaggy thousands who napped through survey courses, doing just enough to keep the yard-sticks moving and the Regents checks coming each quarter. That, too, was, I guessed, a sort of life, the kind most students wound up settling for later, going station to station, single file. It had no sweep or soaring runs, the bold step up onto a bigger stage and a voice that carried to the rafters. *That* world — of books and complex thought, the *I* that insisted on being heard — seemed so beyond my present reach that it was nice to imagine it gone. Who needed the hardship of his father's shadow and the weight of his puissant name? Already I had a teacher buttering me up so that a month down the road, he could hand me his novel and ask if I'd give it to Dad. He'd even made the "mistake" of calling me Ted, my father's name, a slip clearly intended to flatter. I could live quite nicely without all that, the not-so-subtle tokens of my birthright.

"Anyhow, why'd you ask?" said Nathan. "Is that something you'd actually *want,* to be that big?"

"No, of course not — not like *that*. The guy's a circus act, right?"

"I don't know," he said. "You see the girls hanging around here, try-ing to scope him out? If he wanted to just stand there in his Jockey shorts, the line to buy a ticket would be out the door."

"Well, I wouldn't go *that* far. The need to be looked at, day and night...You just wonder what kind of childhood he had."

The glance Nathan shot back — one eyebrow raised, the other stoop-ing to frown — retired the subject for good. It also cast doubt on my sanity and my acquaintance with the developments of the past century.

"Look," he said, "why don't you knock on his door and see if he'll take you lifting? I'll bet he's like, sure, whatever. And I tell you something else: I'll go to the gym *with* you. It'll be the start of my no-dope era."

STONY BROOK'S FIELD HOUSE WAS PLUSHER THAN YOU'D HAVE expected of a Division III program with no history. A cement and steel hangar at the east end of campus, within a ten-minute walk of my dorm, it was large and well lit and had more than enough floor space for the several hundred kids who bothered to use it. On nights when there weren't intramurals scheduled or a volleyball game in progress, you'd find a raucous fraction of the black student body playing end-to-end, racehorse basketball. The racquetball courts had an hour-long wait, the Olympic-size pool was crowded for open swim, and one night a week, after a crew of upperclassmen built a concert stage, five thousand kids poured in, pre-stoned, for acts like Billy Joel and Steely Dan.

But at the bottom of the place, behind airshafts and pump rooms, was a tiny space, no bigger than an attic, that constituted the campus weight room. It reeked of old mold and stagnant air, and the sum total of its apparatus—two aged Universals—had oxidized a rusty amber-gris. This, in dank decrepitude, was what the state board of bursars had deemed sufficient for a school of twenty thousand. As it turned out, they'd probably overbought. There was a sign on the door announcing that Intro to Weight Training had been canceled due to lack of student sign-ups.

After several days of stalling, I'd finally found the nerve to impose myself on Mark. My timing was, per usual, less than Swiss. He answered the door naked, his chest beet red from exertion. Behind him, a girl yanked a bedsheet up. After slipping on a robe and slippers and joining me in the hall, Mark proved surprisingly gracious. He listened to my spiel about being a sickly kid who'd grown up skinny and phobic, and allowed that he himself had been tall and gangly till the summer before his senior year of high school. "What," he asked me, "do you want at the gym? Do you want to get big, or do you want to get strong?"

I thought it over briefly, or attempted to; my brain suddenly juddered to a halt. "What I really want is...to get laid."

And so here I was now, with Nate in tow, fresh off the bus from the Smith Haven Mall, where we'd both bought our first pair of Nikes. As we stretched in the mat room, we glanced in the mirror and saw two gangly, big-haired kids in snow-white sneakers. From somewhere down the hall, we heard a racket that sounded like a derrick drill. Tracking it to the weight room, we found Mark shirtless and benching *warm-ups* with the entire stack. *Clink* went the cadence of cast-iron plates being tossed like poker chips. *BLUNNNG!* was the din at the other end, when the stack came down at double speed and bounced against the stanchion pegs. It was a savagely graceful show of strength, like watching killer whales toss seals up for sport before they gobble them whole.

"What's *he* doing here?" Mark glared at Nathan, whom I'd forgotten to mention I was bringing.

"Um, I told him I was coming, and, well, he wanted to watch. He's interested in maybe starting out, too."

"Hi," said Nathan. "I just want a little tone. Getting *your* size is too much work."

"And did I *say* you could bring someone else to train?"

"Well, no, but I—I thought if he learned, too, we wouldn't have to hassle you again."

"Again!" Mark arched his brows in disbelief. "Look, this is a one-shot here. No tomorrow for back or Friday for triceps. You get an hour, start to finish, so *write it down.*"

We followed him back to the rear machine, where he stood by the bench-press station. Hands on hips, he launched into a screed about "having respect for the room." You didn't bop in there in deck shoes and khakis to half-ass some reps and leave. You didn't put in work for three days straight, then drop out of sight till March. You didn't stand around and yak between sets or flip through *Hit Parader.* And as bad as the gear looked, you didn't mistreat it by dropping the weight at set's end. This place was a *temple*, a serious shrine where miracles sometimes happened. If we were ready to come in and bust our bony asses four or five days a week, we could get something done — go home in May with a half-decent chest and a *chance* to get laid by graduation. If not, we should both get the hell out now and save everyone there the trouble.

I glanced around the room. We were the only ones present, discounting the dog-size dust bunnies.

"And another thing," he said. "You're gonna hurt tomorrow. Any questions before we start?"

"Um, yeah," said Nathan. "What if I just want shoulders? Could I come, like, *two* days a week?"

"Get *over* here," Mark growled. "Lay down on the bench, and don't say a word for the next hour."

Nathan did as told, at least the lying-down part. Keeping his mouth shut was a taller order. A loose, floppy kid with newscaster hair and jeans that rode down his hips, he was perpetually posing questions about abstruse matters, often at the worst possible times. I'd be drifting off to sleep or gargling a mouthful of Scope, when he'd ask, "If a tree falls in the woods and no one hears it, is Hume saying that owls are deaf?" He had an antic mind he couldn't switch off, and it was often hard to tell whether he was really seeking answers or trying material out. I found his shtick charming, if a bit jejune, though our hallmates were less endeared. They referred to him, curtly, as Sleepy or Goofy and to me as "the fag from Manhattan." It's worth noting that, to those sons of mechanics and roofers from Hicksville and Lake Ronkonkoma, the words *fag* and *Manhattan* were interchangeable and, in any case, redundant.

Nathan did his set and got up, grinning. "Wow, that's weird. Are you *supposed* to get dizzy, or does that stop when you—"

"Shut up," Mark explained. "Paul's turn now. Breathe out when the weight goes up, then in on the down."

I stretched myself lengthwise across the bench, planting my hands at shoulder width. Behind me loomed the rusty stack. I was suddenly stricken with the crackpot fear that it would fall and crush my skull.

Why not, after all? This stuff was from hunger and hadn't been serviced in years. A cable could snap; a bolt could shear off. *Why was I here in the first place?* Surely, there were girls in the world with an eye for cadaverous Jews. Hell, Kafka found *two* of them.

"*C'mon, already*—while we're still young yet. Between you, I'll be a sixth-year senior."

Drawing a breath in, I whistled it out and hefted seventy pounds in the air. They hung there a moment, eyeing the view, then came down much too fast.

"*Slowly!*" Mark yelled at me. "*You* lift the weight; the weight isn't s'posed to lift you!" He cast his eyes skyward, to the gods of iron. "You *believe* what Myrons these two are?"

"What's a Myron?" asked Nathan, laughing his horsey laugh. "You saying we're like those pocket-protector—"

Mark fastened him with a glare.

"Never mind," said Nathan. "Got it."

Deeply chagrined, I shoved the bar up again and offered some push-back when it dropped. I did a second rep, which went no smoother, and a third, when something strange happened. A radiant heat began filling my chest, as if someone had draped a compress across it. I did another rep and the feeling spread, inching past my collarbone toward my throat. By the sixth or seventh stroke, my forehead tingled and my sinuses hummed with air. I kept on going, losing track of reps, attuned to the muzzy, pins-and-needles buzz that was setting up in my ears. It was sharp and soft, then hot and cool, a multivalent high that kept building. I forgot who I was and even *what* I was, imagining myself as a two-stroke engine and my arms as pistons firing. Dropping that last rep, I was clinically stoned. I lay there, wrists hanging limp at my sides, watching fireworks on the back of my lids.

"Up," Mark ordered. "No sleeping between sets. If you want to take a nap, go to class."

"You all right?" Nathan asked me. "You're all red and whatnot."

"I-I'm fine." I grinned at the whitewashed brick. "That—that thing is *amazing.*"

Nathan gave a look and replaced me on the bench. I watched in a daze till my turn came, savoring the blood-rich burn in my chest and the wash of lactic acid down my arms. The light show had knocked off behind my eyes, and I was once more sensible of where I was, smelling the odor of damp cement and under-lubricated chrome. It was cold enough to see my exhaled breath, and the only noise that broke the workaday silence was Mark's bellicose grunts while benching. But when I looked at myself in the unframed mirror mounted crookedly on the wall, I thought, *This is the thing I've been searching for. I've found it, and I'm not leaving.*

My next set wasn't as long as the first; I tired before I caught a deep groove. But when I got up again, my chest was crackling, oxygen swamping the short-twitch fibers and pop-pop-popping like flashbulbs. I was so flush with pleasure that I burst out laughing. Mark dropped the bar and sat up.

"I just finished saying this is a *temple.*"

He glared bloody murder, then flopped back down and snorted like a bull in a chute. This was his signature before each set, making a racket that primed his lungs and *scared* the plates off the pegs. When he finished throwing the weight up, he leapt to his feet and gave out a barnyard bellow. It seemed to emanate from below his chest or, for that matter, from below his waist, a ruminant combination of high aggression and the animal joy of a good dump. I couldn't decide whether he was pissed or pleased, and made a note not to smile again.

FOR THE NEXT NINETY MINUTES, Mark led us around, presenting the stations of the cross. Despite his gruffness, he was a natural showman and eventually warmed a bit. He had me climb on the leg-press sled and add my weight to the entire stack as he forced up six slow reps. He used us for anchors during lateral rows, perched like pilot birds on his shoulders while he drew back 245. Bits and pieces of his story surfaced as we went along. A stick-thin boy in a Great Neck enclave who'd gobbled up Hercules movies, he'd begun to lift seriously as a high school senior, eating six meals a day to add mass. In less than a year, he'd gained fifty pounds of muscle and forced his way onto the football team, blowing up receivers in the middle of the field as a 210-pound linebacker. Girls came calling, but he didn't much trust them, because where had they been when he was small? What he wanted was someone who saw past the size, who got that he was special, through and through.

He was also, it turned out, a painstaking teacher, staying past his lunch hour to demonstrate wrist curls and to harp on proper technique. We dutifully jotted instructions on scraps of paper, even drawing maps of the Universal, with notes about what to train when. All in all, it was magic time, one of those days when the big wheels turn and your life suddenly moves out from its siding. But what I most remember about that first-ever Pump was wanting it to end—wanting the three of us to split and walk to class, so that I could double back behind them and bench alone.

That, more or less, is what I did, though I waited till after dinner to return. I was sore already through the chest and back, the leading edge of the horror to come, pain so sharp that my eyelids ached from squinting when I breathed. But I wasn't much worried about the bad week ahead or the chances of fraying a tendon. For the first time in ages, I wasn't worried at all. I was head over heels in love. You can talk all you want about sensual pleasure and the beaten pathways to it: tantric sex or the powder in Vail or the nose of a great Bordeaux. For my money, there's nothing like that first set of benches after a three-day layoff. You load out a weight in the low-middle range, enough to get the blood moving on ignition but not so much that you overwork your joints. Closing your eyes, you bring the bar to your sternum and feel that whoosh of current fan your chest. Air, injected in metered breaths, catalyzes the blood like high-test gas, and soon the machinery of muscle and cartilage is humming through the turns. In the heat exchanger at the base of the brain, a flush of dopamine gets released and bathes the skull in warmth. Pain and exhaustion melt away, carried out of the body in exhalations and dispelled for the course of the next hour. As you race down the stretch, The Pump gets stronger, even as you start to lose power. Those last couple of reps are soft explosions, the pulse in your eardrums roaring up as you rack the bar, depleted. You lay there, tingling from the tips of your fingers to the hair at the edge of your crown, spent but whole again, alive in a deep way, waiting for the next set to start. Sadly, it's never as transformative as the one that you've just finished.

Of course, you only get the high after a three-day layoff if you actually take three days off. For a good year and a half after I started lifting, I never went two full days without benching and rarely went more than one. I knew nothing about rest periods or tissue synthesis or the dispersal of cellular waste, and I wouldn't have paid attention if someone had made the point while standing on my chest. Rules were for guys with the time and patience to get big strand by strand, duly marking progress in ten-pound plates and steady, two-rep gains. Put differently, it was for men who'd gotten *laid* in adolescence and didn't have a string of dateless weekends tied to their rears like tin cans. When you're a twenty-year-old male around thousands of girls, none of whom evince even the slightest interest in seeing what you look like with no shirt on, the only anatomy you have the patience to study is your own in the weight-room mirror. And for *that* you'll make all the time in the world—even if it conflicts with your Physics for Poets class.

That first night back, I was in too much agony to get much benching done; the soreness encircling my chest and arms made it hard even to doff my coat. But there were a handful of kids on hand to lift, and I was thrilled just to half-speed a couple of sets and watch them in the mirror. One guy I paid particular mind to was a poor man's version of Mark. He was five-nine at most and slim through the thighs, but strained the seams of his nylon tank top with a splendid, slant-V trunk. Limp brown bangs overhung his eyes, and a funk came off him when

I angled past, the whiff of a kid indifferent—or worse—to the comfort of other people. Still, I found myself fixed on him, struck by his maniacal concentration and the comet's tail of pimples on his back. He was doing a combination of wide-grip pull-ups and high-weight lateral pulls, and at one point turned around and caught me gawking. "Hey, mind giving a spot?"

"Me? Um...yeah. No problem."

I lurched up off the calf-raise bench with no clue as to what that might mean.

"I'm going for four here, so hold me on the neg. This is sixty pounds more than I weigh."

He was facing away from me, gripping the bar. I eyed his pneumatic back and rump, wondering which part of him to latch onto. Tentatively, I reached for his hips.

"Hey, what the *hell*?" He spun around, glaring. "That's not how you give a spot!"

"Sorry. I—I didn't know. This is my first time here."

"Then *ask* a person what you're supposed to do. You don't just *grab* him wherever you feel. That's how people get *hurt*."

He had pockmarked skin and a sparse mustache the color of salt-stained rope. It was his eyes, however, that worried me. They seemed to pulse inside their sockets.

"I apologize. I didn't know the rules here. Next time I'll definitely ask."

He glowered a moment and turned away, once more grabbing the bar. "Your hands go *there*," he said, meaning his shoulders, left bare by his thin-strapped top.

I took hold where he showed me and pushed down firmly. Each time the stack rose, he rose with it. "Harder," he ordered. "Get your weight into it. Jam your knee against my spine."

I did as told and now had three of my limbs in direct or proximate contact with his acne. It was gloriously awful, like being licked by a cobra. I thought, *I'm not eating till March.*

"Thanks," he said when the set was over. "I got three more sets. You don't mind, though?"

"Well...," I said, wanting nothing so badly as to soak my hands in bleach. "The thing of it is, I was about to head back. I've got a paper on 'The Pardoner's Tale.'"

"'The Partner's Tale?' Yeah, I remember that. I used to be a business major. But then I switched to clinical psych. I'm all on sound mind/ sound body."

"I see that," I said, though I could also have said, *I smell that.* My eyes were practically tearing as we talked. Fresh off a set, his stink redoubled, as if it had its own blood supply. "What kind of therapy you thinking of doing?"

"Not sure. Probably work with kids. I'm told I have a way with them."

"Ah...ha," I said. "Well, that—yeah, that's special. Children aren't the easiest group to—"

"They're our *future*," he hissed. "They have to be *healed*, or in twenty years they'll crush us like *bugs*." By way of illustration, he made a fist and clenched it so tight the bones mottled. "By the way, man, my name is Kenny."

I gulped—I was breathing through my mouth exclusively—and had a ghastly vision. There was Kenny in his skimpy top, sitting on the floor of a book-lined office beside a school-age child. They were sorting through a deck of Rorschach cards that proved, on closer inspection, to be black-and-white snaps of women in bondage poses. Kenny leaned in, holding them close to the kid's nose, saying, *What's the first word that comes to mind?*

"Hi...yeah...I'm Paul. Good to meet you."

"You said this was your first time down here. Has someone walked you through the circuit? 'Cause if you want, I could show you when I'm done. I got a couple more hours to go, though."

A couple more hours? Who was he, Sisyphus? "What time did you get here?" I asked.

"Well, I had a late jump. I've been sick all week, which is why I'm looking so small. You catch me next month, though, I'll be ripped and stripped. I'm up to three hours, plus calisthenics."

"Three!" I squawked. "I'm sorry, no offense, but what do you *do* in all that time?"

"What do I *do*?" He scowled. "You're kidding, right? Try, how do I fit it all in."

Four

Body Shopping

THE PAIN, AS PROMISED, was gloriously bad, a Cinco de Mayo spree of inflammation. It started in the sheaths of my knobby delts and radiated south through my arms and chest to a perfect, knifepoint edge along the sternum. There were car alarms wailing in my left and right buttocks, waking up the neighbors in my lower quads with their *wah-wah* protest at doing squats. Even my calves clamored, though for attention, mostly. I had never, till that moment, known I *had* calves.

At several points that night I woke up groaning, but was so exhausted that I fell back under and drowsed till the sun's glare woke me. With terrific effort, I raised my head to glimpse the clock on the desk. Twelve, it said, though my eyes throbbed so that I couldn't tell noon from night.

"You up?" I whispered, too racked to look over in the direction of Nathan's bed.

"Stop shouting," he said. "Why did I go? Someone please call me a doctor."

The day ticked by in a fugue of gray, as clouds lowered to blot the mocking sun. We lay stock-still, moaning like drunks who'd been hurled through the windshield of a car. There was an aspect of privilege in

45

hurting so much: we finally had a reason to ditch Modern Philosophy, the one class we'd both, by coincidence, picked for its "See Spot run" reading list. (Husserl, anyone? Merleau-Ponty? Wrong: *Zen and the Art of Motorcycle Maintenance*. Vroom-vroom, we'll take that A minus.) At some point Nathan, in less dire shape, rose to fetch a bottle of Tylenol, augmented by some stiff blond hash. My fingers and toes thickened, I couldn't feel my palms, and I lay back down to investigate the buzz of bilateral tendonitis.

If I could be said to have learned anything of value from my mother in the eight-plus years I lived alone with her, it was how to milk infirmity for all it's worth. Mom could cultivate a three-day cold into a month-long bout of bronchitis, dragging around the house like something dug up in sections and sewn back together on a slab. She was never happier than when deeply oppressed, listing, in a voice filed down to its nub, her ambitiously original and patent-pending symptoms that clinicians couldn't wait to get their hands on. Anyone could cough blood, but Mom claimed to belch it, evidence of a carnivore stomach bug from a pint of bad cottage cheese. Others got migraines, but hers came with Muzak, an endless, earsplitting loop of Neil Diamond singing "Cracklin' Rosie" only to her. I had no knack for whipping up scurvy from a carton of bruised tomatoes, but I shared her relish for being out of commission with an innocuous case of the flu. It was as comfortable as old slippers and nicely regressive, a kid playing the one small trump he had, which was to pick up his toys and take to bed.

After a whiny day in bed, Nate got up and showered, then dragged himself off to class. With him went the only consolation I had, our brotherhood of grinding pain. Nor did my suffering suggest great things lay in store for me at the gym. Soreness was one thing, but this was absurd, a firestorm in my "pectoral majoris." (I'd admired the phrase when it rolled off Mark's tongue. It made him sound like Ovid's strength coach.)

Still, I couldn't ignore the exaltation of those four or five sets of bench. That was a fact, not some fever-induced dream during the past two nights of torment. In it lay some larger, unseen truth about who and what I was, a reserve of strength I could only intuit from one faint brush at the gym. If you're lucky, you catch a glimpse every decade or so of the person you'd hoped to become, the robust, clear-eyed, thoughtful guy whom life had cut off at the knees. Sometimes it's art that opens the prism and lets you look into your heart: the phrase that reads true, the voice from the stage, the play of light on a canvas. Sometimes it's nature, with its heart-stopping vastness, or a night of peyote and 'shrooms. And sometimes it's a bench in a utility room at the bottom of a college field house. You take your levers where you happen to find them, and if you're smart, use them to crack something open.

And so, three days after I awoke in agony, I marched myself back to the gym. No Nathan this time, and no waiting till after dinner, when other kids would be there to roll their eyes. Instead, I went straight after morning classes and found the place empty and so poorly heated that I had to keep my coat on while I trained. I started off slowly, lowering the pin ten pounds so I could concentrate on technique. In the notes I'd jotted during the session with Mark was the same word *Style!* in three places. There was art in what he did and art in what he got, a body as deftly wrought as da Vinci's nudes. In my Fat Goose parka and boiled-wool mittens, I looked less like a beau ideal than a bear nosing trash cans for a snack. Still, I'd tramped in there when no one else had, and that, to paraphrase Mark, was a start.

Lifting alone proved to be a major boon, letting me figure things out at leisure and unlock the hidden code of the machine. You say, *What's the big deal; it's a fixed-arm rotor. How many different ways can you move a stack?* But this would omit the thousand-and-one niceties that constituted that grand thing, *form.* The pinning of your elbows to your bottom ribs when doing strict arm curls; the tilt of your jaw during a set of shrugs, your eyes fixed at twelve o'clock — it was endlessly variable and counterintuitive, like learning to speak Mandarin or keep kosher. The things you wanted to do, like bend your knees, were the very idiocies that hindered progress and threatened injury. Worse, they betrayed you as a hapless dork to guys who knew the room—the kind of feeb who trained in his overcoat.

From station to station, then, and rep to rep, I set about the task of gaining form. Squinting at the dog-eared sketches I'd scribbled, I strained to keep my heels down and my rear end planted when trying for that last rep on bench. I rolled up my rhomboids and pulled in my lats on close-grip upright rows, then forgot what I was doing and reversed myself on the very next repetition. It was hell trying to keep the right parts moving and the wrong ones from muscling in on the act, while at the same time remembering to breathe out on the upstroke and in on the down, full stop. It got so screwy that I'd go back to the dorm and do practice reps in the john, breathing and manipulating phantom plates while tapping my foot for time. Guys would walk in there, see me air-benching fiercely, and laugh themselves stupid on the can.

Alas—and there was always an *alas* with me, fate hoisting its merry middle finger—I learned that you can't build A-one pectorals from scraps of skin and bone. What's required to make marbleized, long-strand muscle is the oven-ready clay of loose flesh, and for the life of me, I couldn't pack it on. Despite breakfasts so dense in complex carbs—pancakes, waffles, and a stack of toast—that I'd fart my way through French class (*Non pain, non gagne,* say Cannes bakers), and pig-outs at lunch of pork and beans over heaps of chili fries, all I seemed to get for my gluttony was a series of bowl-busting dumps. At the start of January, I weighed 146. By the end of the month, I was 148. Neither of those pounds waved back at me when I stood in the bathroom mirror.

It's at this point that most men pull up a chair, take a long look at their skunked genetics, and draft plans for a career in botany. But if I'd been most men, I wouldn't have nursed dreams of a night with Barbara Eden in genie pants. Instead of giving up, then, I went harder, bringing my workouts home. Each day, after a two-hour blitz at the gym, I cranked set after set of calisthenics, training chest and arms with exotic stunts, while Nathan kibitzed from his bed. With my feet on the desk and my hands on facing chairs, I'd risk paraplegia with dive-bomb push-ups in an effort to carve a midline down my chest. This seemed to get results, at least the short-term kind. After many a pained rep, I'd run to our little mirror and see the first outcrop of cuts—the indent where the triceps and the deltoid divide; the squared-circle band of an outer pec. That inspired sets from increasingly dafter angles, clearing books from the sill so I could put my feet there and do suicide shoulder stands. But moments later, the blood dispersed from limbs that I'd just trained, and with it went the modest little biceps bulge that had set my heart aflutter. It was there one minute and gone the next, a sadistic frat-house prank on the skinny Jew. I was qualified to rent muscle, but not to keep it. Somewhere, the gods of iron clinked their beer steins.

DESPITE ITS HYPE IN THE LOCAL DAILIES as a charnel house of sex and drugs, Stony Brook was, in fact, a commuter school that emptied on Friday mornings, when a broad majority of the kids on campus went home to their moms in Deer Park. This, to my mind, was dispositive proof that the place needed firebombing. Any institution so aggressively dull that its students preferred their parents' to each other's company had, perforce, to be burned to the ground, in favor of an alpaca farm. But one bitter weeknight at the end of February, I came home to Benedict dorm and saw a crowd of raucous kids in the lobby. In my head-down malaise, I had missed the fliers for the quad's first Mega-Blast and was stunned to find scores of girls in tight bell-bottoms thronging the first-floor lounge.

The room, a hitherto unused space now furnished in church-table chic, was dark and dense with churning hips and the heat-flash shimmer of silk shirts. Above it, a short flight up three stairs to a balustrade and service kitchen, stood a tall kid in headphones who was bobbing suavely over a pair of Technics platters. The song he blared was "Love to Love You Baby," all eighteen minutes of postcoital melting from that fallen former choir singer Donna Summer. It was the first disco record I ever heard, and I fell instantly and fatefully in love with it.

I stuffed my down coat under a vacant chair, bought myself a cup of room-temp foam from the kid manning the closest keg, and found a perch on the three-step landing overlooking the sunken floor. What light there was crept in on dun feet from the overheads down the hall, and in the close tumult I creased my eyes to make out form from form. Shapes glimpsed dimly slid groin to groin through the pitchblende basement dusk, disembodied parts picked out and lost in the moaning, bedlam scrum. The music—a bass line and molten voice; a woman gone groggy from sex—spun the room sideways on a free-for-all axis of grinding, dry-hump funk. No words, no chords, no mental dimension or movement above the waist, just the fuck-me confection of fatback beat and deep-in-the-coin-pocket bass. My legs and groin moved of their own volition.

At some point—minutes, hours, what-have-you—the string section came back up. A light went on at the deejay table, a handheld spot singling dancers out with a firebolt of hot, blue glare. Guitars kicked in and other spots blinked on, crisscrossing shafts of pastel light that T-boned a mirror ball. The light blew up into brittle shards of pink, as if a bomb had gone off in a confetti factory. There was a smattering of *oohs* from rubes like me who hadn't seen a strobe refract, but the rest of the crowd kept keeping on, lost in its carnal frieze.

I stayed for two hours, neglecting my push-ups, as the maestro mercilessly worked the crowd, dropping bombs from the Trammps and the Ohio Players. Finally, around midnight, the room began to clear, as kids with early classes took their leave. I was too wired to split, though, and clung to the rail, sopping up any late-coming clues to the phenomenon I'd just witnessed. There were a couple of dozen stragglers waiting out the end, using the open floor space to polish their spins or get some petting in. One of the dancers, a brick-chested guy in a shrink-wrapped Huk-a-Poo shirt, nodded in my direction, then waved when I didn't respond. I shrugged at him, befuddled, and waved back.

"Kenny!" he yelled. "From the weight room, remember? You gave me that weird-ass spot."

I recognized him now as the short, strong kid I'd offended my first night there. He was motioning me over to join his group, which included a bruiser with barn-door shoulders and two underage girls in thick makeup. I wavered but went glumly, coaxed from hiding.

"What's *up?*" cried Kenny, clapping my shoulder. "How you comin' along at the gym?"

"Yeah, good," I said, unable to meet his gaze. "I'm there almost every day now, except Sunday."

"No shit!" he yelled for no good reason, as the deejay had finally stopped spinning. "I'm there, too, like every other day. How come I never run into you?"

"I train in the afternoon, when the place is empty. I prefer it when no one's around."

Kenny grinned at his friend. "Ah, a closet lifter — we were like that, too, right, Jerry?"

Jerry eyed me with vast indifference. "Where we gonna get some beer at this hour? The ladies are *thirsty*, man."

I checked out the "ladies," two Syosset types who, on their best day, couldn't have passed for seventeen. They both sported Farrah Fawcett bottle perms and eyes done up like Roman candles. The tall one *might* have reached the age of consent; the other looked like her kid sister.

"Dude, I'm talkin'," Kenny said to Jerry. "You like it when I interrupt you?"

He clapped my arm again and said I was filling out. He could tell, even through my two shirts. "But what're you taking, 'cause you got those *hard*-grow genes. I was the same way till I blasted through 'em."

"Um...wheat germ," I said, not quite getting the question. "And half a thing of bee pollen, twice a day."

He looked at me blankly, then gave a wink. "No, really, man. What're you bumping?"

"What am I bumping?" I scrolled my brief syntax of iron. "Wait, do you mean *benching?*"

He sent a grin back to the other guy, who was angrily checking his watch. "You believe this noise? He thinks you get big by sprinkling some shit on your Wheaties."

"Yo, we leaving?" Jerry asked. "I'm fuckin' shtahved. Let's do a Jack in the Box run."

The younger girl giggled and bounced on her toes. "Yay, we're going to Gag in the Bag!"

"Hold your water," said Kenny, with a trace of menace. "I'm talking to my *college friend* here."

He looped a sweaty arm around my neck and drew me several paces toward the stairs. "This is the last time I ever date a townie," he groused. "All they friggin' know is pot and fast food. I'm lookin' for a chick who's got some class, who doesn't think 'the big town' is Port Jeff."

I chafed in his hold, which was more headlock than hug and afforded me a whiff of his pits. "Aren't you a little worried about their parents? It's after midnight on a school night, no?"

"Eh, later for them, bro. What about *you*? You seriously think you'll grow takin' health-food crap?"

By now I was roundly and glumly stumped, wondering whether I was being pitched yet another diet, one based, perhaps, on the flesh of high school girls. I wanted to wrench free of him and run upstairs, preserve the excitement of the night's discovery and plot my disco debut. There was so much to savor and ponder on: the sight of those lovely asses moving in tandem; the strange, snap appearance of female wildness. But I didn't pull loose from him. Instead I bent closer. He was, after all, talking about getting *bigger*.

"It isn't about eating," he said. "You could eat till you burst, and the only thing you'll get is a pooch. And it ain't about lifting more hours a day, or banging out the push-ups after dinner. If you really want size—I'm sayin' *really* fuckin' want it—come talk to me at the gym sometime. No, better yet, stay a second."

He returned to his friends and came back after a moment with a matchbook he'd scribbled something on. "That's my number," he said. "I'm two blocks from campus, if you know where the train station is.

Call me tomorrow, and I'll totally get you started. A month from now, you'll be busting out of your shirt. Oh, and one other thing: I don't take checks, so stop by the bank before you come."

UNLESS YOU GROW AND TRAFFIC BLACK TAR heroin from your family's poppy compound in Karachi, there's no good time to go courting addiction, although certain preconditions are better than others. It will be helpful, first, to arrange a stream of passive income that no act of bad behavior can impeach — a trust fund without a sturdy morals clause, say, or, in my case, a modest but open-ended stretch of unemployment insurance benefits. You'll also find it useful to surround yourself with people who couldn't tell a junkie from a jug band, being themselves bedeviled and rendered oblivious by their own narcotic consumption. And third, you'll be rewarded by your selection of a substance whose abuse rate has not yet spiraled and whose telltale markers (the sudden outcrop of "backne" and a hair-trigger temper around inanimate objects) aren't already fodder for Page Six jokes.

Such was the lay of the land when I got off the bus at Stony Brook's railroad station and followed Kenny's directions up the hill. I'd had the dumb luck to have been fired in a year when Unemployment clerks were being swamped with claims, and I was surprised and delighted to find the $100-a-week checks follow me — in error — to school. For a while I'd slipped them in a drawer, uncashed, fretful of being popped for fraud. Then I went home for a rare weekend visit, saw a leather blazer in the window at Macy's, and there went my compunction, if not my fear. Still, like the master criminal I was, I'd stashed most of the ill-gotten jobless money in a slit of the stuffed Eeyore I'd had since childhood and now kept for safekeeping in a padlocked steamer underneath my single bed. It was thence that I'd culled the new-cut twenties now tucked in my shin-high tube sock.

Kenny lived up a little snow-slick rise, in the mother-in-law flat of a brick Colonial. I rang the bell expecting to find tawdry squalor, his pad done up in early *Hustler.* Instead he ushered me into a living room boasting a supple, overplump leather sofa, a smoked-glass troika of cocktail tables, and the honey-maple wall unit of my dreams. It harbored a monster system with McIntosh drivers, a reel-to-reel tape deck of enameled teak, and JBLs tall enough to land a chopper on — or to replicate the din of one taking off. Kenny marked my awe at his big (for then) TV and clapped me on the back for my good breeding.

"I could tell, just looking at you, that you knew from class. I said, 'He's not one of these clowns who sponge off me. Here's a guy who's really, like, well traveled.'"

He thwacked my shoulder hard in approbation. "Thanks," I said, wincing. "I don't know about traveled, though I've eaten in Chinatown."

Kenny looked at me and made a face. Suddenly, he burst out laughing. "See, that's that New York humor I love. Dry, ya know? Dry as a fuckin' bone!"

He bade me sit while he hit the fridge for bottles of "liquid cheer," though it was not yet ten on a Friday morning and I had barely eaten. Sitting there, the cash burning a hole in my sock, my anxiety pitched to cliff-dive quavers, it struck me that he could come back with an ax, butcher me at leisure, and drink my blood for cheer, and no one would be any the wiser. I hadn't told Nathan where I was off to that morning — the beginning of a long and shame-filled silence concerning my dark-world ventures. The cutting of class — again — in pursuit of muscle; the covert appointment with a crib-robbing perv who smelled like ripe Havarti: it smacked to me, frankly, of desperation, and desperation smacked to me of Mom. In my lifelong effort to remake myself as someone who couldn't have possibly been her son, I'd have paid steep sums and braved great risks to emerge as my own creation. My third eye caught glimpses of the man I longed to be — a tall block of granite tanned the color of Scotch in a black silk blazer and cuffed shirt. He stood at a bar basking in the refracted shimmer of light bouncing off leaded glass, and effused the lordly essence of sexual privilege with a come-hither flick of his heavy lashes. Think the young Sean Connery and his carnal smarts on the travertine torso of Steve Reeves, a sword-and-sandals stud with a master's in Chaucer who traveled with a butler and a Hong Kong tailor—that was the polestar I was steering by, the template of a new-style man of words. To get there, nothing was beneath my scruples except admitting how much it all meant to me or how low I was prepared to stoop.

Kenny came back not with longnecks of Bud but two Rubbermaid pints of pink sludge. "Check *this* out," he said, holding mine up, as if somewhere in that glop was a mighty pearl. "Forty grams of protein in a single serving. Drink two of these a day, and you'll split your shorts!"

He popped the spout on his and took a gulp. A stringer of fluid dribbled down his chin.

"What's in it?" I asked, watching the runoff closely to see if it ate his flesh. When no harm came to him, I sipped from mine. It reeked of violent night sweats in a Circle K men's room.

"That's real cinnamon," he boasted. "I grind it myself, to cover up the flavor of liver powder."

I was working through a mouthful when the back-taste hit me. I closed my eyes and swallowed, fighting tears.

"Damn, dude, you're sweating. See, it's working already. You want me to get some water with brewer's yeast?"

"No!" I croaked. "I mean, do you have a soda, or something in a bottle that isn't open?"

"*Soda?*" he snorted. "You drink that crap? No wonder you're so thin; you've fried your colon."

He seized my wrist and checked my pulse, a brusquely impersonal thing to do. "Look how fast for someone your weight. Should be fifty beats a minute and...whoa, you're zooming!"

This made me conscious of my chugging heart, which seemed to want to vault itself clear of my chest, bolt the short staircase back to the street, and hop the first thing smoking to Manhattan. As Kenny dissertated about healthy bowels and the "anabolic blast from a good enema," I could feel my throat pucker and my fingers thicken; my feet wouldn't follow a direct order. *He's drugged me. I'm paralyzed!* screamed a tiny voice. *I have to break free, or he'll chain me up!*

"The — this — you know, it's great. I feel the burn," I said. "How much for a week of it, or is it by the pint?"

He looked at me, befuddled. "Pint of what?"

"No, the whole thing — the drink, the powder, whatever. I brought cash, but then I-I've got to split."

He continued staring in mystification. "Hold up, dude. You think I'm selling *weight drinks?*"

"Um...yeah. I mean, *no,*" I said, reading his gaze. "Not the drink so much as the, uh, you know, stuff that's in it. I assume, of course, that I'd just add milk?"

A laugh like an ischemic seizure overtook him. "Dude," he said, "you just made my week! Stay here a second; I'll be right back in...Holy fuck, he thinks I'm hawkin' weight drinks!"

I heard his cackle from down the hall, disrupted by the bang of metal drawers. Surely now, the bone saw would make its debut, and lawn shears for those trickier organ cuts. *Leave!* I thought-shrieked. *Run while you can!* But my brain-body connection was on the fritz. My legs still functioned, as I assured myself by taking a stumbling tour of his etagere. On the top shelf, enjoying clear pride of place, was a loving sacrament to Ozzy Osbourne: a foot-tall replica of the Sabbath front man, half-naked she-wraiths encircling his knee, and a silk screen of the Ozzman glaring down from a throne of flame-tongued blood. The shelves below held an album trove fit for an abattoir, with early Sabbath, Uriah Heep, and the moist debut of Judas Priest. (The murder of British blues-rock! Film at eleven!) Two truths emerged for me in high relief as I scanned the back cover of *Rocka Rolla*: one, the secret of the zillion-selling Eagles, who for all their crappiness and fake *duende* had never recorded three songs back-to-back called "Winter," "Deep Freeze," and "Winter Retreat"; and two, it was possible to be a full-time student and still make pots of money. *Whatever* Kenny was selling me in the service of bigger arms, it clearly had a market out there and a roster of repeat business. Maybe, I thought, admiring his Teac headphones, I could be a rep for him, like Amway.

He came back cradling a large display case of fine-grained oak and ash. It was footed with plush, like a jewelry chest, and locked with a key he kept on a ring attached to his chunky belt. "You ready?" he said before raising the lid. "You man enough, 'cause this will make you king."

"Yeah," I said. "I guess. If I can afford it."

"*Wrong,*" he said. "Wrong answer. You can't afford *not* to."

I ducked his glare by eyeing the box. For all I knew, it housed a tiny wizard.

He gave me one last baleful look and threw the hasp on the lock. Within, bizarrely, was an antique pistol that looked like a pearl-knobbed toy. But the voile panel beneath it lifted out, baring a stash box lined with felt, with custom-fitted slots for the goods on offer. And what goods they were, those vials and bottles and old-style chrome syringes—a sales kit arrayed like a centrifuge that melded the black and white arts. I caught myself gaping at the thin-gauge sharps and unsayable, all-capped names, the DECANOATES and OXANDROLONES that read like a Runic chant. A shiver went through me, deep and wide: I knew in that spectral moment I'd crossed a line. Whatever else happened in this half-lit room, I'd been brought face-to-face with hard fixation. That I hadn't acquiesced yet missed the point. I was *there,* rendered up to it in grasping need.

Kenny uncorked a cultic spiel about steroids and their "health potential," calling them drugs that "could wipe out sickness if the crooks at the AMA stopped printing lies." He explained that steroids had been "slanderized" since their creation in Hitler's labs, developed by the führer to make super-soldiers out of "faggy soccer players." Alas, in Nazi hands the drugs had worked *too well,* turning hops farmers into SS killers. But for guys like us, he said, "decent dudes who got the short end of the shaft," steroids were a "fair but nonlegal" chance at what endomorphs gained at birth. "DNA," he sneered. "What a crock of shit. How can I help that my pops was five foot six?"

"Yeah, and mine's six-one and solid," I offered, to back his point about nature's pretzel logic.

"Well, he probably didn't up and book to New Hampshire with some slit he met on his truck route. I'm guessing you hear from yours more than once a year, and *forget* about getting a postcard on your birthday."

The abruptness of the disclosure, and its acrid sadness, brought our dealings to a halt.

"How old were you when he left?" I asked. "I was ten, and we haven't spoken since November."

"No?" he said. "I never would've thought it. You seem too stuck-up to have just your mom."

"Who said I had *her*?" I said. "My dad, at least, is sane, but Mom, she thinks the pizza guy's coming to kill her."

"You serious?" His eyes widened. "Mine's bat-shit, too. Our house was like the Museum of Liberace. She's probably been to Vegas twenty times to see him, and there's pictures of him on every goddamn wall. When I was little, I used to think *he* was my dad, but gradually I got older, and, you know..."

"He got gayer."

"Or something."

I looked at him a moment. "You really think I'm stuck-up?"

He colored. "Well, yeah, as a matter of fact. That or queer."

Now I blushed. "Why do people keep *saying* that? Maybe if I stopped dressing like Gary Glitter..."

"That would help." He nodded fiercely. "And how's a Jew, if I can say so, get all caught up in the glam-rock thing? I would think that that's against the Sabbath rules."

"As opposed to the *Black* Sabbath rules? Trust me, Ozzy ain't playing Tel Aviv."

He broke out his startled, rat-a-tat laugh, turning around to share it with Osbourne's likeness. "Ozzy in Israel? Man, that'd kill! He'd bite the fuckin' heads off kosher bats!"

And so it went for the next couple of hours, our newfound kinship of lost-boy loners trying to make their way in life. Kenny, like me, was an oldest child who'd been deputized much too young and, also like me, couldn't wait to abandon his mother and live like a free-and-clear orphan. His latest plan involved saving the money he made from steroids to found a chain of gyms for chemical lifters. "My message to the world is, it doesn't really matter. What you were born with, or *without* it, you can fix there. Because that's what the gym is, when you think about it: a car repair place for people. And check it out, dude, I got the *perfect* name for it. You ready for this? The Body Shop."

"You know, I like that," I mused. "In fact, I like that a lot. When you get that all together, I want to work there."

"Good," he said. "I'll need you, 'cause it'll be *strengthy*. There'll be guys there — serious *monsters* — who'll design your workouts and come to your house and *punch* you if you don't show up. There'll be people to help you eat right, and a dentist to fix your teeth up, and a hot-chick skin doc to fix your dermal needs. And of course — of *course,* man — there'll be guys in white lab coats to write you out a scrip and get it filled. That'll be the slogan of the Body Shop: Better Lifting Through Chemistry."

"Ah," I said. "Interest—"

"Get it? *Lifting,* not *Living.* I think that's killer!"

By now I'd settled back for his *killer*s and *strengthy*s, the free-jazz locutions of a kid who'd written his own playbook. He had, in his element, a kind of wonkish charisma, sounding like someone who'd taken first prize for the science project he'd made of his upper body. I could envision him, years hence, giving talks at middle schools, explaining, in the tuned-down lingo of his preteen crowds, why it was essential to begin juicing before puberty.

But there was also, in his fervor, more than a hint of megalomania. It scared and repelled me even as it gave me hope. Would I, too, start street-preaching the gospel of Winstrol once I'd dosed my way up to killer delts? Did steroids make you grow a messiah streak and talk in outdoor voices to the unconverted? And what of Kenny's slew-footing changes of mood, the sudden shift from pissed off to impassioned? Was that part of the package deal he'd signed with Satan — big arms in exchange for male PMS?

"So what do you think?" I asked, tapping the case. "If I started out now with just some basic stuff—"

"A cycle's what we call it. Or a stack, if you're doing a combo. Why don't we hook you up right now?"

"What, you mean shoot up here?"

"Why not?" he said. "No extra charge. You seem like good people, and we got some shit in common. Also, you know, it's nice to give back. Maybe down the road, you'll do something for me."

I shriveled in his gaze. "Um...all right."

He led me down the hall to a bonus space off the galley kitchen. Kenny had fixed it up as a mini-gym, with a flat bench, dumbbells, and facing mirrors. "I like to shoot here," he said, "where I can see behind me, really focus in on where I spike. Shooting in a bathroom is just fuckin' wrong. You got little spores of shit and, like, foreign matter all floatin' in the air around you. I don't need *that* in my ass."

"Um, no," I said, shaking. "Neither do I."

I watched as he unwrapped a needle and filled it with an amp of Deca-Durabolin. "Don't worry, dude, I don't sell beaters — that skank-ass slag from Mexico. This is top-grade gear from Europe, man. The finest labs in Moscow and East Berlin."

Holding up the needle, he tapped the barrel, forcing little bubbles to the top. "Now watch," he said, finessing the plunger a skosh, "the air goes out, and you coat the sharp with juice. That way, it goes in a whole bunch smoother and you don't wind up with as many bruises."

He handed over the syringe and undid his belt; I thought he'd use it to tie my vein off. Instead he dropped trou and turned around, presenting his naked rump in its many splendors. I gaped, unable to credit my eyes: the skin was a crazy quilt of grays and mauves and hardened lumps that looked like topped-out landfills. "Don't worry about the welts; I'm doing a big stack now. It's just to show where you start out spiking."

He sketched his cheek in quarters with an index finger and grabbed the toughened meat of the northeast quadrant. "You jab it in quick but not *too* quick, hear, and only go three-fourths in. That way, if the needle breaks off in your butt, you still got a piece to pull out with your pliers."

"*P-p-pliers?*" I squawked. "But why's the needle break?"

"Hey, it happens. Your butt's thick and the needle's thin."

He gestured for me to face the wall and reached for the snap on my jeans.

"Whoa, I got it," I said, pushing his hand away. As I bent to drop my jeans, though, his palm was on me, showing how to pulp the cheek for shooting.

"Put your weight on your off foot so the skin hangs loose and lean against the wall there for balance. The reason you shoot it here and not there or there is, no major veins to jam you up. You ready?"

I felt his stink-cheese breath upon my neck. "I—I...yeah, I s'pose."

"'Cause if you want, I'll do ya this first time out. Spare you the risk of swelling up."

"No, I've gotta learn. Just give me a little room to swing my arm."

He moved to the side a foot and knelt to guide my hand, his nose mere inches from my ass. But just before I jabbed the needle in, I stopped and drew it back. On the one hand, this serum, for all its short-term bang, might possibly—i.e., *definitely*—cause me long-range grief whose nature I'd no way to foretell: the onset of cancer in my thirties, say, or a disfiguring outcrop, on the day I turned fifty, of warts and boils that spelled out *Ozzie Rules!* On the other hand, fifty was a long way off, and by then some nuclear madman could have dropped all his bombs and lumps would be the least of my troubles. In the meantime— *My God,* I thought, eyeing Kenny's forearm, the veins of which bulked like snakes in bedsheets—in the meantime, life was blowing by me going eighty, its arm around the hot girl riding shotgun.

I was still puttering around in my moral lab when a white jolt brought me to. Kenny, having taken my pause for weakness, had shoved the needle in and pressed the plunger. Stunned, I shifted weight to my right (i.e., wrong) foot, and the knotted fibers of my buttock yowled, bruising right before my eyes. A ripple of fuchsia was fanning out. For a dopey moment, I thought I'd hemorrhaged.

"*Ow-ow-owwww!*" I yelped as the pain bit back, its second pass no gentler than the first. From hip to tailbone, I felt a sprawl of heat, as if someone had scattered buckshot in my ass.

"See? You fucked up." Kenny gave a grin, taking wolfish pleasure in the fact. "Next time, *listen* when someone tells you stuff. It might just save you a *hebe-a-toma*."

"*What?*" I glared, not game for Jew jokes, not with a seam of lava in my rear.

"Nothing," he said. "It's a word I learned in Bio. It means 'bruise,' and that one there'll be a smoker."

Five

Lead Me Not Unto Penn Station

Three months later

IT WAS THE BEST PART OF THE DAY for me without exception, an event
rich in perverse vindication. I'd get back to the dorm around five
o'clock, when, in the hour before dinner, the hall was alive with kids
congregating in doorways, kvetching or boasting or letting off steam
as the term wound down toward finals. Fresh from the gym, arms polished as chrome, my chest and back swollen with glycogen chaff, I'd
yank off my clothes, cinch a towel at my waist, and strut the forty feet
to the hall john.

Three steps in, I'd feel their eyes upon me and mark the sudden halt
in conversation. Pretending to check the contents of my shaving kit,
I'd lift my gaze slowly as I strode along, giving them the chance to look
away. To a man, they all went right on staring, trying to connect the
carved specimen going by them with the skeletal, sexless wreck they'd
met in January. A few kids mouthed *hey* or inquired if I'd come from
lifting, noting my answer with a solemn nod, as if they were keeping a log. Once, someone asked me if I trained each day, implying,
in a pinched and hesitant voice, that maybe, *heh-heh,* I should take

a week off. For the most part, though, that twenty-second stroll was met with baffled silence. Given the Jew jokes I'd weathered from those kids, their speechlessness now rang out, to my ears, like a round of wild applause.

Once in the john, I'd take a long shower, rubbing lats sore from pull-downs and a cock so insistent it practically seized the cream rinse and jerked itself. I'd been slow to connect my won't-quit erections to the Deca I now spiked daily and the blasts, twice a week (or as often as I could get an ampule), of soft-shooting Winstrol Depot. Winny, as it was lovingly called by juicers, produced little bruising at the injection site, carved like an ice pick the mass you'd gained on Deca, and made the veins in your forearms bulge hours after you'd done your last curls. Between those two serums, I had weaned myself off D-Bol, the Molotov-cocktail tablets I'd gulped four of a day till the acne on my shoulders grew its *own* muscles. With that off the menu, I had but two symptoms: thirty-odd pounds of brand-new muscle and a dick that wouldn't take no for an answer.

Exiting the shower with my hair slicked back, I'd clasp hands before me and press my palms together to goose the fast-twitch fibers in my chest. Then, and only then, would I step to the mirror and gape at the stranger that was me. The dockworker arms, with their bell-curve lines and vascular, shrink-wrapped skin; the rounded corners where the pectorals met and stood a little taller by the day—I had to keep checking my own reflection, touching and poking, rejoicing. Even my face broadened, filled its own hollows, looked hand-carved, confident, *ready*. What a thrill it was to wake up each morning and lope down the hall for a glimpse, admiring the crescent of a medial delt when I struck a side-chest pose, or the brand-new bulge of a lower lat, which I could see by torquing my back. It was Christmas in springtime when I strolled the oval, startling the girls (and more than a handful of guys) from their head-down, get-to-class trance. And all that was prologue to the late-day jackpot of racing the stairs of the empty field house, shoving my bag under the calf-raise station, and installing myself on the

Universal to fire off a set of benches. The rush that went through me then was more stacked a high than any I've had since. There were times I literally couldn't stand the bliss and had to walk the practice field behind the building till my heartbeat slowed to a sprint.

I had trimmed my hair back to a manageable shag, ditched the glitter T-shirts for tight Lacostes, and consigned my heels to the back of the closet, in exchange for high-top Nikes. The size came in steady, insistent gains—two to three pounds of mass a week, most of it above the waist—and no one seemed to notice till the weather turned warm the third or fourth week of April. The coats came off then, girls lolled on the grass, and heads started spinning when I passed. My English teachers gaped when they called on me, used to my prolix take on Hawthorne but not the suntanned hulk who raised his hand. Kids in the dining hall asked me where I'd been and why I'd avoided their table. Even Nate didn't know what to make of me, grinning in mystification. "Who *are* you?" he asked at the deli counter, after a line parted to let us through. "Are you some kind of pod person who ate my roomie, and if so, could you eat my teachers?"

But walking the walk only gets you so far; at some point you've got to talk the talk. Two nights a week, I'd pull a tight tee on, head across campus to a disco kegger, and ask a stranger to dance to "Love Machine." Often the girl obliged me, we'd do the Latin Hustle, and after three or four songs' worth of spins and box steps, she'd give me a look that said, *Well?* I'd open my mouth, state my name and major, and realize, with the same sickening flush each time, that I'd emptied my store of conversation. She'd tell me her name and shout something back at me that I could or couldn't make out over the din, and I'd grin and say, "Cool!" or—drumroll—"Really!" then lapse into end-stage aphasia. A moment of blank horror would pass between us, and soon she'd remember that her friends were ready to split or that she'd left the iron on in her end-hall lounge, and I'd find myself alone on the crowded floor.

Back in the room again, I'd lie awake stricken, playing the film over in my head. I'd always been anxious and blocky around girls, talking to them in a stilted tone, as if they spoke only high school French. Was it possible, I fretted, to be *sexually* stupid, capable of communing with Yeats and Pound and even the most purposefully recondite Joyce, but not with Joyce from Ronkonkoma? I was miserable at science and brain-broke in math, so literacy had its hard limits. Were females the equivalent of quadratic equations, impenetrable to the kind of men who read *Ulysses*? And where were the *women* who read *Ulysses*—didn't they like to shake their groove thang, too? Surely, at one of these dances was a word-drunk girl with a body by Frederick's of Hollywood, an alien like me in this right-brain barren on the hunt for her bookish twin. I'd know her when I saw her; there'd be something in her eyes: the glint of playful cunning. She needed to come soon, though. I was running short on cream rinse, and the grout in the shower was starting to chip.

FOR WEEKS I'D BEEN PUTTING OFF KENNY'S request to go clubbing with him and his crew, saying I couldn't party till finals were done and all my papers turned in. But he kept after me when I copped from him, griping that I owed him for getting me big. The last week of school I finally relented, though my essay on the *Decameron* was badly stalled, in part because I hadn't read the book. Generally, this didn't matter—I'd simply crib the critics—but while Boccaccio was translated, his scholars were not, and my Italian ran to *Ronzoni, sono buono*. Lilting though that was, it didn't gild my thesis about the rise of bourgeois mores in the Middle Ages.

I was pulling on a new pair of low-heeled Fryes and trying to goad Nate into tagging along when the phone on his desk started ringing. At that hour, generally, it was his mother calling to inveigle him about her health. Sandy was a woman in her late-ish forties who had the piercing croak of a Palm Beach harpy and was always in the throes of some self-named plague, coming down with cancers previously unknown to science and *spiral,* as opposed to spinal, meningitis. Since Nate rarely answered, I'd sometimes man the phone with her as a proxy-resentful son, getting treated to a spiel about the Asian flu and the millions it had killed in Pyongyang.

That night, neither of us was in the mood, and we let the phone ring till it stopped. A couple of minutes later, it started again, and Nate grabbed the receiver, incensed. "What's the crisis *this* time, Mom?"

He listened for a moment, then hung a grin. "Uh, sorry, I thought you were..." He cupped the mouthpiece with his palm. "Fuck, I think it's your father."

"My *who*?"

I hadn't spoken to Dad since the day I'd left town, when, with minutes to kill, I'd called him from the train. It had been a tense chat, his tone remote, saying he thought it best that we take a break. "I know I've always been your mom's bull's-eye," he'd said then, "the one who ruined her life, or some such nonsense. But I don't have to take it from my oldest son, whom I've worked like crazy to support. When you're ready to be a mensch and not a grievance collector, then I'll be happy to talk. But until then—and it starts with an earnest 'I'm sorry'—I'll settle for some peace around here."

"What's *he* want?" I whispered. "He sound pissed?"

Nathan shrugged, cupping the mouthpiece. "Should I tell him you're at the gym?"

I thought it over a moment. "He'd never believe you."

I took the phone warily. "Yeah, this is Paul."

"Hey, it's Dad," he said blithely. "Who was *that*?"

"Uh, my roommate. He's going through a phase with his mom."

"So I gather," he said, laughing. "Well, at least you're not alone with mother hassles."

Or father hassles, I didn't say. "Yeah, his calls a lot and mine never does, so..."

"So be grateful for small favors," he said. "I still get calls from her once a week. Whether I like it or not."

"Right," I said, unsure what to make of his strangely convivial tone. "Look, I thought we were on hiatus. Wasn't that how we left it?"

"Well, time wounds all heels, as they say at Florsheim, and it's been months since our little blowup. I have some thoughts on what went on then, but they can..."

There was static on the line. "Yes, hello?"

"I'm here," he said, his voice back in range. This was an old tic of his—starting a sentence clearly, then fading out by the comma. "As I say, I've done some thinking, but that can keep till later. How's your grand return to college life?"

"All right. Lots of reading. Still a ton to do."

"Well, good," he said. "So the time off helped. There's nothing like getting knocked on your butt to bring the mind around."

"I guess."

"Pardon?"

"No, nothing. I was agreeing with you."

More noisy silence.

"Anything else you care to share with a father? How's the *scene,* as they say now? You dating much?"

My ears reddened. "Um, sure, you know. Hand over fist."

"Aha." He brightened. "Anyone special?"

I winced. "Not so you'd notice."

"Well, there's something to be said for that, too. At your age, sex should be a pastry table. 'I'll hev a little Danish, a little strudel.'"

This last was uttered with a borscht belt lilt, and I stared at the earpiece in horror. Who was this tummler on the other end, and what had he done with my father?

"So, let's see then: classwork, your love life—what's that leave? Playing any ball in your spare time?"

Now my heart stood in pride. "Yeah, I get to the gym a bit. I've put a couple of pounds on since I left."

"Oh, *there's* good news," he said as Nate guffawed, shooting me a puzzled frown. "I've been worried about you; you were gnawed to the bone. You needed to be back in school for *lots* of reasons."

"No, I'm glad I... Wait—what's *that* mean?"

"I'm sorry, it's hard to hear you. What was...?"

Again he sank beneath the buzz, competing with the tumult of the hall. I feared we'd been disconnected, but then he came back up, asking how I planned to get home. I had a week left on campus and then a loose arrangement to share a summer sublet with my brother. It was up near Columbia, where the *cucinas* and dive bars would be full of foreign-exchange girls from Montmartre. Dad disclosed that he'd spoken to Ivan and said I'd been smart to find a share; the "landscape" over at his house wasn't the best now. "Besides," he said, "I'm sure you'll want your freedom, with all the half-dressed women walking Broadway."

By this point the remnants of a protein shake were backing up in my craw. Still, he *was* dangling a lift to New York, and I dreaded having to board a train to Penn Station with all my worldly store on the seat beside me. "Everyone's leaving next Friday," I said. "You think you could make it out here that night?"

He wasn't optimistic; Friday traffic was hellish, and Saturday he had his son from his second marriage. "But Sunday's free," he said, "and you can probably use the time there to wrap up your affairs. Broadly speaking."

Of course, I thought. *Fathering on his terms and schedule.* He asked for directions from the campus gate and was about to hang up when he caught himself. "Wait, I almost forgot."

Christ, almost off. "Yes, Dad?"

"Well, a funny thing happened. My typewriter broke, and I had to use your old one while it was getting fixed. And when I brought it upstairs from our storage space, I came across some things you'd left in the case."

My chest wall tightened. The journal I'd kept in high school? That green marble hash pipe that had gone missing? "Like what?"

"Well, some art history papers from your first year of college. And the thing is, a couple are quite good."

I almost dropped the receiver. "Say again?"

"Yeah, there's one on Michelangelo called 'Slings and Eros' that gets at the porn in his *Pietà*. It's a little heavy-handed in scoring its points, and from the drift of it, the whole Renaissance was queer, but you've certainly begun to string your words together."

A gulping pause. "Really?"

"Yes, really. In fact, not to load you with cheap advice, but you've got, I think, the makings of a fine art critic, and they don't grow on trees, as you probably know."

"I—actually no, I didn't," I stammered.

"Well, pick up a copy of *ARTnews* sometime. Most of it's just trained chimps typing. Anyway, I wanted to pass that along and thought you could maybe use a boost."

"Yeah, thanks," I said to him. "Thanks very much. I guess I'll see you Sunday, around noon."

I put the phone down, gave Nathan the headline, then went out and strutted the quad in manic glee. *Yes! I have talent!* I wanted to shout at the parked Chevelles. *I'm practically an art critic already! While you mouth breathers get degrees in criminal justice and spend the next decade walking a beat, I'll be at openings with Lucian Freud, debating which of us will bang the Danish girl! So yes, I'll have a* big life, *based on this* very rare gift, *which I knew I possessed all along!*

Alas, while walking back to my room, I remembered that art crit bored me and that I'd only taken the courses because they reprised soft high school classes. This left me, in the scheme of things, worse for wear, a misfit for my one true skill set. It also ratified a trend so old it might simply have been joint fate: my father and I couldn't stage a conversation without one or the other coming away bruised. Even the best intentions seemed to raise a welt, leave their recipient mouse-eyed. We could wave to each other from across the gorge and send platitudes about patching things up. But whenever we spoke, the wind blew hard, turning words into blunt projectiles.

THE CLUB, ITS NAME FORGOTTEN NOW, was on Montauk Highway in the beach town of Freeport, Long Island. Big, round, and dark, it was raked like an arena, with a bowl-shaped dance floor, bars on three levels, and seats going up the velvet aisles. Kenny loved the place, and it was easy to see why: there were five hundred girls there on a Wednesday. We walked through the foyer, and my breath stopped short. They were *everywhere,* in fragrant, suntanned knots.

"What I tell you?" He grinned, wrapping an arm around me. "There's more box here than UPS."

Maybe it was nerves, but I doubled in laughter, high off the whiff of pheromones. You could smell it in the air: the mass perfume of sex; a thousand kids vying to get naked first. I turned a slow circle, clocking the freak tableau with a dazzled, capering grin. Hallucinatory strobes ran wild above us, cracking the dark like summer lightning. Fridge-size speakers kicked bass so big, it set my heartbeat bucking: *DO IT ANY **WAY** YOU **WAAANNA** DO IT, DO IT ANY WAY YOU **WANT**...*Kenny shouted something that was lost to me, and I followed him down the stairs of the unlit aisle. With each step, the sound gained and filled. At the bottom, it was like a gale that pushed against us.

Kenny ordered beers from a guy with cantaloupe delts who wore a gray polo that read SECURITY. They hugged, and Kenny slipped him an amber vial in lieu of a five-dollar bill. "Happy hunting!" shouted the guy when Kenny introduced us. "Anything you need, you come see me!"

"Thanks," I yelled as we walked away. "Nice to have friends in high places."

"That's no friend; he's a Smoke," said Kenny. "Half the guys I deal to are cops and staties."

"Really!" I said. "Who're the other half, mob hitters?"

He gave me a look that retired the topic. "I only go for blondes. What's your preference?"

We got to the dance floor as a song set ended. On the track's last note a strobe exploded, and a thousand laser sapphires fell to earth. They drifted in silence, threading the air, then a cat-scratch guitar loop came in. It was the opening chimes of "Love Rollercoaster." I hugged myself in helpless, giddy joy.

KENNY FOUND THE GIRLS, or maybe they found us. In the scrum of unheard come-ons, it was hard to know. There were four of them, then two, the others melting away, taken by the tide of arms and legs. We were bunched up together, brought belly to belly by the crush of bodies around us. The girl I was paired with shrugged and smiled, as if to say, *When in war...*

I strained to make her out in the booming dark: a gleam of pink lip gloss, newly freshened; full hips snug in pin-striped jeans; and tan shoulders bared by a Lurex top that glittered Day-Glo purple and mauve. We could barely move our feet without kneeing each other and danced in place till a track came on that opened the floor a bit. With nowhere else to put them, she had her hands around me, one draped languidly over my neck, the other in the small of my back. I clasped mine primly between her waist and rib cage and arched to hide from her my frothing hard-on, which thrashed and lunged through layers of cotton like a crazy uncle chained up in the basement.

One groove led to the next, the rain-forest heat soaked my shirt clear through, and at some point my thigh wedged between her legs, grinding strong to "Lady Marmalade." We didn't make out—it was a bridge too far with someone whose acquaintance I hadn't made—or put much effort into conversation after a couple of tries to shout above the din. But after one song she tugged my shirttail up, miming for me to flex: a grin of approval, and then she took my hand and pulled me off the dance floor toward the stairs.

Christina drove a Bug, an old Super Beetle that someone had jazzed up with lime paint. We sat in its unconducive cloth front seats, still panting from our strenuous mock coitus. In the quiet of closed windows, we both turned shy, and she reached for a joint in the flap of her purse as she talked about life in Cedarhurst. I didn't catch much of it—my ears were stoppered, after an hour or so of bomb-blast entertainment—but managed to ascertain that she worked for a dentist and resided with a woman who may have been her stepmom and a misbehaving Yorkie called Fribble. She had an accent I found jarring—part Brooklyn, part Yarmouth—and a habit of ending clauses with nervous tropes like *you see what I'm saying here?* It was a little like chatting with a building inspector, but as the dope did its work, she softened in stages, sanding down to sidelong girlishness. "I have to tell you," she admitted, "I'm kinda nervous. My girlfriend's actually the wild one. I'm more shyer."

"Really? Me, too," I said. "I might look like I've got it together, but once that music stops, I'm just..."

I held up my hand, exaggerating a tremble. She took it in hers and laughed, giving a squeeze. "Oh, thank God."

We both let out an extravagant laugh, though mine rang the least bit hollow. She took no notice, or affected not to, talking about her vastly less inhibited friend and her haste to hop in bed. "It's like three, four dances and she's out the door gone, then comes back an hour later with her bra backwards. I mean, I know times have changed, but we *are* both still Catholic, and there *is* still a person called the Devil."

This seemed a lousy time to raise my Jewishness, though it would surely come up if we stayed on subject or if she thought to ask my last name. It occurred to me to lie, but she had my hand in both her palms and was pressing it in good-girl apprehension. Between her earnest perfume and the white-blond down on the back of her sunburned shoulders, I was beginning to feel awful about my angry erection, the bulge of which I covered with my wrist. Yes, she was pretty beneath the layers of makeup, her full cheeks burnished by the dashboard glow, a tangle of curls draping her tawny neck. And yes, she was *close* to me, just a stick shift away, her arm brushing mine as she lit a Newport. But she was nervous and chaste and owned a dog named *Fribble*, and it felt drearily unfair of me to reach across the seat and pull her in. How typical, I thought, to have walked into Gomorrah and come out with the one girl who said a novena after having an impure dream about Sly Stallone. Kenny was God knows where now with the carnal Theresa, doubtless doing push-ups with her legs around his neck after hits of amyl nitrite in his Triumph, while I was being treated to a spiel about diseases you could catch from kissing strangers. "My cousin Marnie met this boy at Club Med," she was saying, "and came home with a case of mono. It lasted for like a month, and she missed my sister's wedding, and so now they're not talking, which goes to show."

Then again, her patter saved *me* from speaking and likewise provided an opportunity to map out my escape. I thought of my old friend asthma, but I had been clear for eight years now and was far too stoned to stage a fake attack. I could have mentioned the term paper that needed an ending, but that would necessitate my leaving the club, and I had no inclination to budge. I'd found my little heaven in this pulsing dome, a Kubla Khan of women who roamed in packs, their eyes done up like New Year's Eve. I was staying all night, then coming back Friday if I could swing a ride again with Kenny. And if that panned out, hell, I'd catch the train on Sunday and see about finding a two-month share. I'd be twenty-one in weeks, and the world was finally smiling, spreading its arms in welcome. *Be here now* was its salutation. *Join us,* added the breeze through my rolled-down window.

I was getting good and trashed off her green-stemmed Hawaiian and decided to go on sitting with my hand in hers till a bolt of inspiration lit the way. The night was lovely, with a gold-watch moon, and Christina seemed happy to have an audience. At some point, I thought, she'd simply *have* to stop talking, and maybe then I'd lean in and kiss her softly, if only to get back in practice. It was all experience, and I needed it in droves—good, bad, indifferent, come what might.

"Boy, you don't say much, huh."

I glanced up. "Sorry. I was listening to you."

"No, that's good, I like it. You're not *blah-blah-blah,* like all these guineas bragging on their cars. Twenty-four years old and still living with Mom so they can buy a new door kit for their Firebird."

"I go to school with guys like that, but don't, um, really hang with—"

"They're babies and always will be, but you, you're different. You're a regular man of mystery over there."

She smiled at me, a drowsy, searching smile, and then her hand was under my shirt. "Well, with a body like this, you don't *have* to speak. Your chest does all the talking."

IT TOOK ME FIVE MINUTES to tug off her Calvins in the clowns-in-phonebooth confines of the Bug, and another minute or more to regain the vision in my right eye after I bonked it against the passenger's side visor.

The front seat stymied all attempts at coupling, and the rear wasn't a lot more amenable, with its sharply raked roofline and window crank that kept poking at the crack of my ass. It would've been simpler to wedge a piano back there than two tall, well-proportioned adults, though when she kicked off her heels and Lily of France hipsters, we did manage to achieve a sort of congress. I was nominally on top but kept sliding off sideways onto the hump in the middle of the floor, and between the hard bench seat and the carpet that scraped my kneecap, I'd long since crossed the line from pleasure to pain. She stopped her minimally effective thrusts and asked me if I'd done this before.

"What, you mean screwed in a VW?"

"No, not the car. I'm saying *ever*."

Oh, the horse blanket of shame — the cold, coarse thing she heaved on my startled back. "Of course I've done it. How can you ask me that? It's this *seat*, goddamnit, I can't get any traction!"

"Well, you don't have to take His name in vain. It just seems like you haven't got this...down."

"But that's crazy," I squawked. "It's the car, I swear! You put me in a Lincoln, and I'll fuck you senseless."

She gave a dubious sniff and went radio silent, craning around to see where her Newports went. I half sat up in a furious sulk and was about to say something grossly unmanful when my anger — or the change of angle — reinflamed me. My foot had found a toehold in the right rear door well, and with my left delt wedged against the musty seat back, I finally had some leverage to push and pull with. I started back in, going left as she went right, fucking at a forty-degree rake. She gave a little grunt of muffled surprise, then pushed at me, tilting her hips. Suddenly, there was warmth and a wet, tight fit, and we slid and locked like two snug lengths of track. Now she was whispering, a sibilant spool of words not consistent with the teachings of Vatican II. Inspired, I pushed harder, happy to send her to hell, which I imagined to be a more cramped version of this car, when her byplay turned to insult shtick. "*Fuck* me, you wop bastard. Yes, fuck me *there*. That is so the spot, you dumb greaseball. Yes, I need it there, but harder, *harder*. Give me all your cock, you filthy gweed!"

"Um, I'm Jewish," I muttered, in the general spirit of things. "I'm the big, dumb Jew that's fucking you hard."

Her eyes snapped open in reflexive dread. Small tears sprang up on her lashes.

"Oh, just bang me," she said, and sobbed a little. "Just fuck me really hard, you Jew fuck!"

I FOUND IT VERY TOUGH TO SAY goodbye to Nate, who left the following Friday with his parents. From the first day he'd been more than a kid I shared a sink with. In his hang-loose cheer I'd seen an opening, a chance to break the trap of pessimism and get out there with the rest of the self-haters. Though a child of the seventies, he embodied the yippie koan of *Nothing matters and what if it did,* letting life come at him in all its force and expend itself, blunted, at his feet. It took balls to be that calm in your first year away from home, coolly insisting on going your own speed while everyone else around you scrambled. Then again, it could have been the weed doing the talking. Either way, I found I liked him fiercely.

Perhaps he felt likewise, because he seemed to take all day to pack a single suitcase and a duffel. Plucking a sock out of his drawer, he'd stuff it into the bag, then sit and gab about the resurgent Yankees before stowing the other sock. When his labors overtaxed him, he rolled up a jay and brought out a stash of Hostess Sno Balls. Chewing those pink horrors, with their hairbrush frosting and wet-cement chocolate cake innards, precipitated a beer run at three p.m., and we were both good and plastered when his parents arrived on the dot of six o'clock. Sandy Weisbrod was smaller than I had imagined, a rumpled woman with a ski-bump nose in a skirt that hung as flat as campaign bunting. She sat at his desk, produced a couple of aspirin, and served Nate a lecture on "the value of people's time" as he finished tossing gym shorts into his duffel. "I'll bet you *Paul's* father isn't kept all night when he's good enough to drive here in the rain."

"Actually, he's not coming till Sunday," I said. "I'm stuck for two days here by myself."

"Well, he's obviously an Important Person with things to do, whereas we, like schmucks, raced while this one dawdled. Hey, what're you putting pens in with your shirts? Do you *know* what it's like to get ink out of a collar?"

Nate unloaded the suitcase and repacked it from scratch, an act of such fine-tuned passive aggression that it sent his mother digging for more Bayer. His father stood by, sucking the gap between his molars: a tall, colorless man in starched short sleeves with a wisp of hair that seemed to wave surrender. Finally, around eight, Nate ended his slowdown strike, and the happy family was ready for the road. He turned around, deaf to his parents' prompts, and held his arms out for a hug.

"So Brooklyn, you know—it's two trains away, and you don't need a passport to visit."

"I hear you," I said. "Same goes for Manhattan. Come in and we'll go clubbing one night soon."

"Like hell," said his mother. "No clubbing for this one. He's on a short leash, with those incompletes."

I passed him a look. "We'll figure it out. I'll call as soon as I know my new number."

"Yeah, well, don't count on him *answering*," she shot back. "If a phone rings in *my* house, I pick up."

I glanced at his father, who beetled his brows. "When I sit, I don't like to jump up again," he said. "That's how people trip and hurt themselves."

I AWOKE THE NEXT DAY IN AN empty dorm, spooked by the seclusion and a free-range sadness. Anxious, I called Kenny, who was having a bad time, too, having roughed up his girlfriend the night before. "It was only a half swing—a backhand, really—but she was all crying and whatnot, and then her friend got the owner of the club, and he damn near called the cops. I mean, it wasn't my *fault*, bro. I caught her on the stairs with some dude pressing up on her hard, and you shoulda seen how fast his punk ass ran when he saw me charging up the stairs. But still, that's not me. I don't hit chicks."

"Is she all right?" I asked. "You didn't mention a girlfriend when we went out the other—"

"She's fine," he said, "but not the point. The point is, I'm fuckin' spazzed and need to talk."

He was over in twenty minutes in his TR6, a stubby red ragtop with a fickle shifter that torqued like a crossbow in fourth gear. I had a yen for pancakes, but he grunted and drove, taking the Sunken Meadow at a gallop. The parkways on Long Island are not without their charms, particularly in May, when the poplars knit a fedora overhead, but no one in his right mind takes those contrapuntal curves as a signal to start gunning his engine. Kenny was doing eighty for no obvious reason, holding the wheel with one hand while squeezing a punchball in the other and screechily switching lanes past honking cars. He braked only to downshift for the Northern State, then once again floored it, zooming west. "I'm *upset*," he said when asked to go slower. "Speeding is what calms me down."

He careered around a blind turn and almost rolled us over, leaning on the sides of his tires. I turtled up as we bucked and pitched before angrily settling down on four wheels. "*Whoa!*" he yelled while straightening his steer. "I practically got us *airborne* on that bitch!"

"Let me out," I said when I could speak again. "Just anywhere. I'll take the train back to school."

"Why, because we three-wheeled? Bro, I *so* had that handled. It was—"

"Stop the car *now*, goddamnit!"

He drove till we came to an ample shoulder and pulled up onto the grass. The motor of the small car heaved when he shut it down. I opened my door and was tumbling out when he checked me with a hand on the arm. "Wait," he said. "Give me a second, man. I got something I have to tell you, and..."

He was slouched far down in his bucket seat, his eyes glazing over the wrapped wheel. Cars blew by us, heading west against traffic to the inlying beaches or the city. Whenever one passed, the vibrations of the road plate rattled the bolts in my door.

"I — I was sorta lying about hittin' my chick. Well, not lying exactly. I did grab her wrist, and it did kind of bruise up on her, but that's not why I'm so freaked."

He glanced at me quickly, then looked away. "Did'ya ever have, you know, some totally fucked-up dream that kept coming back and waking you up?"

"Not really," I said. "But I'm sure I will tonight. Besides, aren't *you* the psych major?"

He was worrying a callus on his upper palm, the pad of which was ridged from years of pull-downs. "Just seems like every night now, I'm up at three a.m. I even started throwing down a couple of Tueys, but so far, they're not helping."

My drug education being wildly erratic, I had no great sense of what Tueys were or how they'd mitigate a bad dream. Nor could I guess why a guy I barely knew was poised to air his dirty laundry on a very busy stretch of the Northern State. "Look, could we maybe do this over a beer?"

He gave a slight shrug. "Got a case of Millers in the trunk. They're warm, but there's a chunk of Moroccan there, too, and a pipe in the compartment on your door."

Oh, splendid, I thought. *Let's just arrest ourselves now and save those busy troopers the aggravation.* "Well, go on, then; I'm listening. But please, man — and no offense — but could you sort of tell it...fast?"

"Hey, you think it's easy? I got *knots* in my stomach. Look at this, they're like ropes."

He hiked up his shirt. I saw no ropes, just a long year at Rikers, awaiting trial.

The dream, when he could finally bring himself to share it, started the same way each time. He was walking alone on a country road when someone in a blue car stopped to chat. A man, obscured by shadow, opened the passenger door. The hand he extended sported a mitt. "Sometimes it's a goalie's glove and sometimes a catcher's — but you ever hear of a catcher being *left-handed*? There's never really been one, 'cause you can't throw out a runner if your ball's always tailing into right."

He looked at me intently, as in, *Take that, Freud.* I ventured a nod, sphinxlike. "What's he saying?"

"Well, that's *also* fucked-up, man. He doesn't talk. It's just these eyes looking down at me over the door. And what happens is, I run, and I'm tearing through the forest and getting cut by these stickers in my legs. And I hear him coming behind me, and then I'm digging under a fence and my feet are stickin' out of the hole I dug. He grabs one and I guess he's got a blade or something, and, well, that's when the weird shit starts."

"When it *starts*?"

A sweat sprang up on his hairless arms; it gleamed in the sun like varnish. "I'm wondering if it's diet, all this protein shit. Is it natural to eat four cans of friggin' tuna? Maybe if I got more fiber, it would normal me out. That or had an *apple* once in a while."

I said it couldn't hurt, then posed the obvious questions. Had his dad reentered the picture lately, been heard from via phone or mail? What about someone from the way-back past, an older kid or neighbor who'd roughed him up? None of these rang a bell for him, and because I lack all tact, I asked the thing staring us in the eyes.

He sat in damp, combustible silence, a dozen moods flitting across his face. His chest rose and fell, now blotched a deep roan. I felt, as *he* surely must have, utterly naked.

"No," he said finally in a watery voice, and hastened to turn the key in the ignition. "Look, I need to train, man. You up for doing legs? I know a guy who'll open the gym for us."

WE SPENT THE DAY LIFTING and running the beach, then met up with his friends in Oyster Bay, where I, for the first time ever, got blind-pig drunk. I awoke Sunday morning wearing my egesta in a shower stall of the john in my empty dorm. Stumbling down the hall, I saw it was almost eleven, leaving just an hour for me to pack my things and be ready for Dad's arrival.

Alas, I hadn't picked up extra luggage to accommodate the muscle shirts and straight-legged Levi's I'd bought in the past two months, and I was going to have to make some hard decisions. I could find room for several of the glam-rock tees, but from there it came down to pure sentiment: the faux-satin flash of Huk-a-Poo shirts or my collection of five-inch heels. Both had been fixtures of the past four years, and both felt intrinsic to some version of me that I wasn't quite ready to junk. Pacing the room, I tripped on one of the shoes and almost cracked my skull against the desk. This I took as a sign from on high and hastily tossed the shoes into the trash. Just to make sure, I dropped to the floor and did thirty reps of wide-grip push-ups. I checked my reflection in the lighted mirror. My eyes were glassy and etched in flame, and each of my cheeks throbbed as if slapped. But my fresh-shaved chest? It gleamed like bullion: beveled and drill-pressed. *Money.*

I left to heave the shoes in the parking lot dumpster before I could change my mind. Returning, I saw a man coming down the hall, squinting to read the numbers on the doors. He turned with a smile, coming forward partway. "Ah, hello," he said, scoping my chest and arms, his eyes still adjusting to the indoor dusk. "I got a little lost, coming in through the back there. This *is* floor 1A of Benedict Hall?"

I stared at him a moment. He was smartly tanned, but his steel-wool hair had begun to thin. He was wearing a shirt rather like my white Lacoste, though being my father, he'd adorned his with mementos of meals past—a splotch of mustard here, a bit of bread crumb there. He returned the stare shyly, taking in my grin with mild but growing alarm. "I—I'm sorry, could you tell me where Paul's...?"

He stumbled back a step and reached for the wall. "Oh my Christ," he said, sliding down.

Six

Eight Million Naked Tails in the City

THAT SUMMER, and for several summers to follow, Manhattan seemed ungoverned, a free-range bedlam. It started with the air, which could be seen from Monmouth County—an oleaginous haze overspreading the island like the gas from a chlorine spill. Asthmatics and seniors were trapped by the smog, kept indoors for days at a stretch and going out only after nightfall. The heat, its coconspirator, had substance, too: you could smell and taste it on the back of your tongue, an acrid, ash-tipped thing that left you smudged. The *Post* was packed with tales of brazen murders, people shunned the subways after nine p.m., and Times Square was so prohibitively feral that even the massage parlors and gay porn theaters fled up Eighth Avenue for safety. The sky was falling and no one cared. Everyone was much too busy getting laid.

Because that was the flip side in those death-star days—a town and its natives mad for sex. Lawyers walked to work with shirts half-buttoned, presenting their chests as Exhibit A in the case for mass psychosis. (In clubs like Regine's, a hirsute trunk was shorthand for "Come here much?" In restaurants like Adam's Apple, it was a public health nuisance, and on midtown streets, a plaintive cry for help.) Women fired back by squeezing their rumps into sausage-casing Sasson jeans, then clomp-clomp-clomping around in Kork-Ease sandals, the straps of which cut like willow switches. On billboards, there were nicely gratuitous shots of girls in Maidenform panties and countervailing pics of the pitcher Jim Palmer in low-rise Jockey briefs. Swingers' clubs were thriving in the Flower District, sex tourists from Europe thronged the bathhouse scene, and every other month or so a disco opened, citing, in its breathless mission statement, the glories of ancient Rome. If New York was going down, it was going down *fucking*, a penis or pendulous boob in every hand.

I'd been warned about these changes on the ride home from school by my palpably rattled father. As he drove, he'd glance over, then look away, as if I were a solar eclipse in the next seat. "I-I'm speechless," he repeated, though in point of fact he wasn't, going on at length about my newfound brawn and his hope that I'd wield it with "tact." "It ought to be your ace in the hole," he tutted, "and doesn't need parading in public. You might try looser clothing—or at least button the shirt you're *wearing*—and let it be your secret with some lucky girl."

Out of grudging duty, I tried to thread a button through the hole of my taut Lacoste. It took all manner of tugging and squirming, but I finally got it lodged and settled back. Then I let a breath out and the button *exploded*, clipping the windshield in its flight. Dad shook his head. "Exactly."

He launched into a talk concerning the perils of sex. Chief among the risks of "carving notches on bedposts"—his felicitous phrase that called unhelpfully to mind the oeuvre of Woody Woodpecker—was the chance of my maybe "knocking someone up." This would pose a nightmare on any number of fronts, not least of them that it would be him, not his penniless son, who'd wind up footing the bill for the abortion. And then, of course, the diseases, of which the less said, the better. "Penicillin or not," he said, "the clap is no joke. Just ask our old friends van Gogh, Keats, and Nietzsche."

"Keats died of syphilis? You sure it wasn't Shelley? I always get the Romantics mixed up."

"In *any* case," he harrumphed, "I hope I'm getting through here. You've built yourself a body, but it's no defense."

Beyond the prim lecture, it was hard to get Dad's read on his new and improved first son. He seemed, on the one hand, vexed and appalled that I'd done this yahoo thing, repudiated nuance for Popeye arms and shirts that spit buttons at loved ones. But he also seemed pleased, or in any case intrigued, by the wild left turn I'd taken. If nothing else, his kid had finally shown some gumption, stopped moping around in a passive sulk and become an active agent in the world. It had saddened him to watch me waste my adolescence, parked in front of the tube during weekend visits. While other parents were trying to rein in their teens, he was always noodging me to call a friend and find out where the "wild parties" were.

It was late afternoon by the time we reached the Triborough, and he asked if I'd like to stick around for dinner. My stepmother was out with Isaac at a Disney film, and it would be a chance for us to catch up and "mend fences." (Metaphor dependence was part of our problem. Straight talk isn't literary and shouldn't be.) But I was fatigued by all the fraught air between us, to say nothing of the stuff coming in the window. He dropped me off at Ivan's on 113th Street and tactfully declined to walk me to the door. "I've seen some of Ivan's other apartments, and a few still give me nightmares," he said. "Remember the one on Seventy-third Street that he shared with those stoner kids?"

I did in fact recall that fetid two-bedroom, a furnished flat scented with rotting meat and aromatic mold above the tub. Ivan and one of his roommates were dropping acid like Tic Tacs, brazenly boosting groceries from the A&P, and throwing foodstuff out the window at unsuspecting couples leaving the corner bar at closing time. (The couples were gay, the bar was Boot Hill, and the projectiles uncooked hot dogs. Somewhere in that mix was both an unsolved hate crime and a stunningly gauche use of symbols.) One night the cops showed up at the door; Ivan and his friends cowered in the hall. "We can *hear* you in there, idiots," called an officer. "Open this damn thing up or we'll break it down." Ivan let them in, and they searched the place, taking in the filth with hard-hat scorn. After satisfying themselves that any drugs had been flushed, they huddled in the front room for a minute. "We've decided we're gonna teach you a lesson," said the sergeant. "We're gonna stay all night, if that's what it takes, and make you clean this filthy shit hole up."

"Well, that was a while ago, but I'll guard the windows," I said. "I'm sure you don't need the aggravation."

"No, I don't." He nodded bleakly. "I really don't. Life on Seventy-eighth Street has gotten..." He twirled his hand, struggling to end a sentence that had said plenty already.

Here, then, was the subject, if not the occasion, for dinner: he and his third wife, G., were on the ropes. It shouldn't have been a shock: she was twenty years his junior and liked to make her point by slamming doors, while he, an avoider of domestic strife, beat a retreat to his air-locked study and knocked off a review of samizdat fiction. It was, like his first two, a head-scratcher marriage—the selection of a woman with whom he shared little but a zip code and an advanced degree—and supported my theory about sexual blindness, that smart people make dumb lovers. You saw it all over the literary harem that was then the Upper West Side: brand-name writers and critics and editors churning through spouses and children. I always knew it was Friday at IS 44 by the overnight bags the Jewish kids schlepped on their way to custody weekends. And then we'd get stoned on the walk home from school and forget which parent to report to. For years my mother and first two stepmoms lived three short blocks apart. Once I rang the doorbell of stepmom number one and was reminded, through the garble of intercom static, that not only was she not married to my father, she wasn't currently *speaking* to him either.

"Are you two going to...?"

"I don't know, Paul," he said. "I shouldn't have raised the subject. No one wants to hear their old man's problems. But it does, I think, go to the point I've been trying to make. Be *careful* out there. Please: use your wits."

He said this last with such rueful frankness that I thought, for a moment, he might cry. It occurred to me, through the dull lens of filial shock, that I ought to reach out and render comfort; take his arm or his wrist or—no, not his hand. But uncertainty seized me and froze my limbs; I stared off in a rictus of panic. My father loathed sentiment in all its forms, detested its deeply American falseness, the cued violins and concocted tears and patriotic *schnorring*. I shared his contempt but was broadly confused: I couldn't tell sentiment from feeling.

"I'm sorry, I didn't know you were—"

"Well, don't be," he said, stoutly bucking himself up. "These things have a way of working out. And if they don't...well, I'll jump off that bridge when I come to it. The Jews, as they say, have had it worse."

And there we were: the double-metaphor dismount. I let myself out and popped the trunk.

IVAN'S SUBLET, TO MY AMAZEMENT, was a Shangri-la: a classic-six apartment with an eat-in kitchen and views of the Hudson from its windowed den. I walked the rooms with him, asking how he'd swung it, but he, as per his way then, was oblique. "Belongs to some Marxist," he murmured and shrugged, then wandered off to roll himself a Drum. In those days that constituted a monologue; Ivan was a cipher in plain sight.

Our third man, David, was a childhood friend and a bit of a Marxist himself. He'd taught himself Russian, joined the Workers Party, and was driving a cab while he earned a degree in international affairs. It was dicey to work nights or to pick up fares going north of Morningside Heights, but David had the courage of his commie convictions and braked for crazies and dope boys. He was streetwise and funny on every subject but power, and to prove his bona fides on social justice, he played host to a string of fellow travelers. The one who stayed the longest, a Nigerian kid named Edson, took a fierce shine to Lola Falana and "the great nationalist singer, Elting John." I'd hear him in the kitchen, mashing chickpeas and croaking, in his wind-whipped reed of a voice, "Phil-a-delphia free-dom, I luh-uh-uh-uv you...yes, I do." By the end of his visit he had latched onto jingles, absently ironing his one good shirt while singing, "Don't cook tonight...call Chicken Delight."

I dropped my bags in the smallest of three bedrooms; checked the fridge, whose only holding was a jar of pickled herring (David, espousing the views of a Soviet dissident, also chose to eat like one); and rifled the kitchen cabinets for a phone book. Thirty hours after my last set of benches, I found myself in acute withdrawal. But the white pages were useless and the yellow had next to nothing, even under "fitness" and "health clubs." For all the sudden license to parade their flesh, New Yorkers weren't rushing out to *tone* said flesh or to profit from the fad by opening gyms. I turned up only listings for the branches of the Y and a single, self-dubbed "men's spa" on Columbus. As the only Pump I was likely to get at the latter was a bungled hand job in the sauna, I called the McBurney Y about Sunday hours.

"Where you off to?" called Ivan as I passed the parlor, where he and David sat talking. I'd slung my weight belt over a shoulder and was clad in a black wife beater and the too-short cutoffs I wore when I did squats. "Wait, you're going out like *that?*"

"Yeah, it's my workout gear."

He traded glances with David. "I'd think again."

"What for?" I said, sidling a couple of steps over to check myself in the mirror. I looked, I thought, imposing in my Leg-Day getup — the quads gleaming nicely after I'd shaved them bare, and the vastus medialis (the muscle above the kneecap) rounding up. "This looks fine. What's the problem?"

"Paul," said David gently, "we're on the border of Harlem. The brothers see you wearing those — those hot pants there, and there's going to be a world of shit."

"And how many times do you want your ass grabbed by the Puerto Rican trannies on a hundred and tenth?" Ivan added. "I see both your butt cheeks, and *I'm* trying *not* to."

I checked the mirror again and pulled the shorts down in back. This did little to protect my rear end but unhoused the tip of my penis for all to see.

"No, *c'mon!*" cried David, averting his eyes.

"This is just wrong in every way," moaned Ivan. "I've lost an older brother and gained a hooker."

I stormed to my room and plucked a pair of jeans from the unpacked duffel on the bed. In the first-of-summer heat, though, the ball-squeezing Calvins clung to my sweaty thighs and barely budged. Able only to pull them over my hips with one great Jaws of Life effort, I marched back to the parlor for inspection. "There now. You two happy?"

Again, an exchange of looks.

"Fuck it," said Ivan. "I hope you took jujitsu in college."

THE MCBURNEY Y PROVED to be a wash for me: a mixed bag of forty-somethings jogging the oval and a collection of elderly war-camp survivors shuffling between pool and sauna. Watching them in the weight room lift a five-pound plate, then sit motionless in the window like Komodo dragons, induced in me an existential panic. On a tip from the janitor, I gathered my things and raced to the Y on Forty-seventh. Instantly, my mood brightened: from the sidewalk I could hear the bellicose grunt of a powerlifter two floors up, and the *clung-ung!* of a heavy bar being reracked at the end of a monster set. I dashed off a check to the membership clerk and ran the two flights up without taking the tour.

Ah, but how, reader, in this age of commoditized fitness, do I render, with anything like full faith and credit, the *Eyeless in Gaza* scene I walked into? The smell alone beggars my power of description, though I can still call it up on command: that sharp, boric musk of air-dried sweat on the ruptured red-vinyl padded benches, mixed with years of grit in the cracks of the gummed floor mats and the rust and sporiferous mold on the leaky pipes. It was weeks before I managed to stop breathing through my mouth there, and at least that till I adjusted to the viscous heat that started my armpits dripping when I entered. The room, a long rectangle with wide-paned windows that no one short of Samson could open or close, was always between five and ten degrees hotter than the temperature on the street, and an ancient AC emitted uncooled air in intervals with puffs of dust.

Perhaps that explained the state of half-nudity that a number of the patrons favored. In the cage nearest the door, a crew of bruisers was training in chalk-smudged Speedos. They wore wrestling boots and cropped-top tees, and as they took turns strict squatting four hundred pounds, I caught myself thinking, *These are the world's strongest gay men*—till I overheard them talk about buy-and-busts. *Aha,* I thought, harking to Kenny's admission that half his steroid clients were cops. Still, it didn't compute for me: *narcs in bikinis?* What Busby Berkeley nightmare had I stumbled into?

THERE WERE FIVE DAILY MEALS I made it my business to eat, and breakfast at Tom's Diner (aka Monk's on *Seinfeld*) should probably have counted as three of them. I'd start with four eggs and a life raft of bacon in a moat of maple syrup, then mop up what flotsam my fork had missed with hunks of maple-walnut muffin. Before I knew what hit me, I'd order a black-and-white shake, a brick-thick decoction of U-bet and Breyers that went straight to my temples and left me sugar-shocked, the happiest man from Harlem to H&H Bagels.

The *Times* and the *Post* before me, I'd savor, with the luxuriant lentor of a sultan, the triple-sweet rebirth of the New York Yankees, who were back where they belonged, at the top of the American League East, after twelve years of penance for their crimes of empire. They were an extravagantly strange cast of kooks and curmudgeons: Mickey Rivers, the minstrel of a leadoff hitter, who was beloved by beat writers and bemoaned by black leaders for his Stepin Fetchit butcheries of the language ("My goals are to hit .300 and stay injury-prone"; "I was brought up in Florida, which ain't different from New York; the climax are about the same"); Dock Ellis, who'd once thrown a no-hit game under the influence of blotter acid; and Graig Nettles, the great but dyspeptic third baseman, who fought his own teammates, sneered at Billy Martin, and openly lobbied for his owner's death ("The more we lose, the more Steinbrenner flies in. And the more he flies in, the better the chances for a plane crash"). God, I loved that team, and not just for its rancor — the sniping and brawling and belligerent bus rides that led Nettles to remark to a writer one night, "When I was a boy, I wanted to be a player *and* join the circus. With the Yankees, I get to do both."

I was hunched over my third set of box scores one morning when a voice going past me said, "They win?" I looked up blurrily, displeased at being pestered by the owlish Greek waitress working breakfast. "Every day you ask that, and every day I —"

But the woman standing before me was neither fifty nor fat-armed. She was, instead, the fine-boned strawberry blonde I'd seen when I walked in. She'd been sitting with a textbook of surpassing heft at a booth two behind mine on the aisle, drowsily ignoring her burnt-brown muffin and cup of well-creamed coffee. I'd noticed, in the flash-bulb way the eye has of storing bits of aberrant information, that she was wearing what appeared to be pajama bottoms over a pair of torn Pro-Keds, and that even in the haggard, smog-dulled light, her lush hair shimmered like foil.

"Yes. Yes, they did," I said, properly dazzled. "And Baltimore, you know, lost, so, um..."

"Aha," she said lightly. "And is that good?"

"Um, well, yeah," I explained, trying to hear myself think over the sudden, lunatic clamor of my heart. "They're the bullies in that division and have been for years, going back to Boog Powell and Frank Robinson. In fact, ever since the Yanks collapsed in 'sixty-five, when they all got old seemingly overnight and CBS, who'd bought them, basically left them to rot..."

But she didn't want to know about the transfer of power down the eastern seaboard of baseball. What she chiefly wished to hear of was the health and well-being of the Yankees' all-star catcher, Thurman Munson, about whom she had been solicitously concerned since she was taken to her first, and last, baseball game and saw Munson knocked cold while blocking the plate. "I thought he was dead, the runner hit him so hard. The whole place just went *ohhh*," she said. "But then he got up and actually stayed in the game, and from then on I'm just, *Be nice to my Thurman, people!*"

"Really?" I said, not quite stifling a giggle of greedy exaltation. "No, yeah, he's fine. In fact, he's having his best season. If he keeps on driving in runs at this rate, they might just have to give him the MVP."

"Well, that's all well and good, but I'm worried about his brain. I used to be a skier till I was twelve years old, when I cracked my head hard on a patch of ice. I had a bad week, then thought I was getting better—but the dizziness came back when I stood up fast, and I *still* get headaches that last days."

"Oh, that's *awful,*" I said, practically knocking over my milk shake in a rush to clear the papers off the table. "How're you feeling now—would you like to sit down? It's terrible when your head hurts. There's no escape."

She wavered for a moment, switching the text from arm to arm. "Well, actually, I was headed out. I'm having one of those days now. But..." She looked me over warily. "Eh—you can walk me to the drugstore."

Telling myself to breathe (and paying scant attention), I dropped a three-buck tip on a breakfast that cost five and rushed ahead to get the door for her. Outside, she blinked against the slanting light, and I impulsively raised the *Post* to block the glare. "That's nice of you," she said, "but now I can't see, and if I fall down a manhole, I'll sue your tail off."

"Oops," I said, "sorry." I offered my shades; these she accepted with a nod. "There," she said. "Now I can *see* your tail, which I'd much rather do than sue it."

It was at this point I had to repurpose the *Post,* using it to shield my fierce erection. I was wearing, to my misfortune, white carpenter pants, which, far from protecting hapless passersby from the contour of my raging schlong, functioned rather as a bully pulpit for that clenched pink fist of Jewish power. "Um, well, thanks." I glanced behind her. "I kind of like *your* tail, too."

"One thing I should mention, though, and take it for what it's worth: never wear zebra-striped bikini briefs if you're going out in sheer white jeans."

"*Fu-uck!*" I cried, changing the paper's position so that now it blocked my *Post*-erior. This negated, however, my earlier work in this matter, and she got a fine glimpse of her little admirer.

"My, you're really having some day." She guffawed. "I don't know whether to thank you or call the cops."

"*Please* just go in front of me so no one sees. *Christ,* I'm such an ass. I'd no idea."

We walked, single file, to the drugstore for Bufferin and from there on to her place off Riverside Drive. I stood with her on the steps, my heart churning butter and my stomach doing triage with the horror of breakfast, gurneying out its dead through my duodenum. By now I'd learned that her name was Kate and that she was taking summer courses at Columbia, trying to steal a march on her bachelor's degree so she could apply to NYU law school in the fall. I'd gleaned, moreover, and without much prompting, that she'd broken up bitterly with a "shit" called Bennett, who'd slept with half her girlfriends back in Dayton, Ohio, in revenge for her having strayed once in New York. "Never date the youngest of three sons," she said. "He tries too hard to compete and doesn't know it."

"Oh," I said, turning this wisdom over. "Well, I'm the oldest of four, so what's that make me?"

Her eyes did the slow-boat tour of me. "Underdressed."

"No, *besides* that already. Take a shot."

This time she studied me above the neck, tilting her jaw in mock earnest. "All right, let's see: you...probably play lacrosse at...C. W. Post and major in something manly, like marketing."

"Pfhah," I hooted. "Stony Brook. Honors English."

"Really?" She dropped back a step in reassessment, her lively, pool blue gaze taking its time. "Well, all right, then, Mr. Literature, who's Volpone?"

"*Volpone?*" I cackled. "That's the best you've got? I can recite his monologues while doing flips."

She folded her arms archly. "Okay, modern fiction: what's the name of the narrator in *Invisible Man?*"

I pretended to think it over, enjoying the game too much to rush. The delay also afforded me time to scope her out, and this I did with relish. She was shorter than I'd have liked, five foot four or five, but had the high waist and swanlike neck of someone a fair bit taller. Her hair, almost orange in the acid sun, fanned like a mane and went a third of the way down her back—a long, lustrous pelt that loved the light. There were caramel freckles on the crowns of her narrow shoulders and a faint pink tint to her porcelain arms, a reaction either to me or the abradant heat. "He *has* no name; he's supposed to signify for every black man who's gone unseen. Got any other trick questions?"

Her brows rose in mild surprise. "Yeah. Why does a guy who reads real books walk around dressed like *that?*"

"I know," I said. "I need new clothes, huh?"

She shrugged. "I'd bet there are women who see you on the street and ask you back to their place, bing-bang-boom."

"Well...yeah. I mean, *you* just did."

She looked over her shoulder and let out a laugh, surprised to find herself on her front stoop.

"Look," I said, "if I go straight down to Morris Brothers and buy myself a decent pair of slacks, do you think I could take you to a flick on Friday, and maybe also a bite before or after?"

"What, you can actually talk about *eating* after that smorgasbord you had for breakfast?"

"Oh," I preened, "I was just warming up. You should see what I devour after training."

She stroked her sharp chin, drawing the drama out. "Yeah, why not," she said. "I've never dated a cyborg; you can show me where you hide the flying saucer. But only on condition you buy a real shirt, too. If they sell one in a store that actually fits you."

WE SAW *The Man Who Fell to Earth,* though I remember nothing of it, other than that it seemed to run six hours. We had dinner at O'Neill's, and that, too, is fuzz now—the bellicose drone of postshow diners shoved together at tiny tables. My memory, however, blinks on in the cab, when I gave the driver directions, scooched in beside Kate, and asked her if she'd had a nice time. Her eyes were bright and almost laughably vivid, as if they'd siphoned all the color from the blue-black night and offered it up for my delectation. Before she could answer, I cupped her face and poured out my heart to her in a kiss.

"Well!" she said, breathless. "You got *that* out of the way. Let me just take a second and count my molars."

"I like you," I burbled. "I mean, I *really* like you. You're beautiful and sweet and charming and funny, and about forty times smarter than the women I've dated."

"Oh. Thanks, I *think.* You're cool yourself, though it isn't the greatest form to trash old lovers."

"No, all I'm saying is, you're in a whole other league. I didn't know girls my age were as smart as you."

"Pardon?" She tittered, her dry smile shrinking. "You're not doing yourself any favors."

"I-I'm...Let me try again. From the top." I took a breath. "What I *thought* I was saying—and I don't know *what's* with my mouth tonight—is, well, I go to college in Nassau County, where the women tend to mostly...Oh, *that's* no better!"

She gazed out the window in barbed amusement, in no great hurry to bail me out.

"Look, I really *like* women and, frankly, prefer them to guys, just in terms of the people I've called my friends." (*The people I've called my friends? Who am I, Mel Tormé? Who the hell speaks like this?*) "I mean,

I've always just been able, you know, to confide in them, to open up about the way-back stuff, my childhood and—and growing up, those types of things." (*And which women, exactly, did I have in mind? The ones slinging hash at Tom's Diner?*) "In fact, to be honest, with the exception of my mom, whom *nobody's* been able to get along with much, I think I've done better than most guys out there when it comes to, you know, um, relating."

Eyes fixed on the potbellied midnight cabs that skimmed Broadway like schooling groupers, she didn't say anything for several seconds, head bobbing as we bounced the washboard street. Then it hit me: she was *shaking*, not bobbing, convulsing under the strain of stifled mirth.

"Wha-at?" I quavered. "What's so funny?"

"You," she said, dabbing her eyes with a wrist. "You're either putting on a hell of an act, or you're the dumbest smart guy I've ever met."

"Huh? I—wait. I don't get—"

"It's all right," she said, tapping the top of my thigh in a provocative act of solace. "It just means I've got my work cut out."

KATE'S REMAKE OF ME started three nights later, in the closet of my too-small bedroom. With a ruthlessness born of mercy, she combed my wardrobe and divided the lot into two piles: the "barely acceptable" tennis shirts that were tight but not sluttishly so, and the "crimes against nature" tees and shorts fit "only for a girl named Vanessa." A regular at thrift stores, she'd staked me to a set of vintage short-sleeve shirts, Arrow button-downs that bloused in back but whose cuffs could be rolled to show my arms. She hocked me to stop taking sun each day on the tar-paper roof of my building, saying the deep tan made me look like a Jew trying to play an Apache on *F Troop*. And she urged me to ditch the high-top Nikes for something grown-up, like suede loafers. "Summer camp's over and not a moment too soon," she said. "There's no Color War, even in state school."

In addition to the shirts, she had schlepped over supper, at least the makings of same. "A guy who's left home," she said, "should be able to

bake a chicken and sauté up some greens in oil and garlic." Hiking my
new sleeves, I was taught to stuff a roaster and to light the previously
untried stove with something called safety matches, although there was
nothing especially safe about the close proximity of my mullet to an
open flame. "You'll thank me when you see how much it saves to cook
a meal at home," she said. "And even one less dinner a week at Tom's,
and your liver and small intestine will thank me, too."

We found a box of tapers over the kitchen sink, wiped a coating of
dust off the dining table, and had a candlelit dinner à deux that might,
in the broadest sense, be called adult. She talked about her girlhood
in eastern Ohio and the yearlong sequence of grim events that grew
her up fast in middle school: the drowning of a cousin at a water hole
that she and several friends snuck out to; her own close shave on a
horse that bolted and threw her into a tree; and the sudden splinter-
ing of her parents' marriage, which neither she nor her sister had seen
coming. "My dad just went bonkers, ran two towns over to shack up
with this woman from his firm, and tried to hide money his grandma
had left him, till my mom hired a lawyer and tracked it down. What's
with fathers now? Are they trying to make up for the sexual revolution
by going all Warren Beatty? I swear, it's like a geezer game of spin the
bottle; not one of my friends' parents are still together."

I countered with tales from the eastern front of marital dissolution: the
hauteur of stepmoms; Mom's slide down the drain; my sense of being a
stranger in Dad's house. She listened raptly, eyes creased in dolor, utter-
ing little grunts of recognition. Here was a flash: around certain women,
my childhood was actually an *asset*. It had to be done properly, of course,
and was all about tone, a calculated mix of bafflement and hurt and a
spritz of comic resolve. And there was, yes, the problem of hating myself
fiercely for acting the doe-eyed orphan. But if nothing else, I now had
a salable rap to go with my new, hard body, a one-two of muscle and
melancholy that hit 'em where they lived: the mother zone.

We finished our wine, put the plates in the sink, and retired to the
couch for dessert. In a summer of firsts, Kate was my course instructor

in Women Better at Sex Than Me. Her kissing, in particular, was virtu-
osic, a skill both ecstatic and enraging. Taking me in hand, she stroked
the side of my face while brushing my mouth with hers, darting in and
out, using one lip, then two, granting only the tip of her tongue. Thinking this a joust, I lunged and lunged, tongue poking at her like a lance.
A tilt of the head, though, and she'd slide away, then recommence the
master class in necking. It was all very artful and post-postmodern and
about as raunchy as a reading at the Y. Finally, I grabbed her by the hips
and spun, giving her a taste of *my* expertise, a little number I liked to
call brute strength.

She submitted to being mounted, hands pinned overhead as her neck
and ears were nuzzled. But when I freed one of my hands and pawed
her groin, she jerked to a stop with a shudder. "Time, time, time," she
gasped. "*Way* too soon. I feel like a calf at a rodeo."

"Sorry," I said, "I apologize. I thought you *liked* it when I—"

"No, I'm fine with being rough, once we've gotten there. But it's not
where a woman starts out."

"Oh," I said, so far past the start line that I was almost finished. I
spied a ring of pre-come on the front of my jeans and was horrified
she'd see it if I stood up. "Well, could we...try again? Without the
roughness?"

"Let's take a break," she said, patting down her skirt. "Why don't you
walk me home, and we'll see what's what."

I excused myself glumly to use the john and skulked to my room
to change. She made no remark when I came back in, offering only a
fractional smile as she shouldered her purse. We were silent much of the
way, holding hands primly, the sympathy spell I'd cast dashed to bits.
She asked me up as far as her apartment door, but there she planted her
feet on the sill and said she'd had a great time. "There's a good guy in
you—I see that now. I wasn't sure, off our first date."

"Well, *thanks*—I think. To quote you."

"But..."

"Yes? I'm listening."

"Well, not sure how to phrase this, and I'm the *last one* to talk. But it seems like what you need now, more than a girlfriend, is a good, solid year with the right person."

My face fell a mile. "You mean a shrink."

"Well, you just seem so...*raw*, you know, like it's right there at the surface. And meanwhile, *I'm* also dealing with family stuff. My father's reached out after three years gone, and damned if I know what to tell him. And I wonder, with all the red flags between us—your crazy mother, my ruthless dad—how we'd ever last a week together."

"I can't argue," I said. "The history's fucked—though it's fucked for all of us. Like you said yourself, whose parents *aren't* split and acting like teenage brats?"

"Point taken."

Suffering her hand to be kissed and held, she blushed right down to the sternum. "We *are* alike in ways that, frankly, make me cringe. Don't you think we'd drive each other loony?"

"Maybe," I said. "But you make me want to atone for the things your father did."

I heard her breath catch. She stared as if a gear had tumbled. "If you're lying to me..."

"Then shame on me. But I'm not, with all my heart."

And with that botched declaration, I pulled Kate in. Her feet came off the floor as I leaned back. The next thing I knew, she was fumbling for her keys, and then we were in her foyer and there were clothes coming off and a phone rang and rang, for all it mattered.

Seven

Hark, the Angel Swings

IT'S HARD, WHEN YOU'VE HAD so little of it in life, to place much stock in joy: the giving, and getting, of route-going pleasure and a sudden, home sense of connection. But you wake up one morning with a woman lying next to you who, even in the dishevelment of sleep and sweat, causes your heart to jump, and you lay back down and, for the first time ever, think those tall words *I'm happy.*

It's a terrifying moment, conjuring, as it does, the dark months and years that came before it. All that awaits outside her fragrant room is the chaos and misrule of an unwell world, a conspiracy of pressures and competing claims that pluck, pluck, pluck at your affections. And so you reach across the bed and reel her in, standing vigil, as she drowses, over this thing you've made together, this bower of enchantment and low-grade terror.

Our Friday night date stretched to Saturday, then Sunday. For sixty-odd hours, we barely stirred from bed, in the grip of the kind of appetite that scoffs at food and is only staved off by light naps. Kate's room, at the rear of a shotgun flat she shared with a friend from Ohio, looked out onto a shaft that housed a roost of pigeons, and every now and then I'd get up and try to shoo them with the business end of a broom. Then

I'd lie down again to renew my cooing and so, after a spell, would they, a feedback loop that riled the couple downstairs, neither of whom we judged to be avid birders.

I did, of course, eat *something*. I hadn't lost my mind or the monster-movie mania to be bigger. She gaped as I bolted a bacon and Swiss omelet in three gargantuan bites, and laughed when, coming back from a trip to the john, she found me hunched over the end of her bed, doing wrist curls with the footboard. *What's* that *about?* she asked in different ways, and each time I cobbled together a sort of answer that amounted to *I dunno*. But I did, of course, know: if I stopped, both the bed and the woman in it would instantly vanish from view. Of that lone truth I was grimly convinced, and I kept counting backward, from the clock on her wall, to the time of my last injection.

AND SO, AFTER TWO-PLUS days of naked Scrabble and a back-from-the-desert binge of sex, I got up Monday, kissed Kate goodbye, and ran the mile home for a shot of Deca. Turning in the mirror, I saw my ribs distend and launched into panicked invective. *Look at you, beanpole, you must've dropped five pounds. That's two weeks of gains out the door! Was it worth it for an extra day of pointless sex when you could've trained Sunday and made up for the missed workout? Which is more important here, a roll in the hay or building something real that you can count on?*

Unnerved by the rhetoric and the loss of bliss, I ran to the train as fast as my legs would take me. The lunch crowd at the Y included no one I knew, just a handful of white-collar types in a hurry and pensioners futzing with modest stacks. I was happy to be the size king for an hour and abused the privilege by seizing most of the dumbbells and piling them at my feet. For a crazed half hour, I fired off supers of four different weights in descending order, then lay there, after the last rep, relieved and spent, my brain and body stoned on phosphate ions.

"Yo, I need those sixties. You almost done?"

I looked up. The noon glare blunted my eyes; the man before me blurred like smoke. "Nope, I need 'em. Come back later."

I lay my head down. He didn't budge.

"Look, in five minutes you can have them all. I'm down to my two last sets here."

A nasal hiss, and then off he stalked, muttering to himself about "mark-ass bitches." Stunned, I sat up and shaded my eyes, squinting in the direction of the voice. A splendidly built black man was walking away, sending a fuck-you glower over his shoulder. There were two men waiting in the dumbbell pit. I gawked from chest to chest in stricken awe.

The black man — Angel, I heard him called by the others — wasn't in fact black but hazel, a square-jawed marvel whose coffee-and-cream skin set off gemstone eyes. He wore a tight Afro treated with some chemical to achieve a low-spark sheen, a pair of suede Pumas in midnight blue that matched his crisp-pressed sweats, and silver wrist cuffs with turquoise baubles that blazed when the hard light hit them. I tried looking away but found it impossible. It was like seeing a lion on your terrace.

The others, both white men, had chiseled trunks and the complicated, quasi-Cubist planes that give away hard-core juicers. Angel, however, was a cut above, muscle from a fourth dimension. I couldn't say why, but I had to talk to him. It felt, in some manic way, like my hopes rode on it.

I watched him do a set of upright rows, then got to my feet, walked a circle around the bench, and heard the word *go!* in my head. He was standing in the mirror, shooting a side-chest pose, when I approached him carrying the pair of sixty-pounders. "Here," I said. "I was kind of in the zone there. I get a little ape-shit doing supers."

He turned around slowly, his emerald eyes blazing, homing in and locking down on mine. He said nothing for a moment, just nodded his head vaguely and chewed on something skinny, his jaw rippling.

"Anyway, I'll just leave 'em. I see you're doing bar work, but maybe you—"

"Get the others."

I blinked, not comprehending. "I'm sorry, what?"

"Go and get the others, then bring them here." He said this in an android drawl, as if addressing a mental defective.

"Oh," I said. "Do you want them all, or just the fifties and forties to switch with?"

Again he fell silent, letting his gaze pour through: impassive, penetrant, cold. Just as I was turning to fetch the weights, he dropped into a gorgeous grin. "No, come on, slick. I'm just *playing*. Lincoln freed the slaves."

"Oh," I said. "Right. I wasn't sure..."

He went on staring, casing my upper body. I flinched but said nothing, transfixed.

"Son, you got some *pipes* there. Working hard, huh?"

"Well, I—yeah, I was away, but I'm trying, thanks. You see me here next week, I'll be ripped and stripped."

"Sure you're right, champ. I know the deal." His eyes, those shiny things, kept dancing.

"You do."

"Of course. You start chasing ass and lose your mind behind it. Poof, four days go by."

"Um...yeah," I said. "Ridiculous, huh?"

"Not really," he said. "It's why we train. But damn, leave some girls for us."

I felt myself color from the hairline down. "Well, *one* girl. But we barely got out of bed."

"Ow! *That* good to you? Maybe I know her."

"I doubt it. No offense."

"You can't be sure. I know a *lotta* girls." Laughing, he glanced at his friends. "Yo, my boy here's getting leg and takin' names."

They stopped what they were doing and stared in challenge. The closeness of the room bore down. "I *did* spend the weekend with this...smoking redhead. Best I've had in a long time."

No sooner were the words out than my stomach shriveled. I wanted to bolt—run the four miles flat and apologize to Kate on bent knee.

"You hear that?" said Angel. "While we were laying back, he was out banging Ann-Margret."

I looked at his friends, who'd been trading sets of furious one-arm rows. Spiro, the tall one, was built in slabs, a rock formation with feet. It started with his head, which was broad and flat, as if placed on his trunk by a crane. He had wide-set cheekbones and a jaw that jumped at you, cleft down the center like Superman's. This was, as I'd learn later, no accident; he'd spent two thousand dollars of his mother's money to achieve the resemblance in surgery. He'd even had his hair dyed comic-book black, with the signature spit curl in front.

The other guy, Tommy, yanked his tank top off, baring marbled rhomboids and the pear-shaped triceps that steal the hearts of judges in competition. Like Spiro, he was tanned a fire-engine red, the kind of burn that builds, layer by layer, and eventually turns purple, not brown. His hair, a bouffant shag, was thick with waves that ended in frizz against his neck. The general effect was of a mercenary whose day job was game-show host. "He can *have* Ann-Margret. I'll take the blonde with big cans. Spiro, who's that broad that I love?"

Spiro answered with a grunt.

"You know who. She was in that flick, the one with all the tennis and fucking."

"What, *Shampoo*?" said Angel. "That had boo-coo fucking, but I *hope* you're not talkin' Goldie Hawn."

"*Hell* no," said Tommy. "*My* tits're bigger than hers. Oh, sucka-mucka-plucka—Diane someone."

After a beat, I ventured, "Diane Keaton?"

"No. Way hotter."

"Diana Rigg?" said Angel.

"What? She's even flatter than Goldie Hawn."

This prompted a round of throat clears and wild guesses. Then Spiro, who'd said nothing and seemed vexed by the whole business, let out, with conviction, "Diana Ross."

Tommy looked at Angel. Angel looked at me. Unable to stop myself, I burst out laughing.

"See? Even *he* laughed, you big Zorba the Greek bastard," said Tommy. "Since when is *she* a *blonde* with big jugs?"

"Diana *Ross*," spat Angel. "How's the leader of the Supremes showin' her coochie on-screen?"

"She been in movies plenty," Spiro said in a voice that still carried timbre from the Adriatic.

"Yeah, *Lady Sings the Blues* and *Mahogany*, period. That's the only two, man. End of list."

Spiro set the bar down with a louder-than-needed clang. "Eh, but that song she sing, 'Touch Me in the Morning'? What you think she mean there—acupressure?"

Angel rubbed his brow with both hands. "So what're you saying? When she sang 'Baby Love,' it was all about sex in preschool?"

"No, but that's different. That's wrote by someone else. 'Touch Me in the Morning,' that's *her*, man."

While Tommy and Spiro considered the matter further, Angel walked me halfway down the mat. "You believe this noise? They say shit so stupid it makes me wanna cry sometimes."

"Sorry to hear it," I said.

"I swear, I get this pain here, behind my eyes. You can't catch cancer from morons, right?"

"I hope not." I stifled a smile. "If so, I'd have tumors from myself."

He grinned, tapping my wrist. "But what's that accent, though? You from England, slick?"

"Nope. Raised in Manhattan, born and bred."

"Really? Whereabouts, you mind me asking."

"The West Side. *Above* Eighty-sixth Street."

"*Bull*shit. That's my spot. The Amsterdam Houses."

"Wow. Park West Village on Ninety-sixth."

"Stop lyin'! You went to PS 87 with the white kids, though?"

"Nope, 163, with all the projects kids. Where do you think I got my taste in shoes?"

Angel glanced at my red-laced Nikes and tossed his head in laughter. "Hey, Tommy, Spiro, meet my new man here. This cat and I go back to *kinder*garten."

"Best of luck," said Tommy. It was unclear whom he meant, Angel or me.

"Forget him," said Angel. "His ass is from *Bayside*. But hey, let me give you my card." He fished from the pocket of his tailored sweatpants a pouch of drawstring velvet. Inside it was a card case, brightly polished, of the same heavy silver as his bracelets. "The girl who bought this won't get me gold," he said. "She says it makes me look like a pimp."

The card read:

Angel Alvarado
Producer/Director/Entertainer

"Ah. That's unusual. I wouldn't have thought to go with red ink."

"That's to let you know that I go all out. Put my heart and blood in every showcase."

He went on to say that he had something coming up soon that he'd keep me in the loop about. I wrote my number down on the back of one of the cards and asked him if he trained this time each day. "Oh, we're not here on the regular. We go downtown or one of the iron dungeons in Brooklyn. We like to keep our thing *grimy*."

"You don't *look* grimy. You're the first guy I've seen in matching sweats."

He knelt to grab the eighties. "Hey, I'm *always* clean. Now you mind goin' and gettin' those fifties?"

For the next couple of hours, I watched from close range as the three of them tore through a back and arms routine. With no wasted motion or water-fountain meanders, they piled one set on top of another: the first man on, the second spotting him, the third switching out the plates. It was part luge team, part pit crew, part messianic rage—three sets of limbs that didn't tire or drop reps, one clean line of power. They were hefting weights beyond my wildest reach—strict arm hammers with sixty-pounders; bent-over rows using hundreds—and badgering and cursing and threatening each other to crank that last rep out. Here was animal strength paired with style and steel, a whole other cosmos of obsession. To raise my game to their grade seemed a forlorn hope and would certainly necessitate a cocktail of drugs that only the most demented would consider. All I really wanted was a fraction of Spiro's mass and—dream a dream—Angel's definition. That and the machine-shopped trim of Tommy's pecs, and then, praise the Lord, I'd be done.

On the dot of three o'clock, they wrapped their day, closing with a blitz of incline crunches. I watched as they patted themselves down with plush towels and zipped their lumbar belts into flight bags. Angel came over, served that million-dollar smile, and held out a fist to bump. "Yo, it was good to meet ya. I got your number on me, and, like I say, I might have something coming up."

"That'd be great," I said. "A party or something?"

"Yeah," he said, still grinning. "Or something."

I RETURNED THE NEXT DAY, but true to his word, Angel wasn't there. So again that Tuesday and Wednesday, and by the end of the week, failing a call from him, I went back to my four o'clock shift. I'd trained each day of the previous week with Richie and his tribe of half-dressed hard hats, and sung my way into the circle a bit with tales of wild girls and mixed dorms. (They especially liked my lies about coed bathrooms and wondered why guys *ever* left for class.) Even the cops took to calling me Joe College and said they'd come visit when I went back to school. "We'll all go," said Richie. "We'll do a panty raid—though it doesn't sound like the chicks there wear any."

When I walked in that Friday, I was met with razzing laughter and an emphatic hug from Richie. "We thought you'd been sex-napped by some chick."

I assured him I was fine and could come and go freely, though I had, I said, met a great girl.

"What I tell you!" he said. "Did I call it, Hank? Two weeks, he'll be rinsing out her bras."

"Tragic," said Sal. "And always the young ones. You try to wise 'em up, but what can ya do?"

"Ignore them," Hank told me. "We should all be so lucky to be getting steady head."

"We do," Richie hooted. "We get it off *you*—and this Valentine's, we'll definitely send a card!"

And thus and suchlike the Socratic discourse of my local Mensa chapter. It bears noting, however, that I was moved and rattled by the warmth of the crew's embrace. Here was further proof that I was on my way, another door opened by my souped-up size and the genie in the steel syringe. Not since the days of my parents' divorce had a prize group of males taken me into the fold and said (without saying), *You're with us*. All the years of eating burgers alone in one student lunchroom after another and the heartsick skein of Saturday nights, sequestered with my comics and black-and-white Sony—the weight of that time suddenly lodged in my throat, and, damp-eyed, I fled to the john. There I stayed, splashing water on my cheeks till the wave of feeling subsided. *What the hell is* this *now?* I gasped through clogged sinuses. *When did I become a guy who cries at nothing?*

"Everything copacetic?" Richie said when I came back. "What, she got you calling every hour?"

I worked in for a night of delts and triceps. It was all very chipper, the guys in great spirits, ready to close the week out with a solid Pump, then head off for a mammoth meal together. They did that some-times—piled over to the Greek place on Lexington Ave and slurped sauce-heavy dishes with side plates and salads, bought round after round of Pabst Blue Ribbon, and swapped war stories with one another. Alas, I'd heard those stories, and they weren't about war or even, after the third beer, about cops and robbers or the hassles of trash pickups in Harlem.

By and large, they were lamentations on life and the sour notes hit with women — a chorus line of love's labor's lost. I'd listen in silence, having no harp to pick, and glean from the drift and tone of the talk that for these men, women meant heaven and hell, and more than that, women meant *work* — work to interpret and try to keep happy, or work simply to remain on speaking terms with after the inevitable fuckup. This saddened me, but made me leery of their mojo. I'd spent twenty years gaining the nerve to approach girls; the last thing I needed now was a sign on my back saying *I'll Only Disappoint You in Bed.*

At the end of the workout, then, I begged off dinner and stopped at a pay phone to ring Angel. He surprised me by answering on a Friday night and said he'd called me earlier, to no avail. "Great minds think alike," he said. "But I'm on my way out now — got some business downtown. We're thinking of doing the Y again tomorrow, though."

"*Great,*" I said, too loudly. "What time were you planning on getting there?"

We agreed on noon, and he signed off suavely, telling me to "go easy on the ladies." "They ain't ready, slick. You're the newest thing out there. A smart college boy with big arms."

I hung up, feeling both flattered and conned, but had hit full swagger by the time I got to Kate's. She'd graciously spent the afternoon preparing a meal, an underpowered (by her lights) jambalaya. She picked at her plate as I bolted down spoonfuls while raving up Angel to her. "He's like a god, a superhero; you've never seen a body this advanced. When he yanked off his top, half the guys there said *Fuck it* and quit on the spot."

"But not you, from the sound of it."

"Oh, God, no. I was zooming. It's like walking through Florence and seeing that twelve-foot *David* in the square."

"Actually, it's more like sixteen, but go on."

I explained that he ran some sort of theater troupe and that he'd hinted he might be able to take me on. I couldn't guess why, as I had no training and he hadn't even asked if I'd acted before. Maybe it didn't involve speaking, just carrying a spear, being the fourth Hessian from the left. In any case, it figured to be an *experience,* and wasn't that the point of being twenty?

"I don't know," said Kate. "Depends on the experience."

"By which you mean...?"

"I mean, you meet him at the gym, he sees you half-naked, and the next thing, he's handing you his card."

"And? So?"

"So how do you know he's not shooting gay porn and you're the fourth convict in the cell?"

I let out a chortle and kept eating.

"Or what if he's running coke and looking to crack a new market, recruit you to sell at school?"

"Please. I couldn't sell vacuums, and they're *legal.*"

"But that's the whole point. You don't know him from Adam, and you aren't exactly the most, you know..."

Now I put my fork down. "The most what?"

"Mmmph," she said, lighting her half-smoked Merit, which she'd been saving till after dinner as a treat. She'd been trying for months to wean herself off them and was down to one low-tar at meals. "Baby, all I'm saying is, you're new to this still—having a body, getting attention, all that stuff. And I think, till you've been around more and learned the ropes, you really need to be careful who you deal with."

"Well, thanks," I said coolly, "but I'll be fine. The first sign of chain gangs, I'll take off."

ANGEL SURPRISED ME BY BEING on time, and thrilled me by coming alone. Spiro and Tommy had punked him, he said, opting to sleep in late. "But you're here," he said, "and that tells me a lot. I might have to kick you some science."

We started, of all places, on the top-floor oval, a great, gloomy hangar of a track. On the wedge-shaped siding that abutted it, an old man pawed at a heavy bag, his jab barely grazing the nap. There were burled-oak dip bars on the wall behind him, a wrist-curl roller stained black by sweat, and a hopscotch of gym mats strewn about, their stitched seams splaying like stubble. Angel dropped mats on a small square of floor space and assumed a knee-down pose. "Stretching," he said. "I thought it was corny till my friends on the Jets showed me how. Then I saw it was their secret weapon, and I *like* knowing things that people don't."

I went to all fours and tried sinking backward. A blaze broke out in my thighs.

"Try it with one leg straight first."

I did as instructed, reclining slowly. There was a soft, pleasurable pop in my knee, then ankle, that blunted the set of steak knives in my groin. "Wow," I grunted, shifting to ease the torque. "This is—"

"*Real* man strength. See, busters think it's all about what you squat, but it's also about how you flow. Someday, they'll hit fifty and not be able to walk, whereas we'll be running the beach in Rio, being chased by some light-skinned *chicas*."

For the next half hour he guided me briskly through a full-strength stretch-and-fetch, a series of postures and calisthenics in search of invisible fruit. "Hopping for apples" entailed lunges and arm swings, reaching for low-lying pomes. "Popped cherries" left me hot-cheeked and puffing, rising up tall with hands held high, then dropping down fast to palms and toes for downward-facing-dog back bridges. I was soaked clear through by the time we stopped. Angel stood and gave his champagne laugh. "Damn, can't handle the stretch-and-fetch? How you gonna get through lunges?"

"Lunges I can manage. But this shit's vicious. For Jews, it's more like stretch-and-kvetch."

"What? You're *Jewish*? Damn, you just get better."

Glancing up. "Sorry, I don't follow."

"Forget it," he said, laughing. "I'll break it down later. For real, though, I thought you were Italian."

"Get in line," I groused. "I start working out, and next thing I'm Sonny Corleone."

"Don't knock it, slick. It might make you some loot."

"How so?" I asked. "And before I forget, who're your friends on the Jets?"

"You ask a lot of questions," he said, folding his mat. "Don't *look* like a Corleone; *act* one, B."

We proceeded downstairs, where for two grim hours he whipped me like a three-legged mule. "Slow and low" was his weekend creed—a light weight lifted at snail's tempo. Each full rep lasted twenty seconds: an eight count up, then twelve on the down. By the sixth rep of sets, tears commenced. (Try it, and have your spotter hold the Kleenex.) The first time he had me attempt preacher curls, my forearms rattled as if a quake rolled through, shaking to heft a fifty-pounder. Then I stood up, and the burn in my biceps made the blood in my head run black.

"You're funny," he chortled. "It's just lactic acid. If I could, I'd spread it on toast."

At the end of an hour he called a break. I wobbled like a soft-boiled egg. But there, in the mirror, was the point of his torture: freakish definition from neck to knees. My upper and lower arms were rudely engorged, the veins between wrist and elbow fat as earthworms. Shooting a double biceps, I saw my lats stand and finally got why gym rats called them wings. Even my skin glistened in fierce salute—the dark, ruddy howl of dammed blood.

Angel backed off some in the second hour, switching to reps at normal speed. "I forget that people don't train like me. It takes some getting used to—but you're doin' great."

There were water breaks now every fifteen minutes, during which he explained his methods. Weekdays lifting big weight was about "making deposits," putting money in the bank to earn and grow on. But Saturday's session? That was straight withdrawal, getting a savage Pump by cutting your poundage so you'd be "top-dollar sharp" for all the girls. "You'll see what I mean when you throw on a shirt and your arms just pop like *blammo!* You'll look and go, 'Damn, that Angel's the *deal.* I should tithe him ten percent of my women.'"

I smiled weakly, too spent to laugh. "Like you don't have twelve of your own."

"Hey—twelve is good, but twenty's better."

"I guess."

"And why stop there? How 'bout thirty—one for each day of the month?"

At my shrug, his brows went up, tipped like tiny swords. "What, I'm wrong? I can't be like that? Shit, I can't *help* being like that."

"No problem," I said. "But with me, even two girls seems...a lot."

He stared in the mirror, shooting a side-chest pose. "Not when you do 'em both together."

HAVING SHOWERED AND DRESSED, I waited for Angel, skimming the *Post* at my locker. It was gashouse hot in that gray-walled oven, and here he finally came now, nude as Zeus. To the shock and delectation of two aging queens who'd lingered at their stalls post-swim, Angel quite leisurely elected to shave his legs, bending and craning with one foot up to moon (and then some) his admirers. Sitting two feet from his uncut cock, I bent to scan the floor for the Jefferson nickel I suddenly remembered having lost. While down there, I scoped the striations of his calf as he shifted from the heel to the ball of his foot. I was thinking of the old masters and how they'd paint that leg—Mantegna, who'd rendered Christ as a deathbed colossus; Carracci, the first portraitist of Bible strongmen—when I glanced at Angel's feet and gasped. The webbing between his toes was thick with bruises. "What's the matter? Don't like my dogs?"

"Um, no, that wasn't what I was—"

"Better there than in the ass—especially with the shit I shoot now."

I blanched, stunned silent by his bluntness. In the four months I'd juiced, I'd only copped to it once, when Richie's crew had jeeringly called me out. I didn't fear arrest as much as ridicule, the mockery mixed with pity I was sure would follow when people learned the cause of my transformation.

When he'd finished his nudist grooming and gotten himself dressed in a pair of Dan Post boots and a knotted scarf, Angel and I left to grab lunch at a diner and talk over the "gig" he had in mind. Standing in front of the Y, we saw a cab pull up and four splendid girls pile out. They were tall and fair, the milkmaid pallor of the North, and walked past us into the Y with the grace of ballerinas. Angel dropped his flight bag and applauded suavely. They turned for a giggly moment and smiled back.

"Wow," I said, as the door closed on them. "What do you think *they're* here for? It's guys only."

"Don't know," he said, "but I'm on the case. You don't speak Swedish, by any chance?"

We learned from the desk clerk that they were with a Dutch dance troupe and that someone had called ahead and gotten permission for them to tan on the roof deck for an hour. Skedaddling to the men's room, we remembered we had no swimsuits and raced up wearing only towels and oil. My fingers and toes tingled as I bounded the stairs, eager and flattered to join Angel in action but also, in some recess, sick for Kate. What would she say if she saw me now, baying like a hound at his heels? One week removed from our feast of love and already I was doing her dirt, out chasing tail with the very guy she'd hectored me to drop. This was crazy wrong, but no time for that now, not with the fire door banging open and the four of them sprawled on plastic chaises in the snuggest string bikinis I'd ever seen.

"Ladies!" hailed Angel, spreading his wings. "Welcome, one and all, to our *voulez-vous!*"

Eight

Zing Went the G-string of My Heart

IT'S EASY ENOUGH, in the flatness of time, to look back and see the pivot points: the two or three places I could have pulled up, saying *Here I'll go, and no further.* That's the Big Lie of survived mistakes, the notion that they're born of haste and rash misjudgment, these derailments from the gentle track we're on. For me the derailments *were* the track, uncouplings that sent me around the bend and down the embankment to somewhere else. It wasn't very pretty when I got to the bottom, waking up to wreckage and diesel smoke, and I certainly wouldn't suggest a course of crash-and-burn folly to anyone seeking to goose his stalled life. Nor am I waving the Jamesian flag, saying *Character is fate,* and tra la la. No, character's what happens *after* the fate, when you scrape yourself up, piece together what's left, and resolve to stop torturing the ones you love, who were, in spirit, along for the crazy ride.

What I'm saying, in other words, is that there are certain disasters that no amount of foresight can prevent—the risk that's too sweet, the deceiver too slick—even if you clearly see him coming. At no point during my time with Angel did I think he meant me well, or that here was someone who could teach me things, if only by negation and hard knocks. The fact of the matter is, I wasn't thinking at all; there was too much fun to be had. Wherever I went with him, wild things happened. Who cared what that augured for my soul?

THE DUTCH GIRLS, in their late teens and prone still to giggles, were no innocents when it came to thirst. Beginning at lunch and through the taillights of evening, they drank their way up and down Lower Manhattan, chasing us from one dive to the next. Margaritas, peach schnapps, champagne cocktails: it was a candy-colored crawl to midnight, with a stop at Ray's Pizza along the way. They had their hearts set on buying leather jackets, "the kind from your *Happy Days*–Fonzie TV," so we started out gamely for Delancey Street but got no farther than Tompkins Square Park. There they saw their first punks with tats and Mohawks and clung to us in terror and excitement. Their English was sketchy, but that didn't stop Angel, whose charm was its own Esperanto. Feeding the jukebox, he taught them how to Hustle, adding loops and dips and swing-out turns, his hand rarely north of their San Juan. He led them in song, old Isaac Hayes jams that they recognized from viewings of *Shaft*. And as we got drunker, he got the girls howling with a foreign-exchange program of slang, teaching them Spanish curse words in return for their Dutch cognates, a great step forward for both cultures. And all of it—the jokes and effortless hip shakes; the reaching for his wallet every round—all of it was overkill. He had the girls eating from his manicured hand long before we ever left the Y.

We wound up back at his place in the Amsterdam Houses, walking past a gauntlet of simmering B-boys, their eyes locked and loaded on the girls. "Don't sweat 'em," said Angel as we tromped through the lobby. "Anyone with me has a ghetto pass." His tenth-floor two-bedroom, passed down to him by his mother, had been plushly done over like a player's lounge, all gold leaf, chrome, and animal prints, the foyer painted stripper-lipstick red. In the hallway I examined his wall of fame while he gave the girls drinks and a quickie tour. There were a number of shots of Angel with minor barrio stars: singers in salsa bands, semipro pitchers, and actress-slash-models with shiny foreheads and zero chance of landing a national ad. Sprinkled in among these were snaps of him from boyhood: the beamish six-year-old in holiday duds, his mother, a light-skinned Caribbean beauty, pressing her cheek tightly to his; Angel at twelve, enfolded by nieces, a magnet even then for female worship. A couple of things struck me as I walked the length of his gilt-framed shrine to himself: one, how plump he had been in childhood, till he'd suddenly dieseled up, post–high school; and two, how barren his life was of men—not a father or doting uncle in the bunch. *No wonder he's so natural around women,* I thought. *He's never had to fight for their attention.*

He was taking his sweet time coming back from the tour, and I seized the chance to do a little snooping. The far wall of the living room held floor-to-ceiling mirrors that I didn't immediately guess hid built-in cabinets. Custom-made for Angel from enough smoked glass to reface an office park, they housed behind their panels a stand of self-help books, a leather-bound edition of the I Ching in Spanish, and the collected works of Iceberg Slim, the best-selling pimp and lifestyle guru to a new generation of hustlers. One shelf down from these was a trove of small statues, Polynesian tribesmen in precoital poses, their preposterously large members pointing up. And on the bottom rack, wedged together in bins, was every funk album of the past ten years, some of them still sealed in plastic wrap.

I sank to my knees and plucked disc after disc that I needed to hear *that instant,* piling Earth Wind & Fire and the Ohio Players onto Graham Central Station and the Bar-Kays. Fumbling with dials I knew I shouldn't be touching, I slipped *Skin Tight* onto the platter and dropped the needle. Out, like a bomb blast, came the title track. The volume shimmied the cabinet shelves, nudging Angel's long-dicked lovers to the edge. One by one, the statuettes plunged; I scrambled to catch them before they landed, bundling each to my chest as I snagged the next. There were five, all told; I managed to save four, the last one falling to a grisly fate, dismembered by the parquet floor.

With a groan, I set the others down and yanked the needle off. A door yammered open; I heard footfalls on the carpet. I dropped to my knees and attempted, with numb hands, to reunite penis and Polynesian. It proved fruitless, however: his pecker was chipped and seemed only to want to point southerly now, aiming its affections at his foot. I had the organ in one hand and its owner in the other when Angel, buck naked, burst in on me. "What the *fuck*?" he yelled, his own pecker pointing skyward. "Can't I leave you alone for two minutes?"

I tried—God knows—not to look at his prick, but I was too drunk and flustered to ignore it. Quite apart from its distinctions—it was thick rather than long, and tinged a most alarming shade of purple—I couldn't see how its sudden appearance was connected to the drinks he'd gone to fix. "Oh God, I shouldn't have touched your system. How much do I owe you for the, uh, thing here?"

"Man, *dead* that," he snapped. "What are you doing in my shit?"

"Well, I thought you were coming back with them, and I was trying to set the mood here and—"

"The *mood*?" he said. "Fool, they're naked already! I got three of 'em in bed now, waitin' on you."

"They're wha-at?" I sputtered. "When did they—I thought you—"

"We've been freakin' for ten minutes. What'd you *think*?"

"I—I didn't know," I said. "I guess I got distracted and...By the way, um, where'd the fourth one go?"

"Say *what*?" He glowered. "Three ain't enough?"

"No, I'm just...How do we divide three between us?"

"There you go with the questions again. Could you please just *put the dick down* and come on?"

I followed him down the hall, feeling ripely unwell, watching myself from somewhere overhead. All day long, I'd been hedging my bets, flirting like mad with the lissome Renata but expecting the girls would return to their hostel after they'd milked us for drinks. Even in the cab up to Angel's place, I'd sloughed off the thought that sex was imminent, ignoring Catje's hand on his inner thigh and the shirt he'd unbuttoned to his waist. At most, I figured, they'd compete to fuck *him* and I'd head over to Kate's, my tin badge of honor lightly dented. But as I learned that night, there was no half-stepping Angel. You either went the whole hog or you went straight home, clutching your stricken conscience to your chest.

It was quite the merry *Decameron* in his sizable room, where the girls had diverted themselves during his absence by raiding his walk-in closet. They met us, otherwise naked, in his gym shorts and Pumas, doing a merry mime show of pumping iron. Angel grabbed Katje and Lidia, slung them over his shoulders, and proceeded to do a set of lockout squats as they begged him, laughing, to stop. Renata insisted on being next; he told me to oblige her. When I didn't strip fast enough, she fumbled with my belt and tugged at my sweat-glued Calvins with such force that she keeled over backward and took both of us down on his fudge brown, high-pile shag.

She was laughing so hard that it sounded like sobbing. We rolled around together, my jeans at my knees, till we somehow toppled Angel and the other girls. There were bodies across my thighs and nausea in my throat, the residue of the daylong drunk and the sausage slices at Ray's. Someone was pulling my jeans the rest of the way off, a hand was cranking my cock like a sailboat jib, and I had a breast in my mouth that I couldn't recall putting there, pressing its claims for attention. But all I could think about was taking small breaths, lest a day's worth of calories crash the party.

Pinned to my back at the bottom of the tussle, I did my best to pitch in, caressing asses and nipples I couldn't quite see and licking what flesh happened by me. As a delivery mode of pleasure, our orgy was inefficient and more closely resembled a ruck in Gaelic football than the Roman sexapaloozas of Suetonius. The profuse arms and legs packed in very tight quarters; the pungent perfume of over-moist groins; and the inadvertent weird-out of guy-on-guy nearness made, for me at least, an experiment in passive suffering. I kept trying to sit up or roll to my side, but there were knees athwart my hips or an ass on my chest, and I stopped, at some point, twisting and just let the thing happen, trying, if nothing else, to get comfortable.

Someone faced the other way was riding me hard, and as I lay there, enduring her sexual favors, I noticed the room-length mural over her shoulder. Rendered in side-by-side Day-Glo panels was Angel's silhouette, enacting, from left to right, the twelve sexual positions of the super-fly zodiac. (I knew it was Angel because each of the male contours sported his high-domed 'fro. As to the women pictured, it was anyone's guess, though at least half favored the young Pam Grier.) The breadth of his vanity, flaunted on every flat surface, was a madness I hadn't encountered before, and it baffled and enthralled me in equal measure. As a Jew brought up in the grand tradition of self-loathing, I was floored by the idea of hiring a painter to splash my naked likeness on the wall. Far from serving as erotic tinder, seeing a dozen versions of my weak-chinned profile would have sent me on such a bender of sobbing and drug use that I might never have mustered a hard-on again. Then there were the process questions to ponder: Was nude silhouette work a staple in the 'hood, like cornrow braiding or curried goat? Did Angel have to pose for each of the panels, and how long could he have held that Pisces position, in which he somehow jackknifed above his beloved and stuck her like a narwhal spearing a cod?

These were the sorts of things I found myself musing as I descended from the clouds and rejoined the fun. Renata had been replaced on my lap by Catje, who in an act of nearly intolerable kindness bent in low for a kiss. She did so gently, brushing her lips against mine, and emitted little puffs of sour-sweet breath that moved me as she gazed into my eyes. I responded by shoving my tongue past her teeth and torquing my hips with vigor. This inflamed her, or roused her from schnapps dreams, and she, in turn, humped me back harder. *Now I* was stirred, my cock firing up its core inside her. What followed was an arousal that built in stages, getting to an outcrop of steady sensation, then going up a notch to the next ledge. Amateur though I was still, I was shrewd enough to wait, letting Katje handle the bulk of the thrusting while I homed in on the heat. In the three or four seconds that preceded the big moment, a jaw-wobbling wildness took me over and turned my fingers to garden weeders. There were no sheets to claw, but I was too gone to know it and dug in whatever came to hand. A moment before I blew, someone grabbed my wrist and shook it. "Ow, mother*fucker*! That's my butt cheek!"

Mouthing *sorry,* or something like it, I came in torrents, riding the wave back to shore.

SEVERAL NIGHTS LATER I took Kate to a show at Lincoln Center for her birthday. She looked especially fetching in her black suede mini and off-the-shoulder, pale silk blouse, and the play we caught, *Streamers,* ravished us both with its powder-keg prose and stagecraft. Afterward, on the garrulous, soul-stirred buzz you only seem to get from great drama, we chatted and nuzzled for hours over dinner, ignoring our eager-to-leave waiter. I was struck again, sharply, by how easy she was to talk to, pulling me out of my clumsy pauses with her droll gift for being herself, and the way she made me feel at least ten percent smarter every time she opened her mouth. As I was just beginning to see, I had an echo intelligence that mimicked both smarties and numskulls. That was the *good* news. The bad was that I seemed to like the company of numskulls. They were much less work to keep up with.

Kate was praising a book she'd begun over the weekend and had barely been able to put down since, a novel so spectral and packed with left turns that, for two days straight, she'd forgotten to bathe, sitting there in her "stink," turning pages. I was only half-listening, though, revisiting Sunday and the long, strange debauch at Angel's place. Much like Kate's book, it seemed to last forever and owed its duration in very large part to the late guest appearance of cocaine. At three a.m., when the girls were sobering up and asking what a cab ride would cost downtown, Angel left the room and came back shortly bearing a cheese board and a rolled-up twenty. "It's high-test," he said, chopping rails with a straightedge, "so go *eaa*-sy. Two lines'll do you."

It was the first time I'd ever seen coke up close, though I'd heard it being tooted in the bathroom stalls at the clubs I'd hit with Kenny, and I'd skimmed a nattering story in *New York* magazine about the storm of it sweeping East Side bars. The girls perked up as he passed the board, awed as much by the coolness conferred as the chance to actually try the drug, but I hung back, going last. What little I remembered of the *New York* piece concerned coke's power to turn bankers into zombies, and given my struggle to kick peanut M&M's, I fretted about instant addiction. No less vexing was any unknown synergy with the Deca and Winstrol I'd been shooting. In my budding paranoia, I had bought myself a copy of the *Physicians' Desk Reference* to study, but saw nothing in it about possible interactions between steroids and stepped-on blow.

"I-I'm just a little freaked about my allergies," I said. "Should I worry about this clogging me up?"

Angel gave a look of bone fatigue. "You should *worry* about sounding like my grandma."

I took the rolled-up twenty and made a pass, hoovering most of a line with my good nostril. A cold fire singed the hairs on my septum and sent stars up the walls of my skull. "Wow," I said, though nothing else happened — no high or sudden transport to Devil's Island.

"Am I right?" said Angel, with a knowing leer. "Don't you just thank God that you met me?"

"I do," I said, and blew a second rail. I started to say it again but stopped and grinned: my head was suddenly a snow globe overturned. I went back, laughing, on my hands and wrists, watching the lovely flakes flit where they might.

"Anyhow, I'm eager to hear your take," Kate said now. "The narrator, Nick D'Urfe, is you all over."

"Huh?" I said, reentering earth's orbit. "I'm sorry, I missed that last part."

"Never mind," she said, and kissed me. "You'll see what I'm saying. *The Magus* is just one of those books you'll think you live in."

IT WAS ANOTHER COUPLE OF DAYS before I heard from Angel, and I began to make myself crazy about it. The broke-dick knickknack; the willies about doing coke—I wondered if I'd loused my chances with him by acting like the rube I was. I also stewed about my cash on hand, watching Eeyore get thinner and flatter as I plucked fifties from his slit to pay for dates. I was getting enough (still!) in unemployment to cover the rent and lights and had stashed away something like twelve hundred bucks during my profitable semester in school. But just a month back in town, I'd burned through half the money and was loath to nose around for an off-the-books job, lest some civic-minded employer call the feds. At the clip I was going, I'd be broke by late July, with six weeks to go till registration.

That Thursday Angel rang and asked where I'd been, wondering why I'd "dogged" him by not calling. "I get your ass laid, feed you half a gram of coke—I'd think my phone be jumpin' off the hook."

"I know, I should've called," I said, relieved.

"Then why didn't you?"

"Fuck, I don't know. I didn't want to seem like I was hocking you."

"Hocking? That another of your Jewish words?"

"Yeah, it means to nag. I was scared you'd think I was hassling you to go again."

"Hey, well, hock away then. That night'll go down as one of the greats."

"Really?" I said. "I didn't totally screw things by breaking your statue?"

"Nah. Just slide me a C-note and we're straight."

"Oh." My heart sank. "I suppose that's fair."

Silence on the line, then his hissing laugh. "I'm fucking with you, slick. You know your money's no good. Besides, if not for you, I wouldn't have tagged a Swedish chick. Let alone three from Norwegia."

He switched gears, saying he had something in the Seventies that would end around three o'clock. How did I feel about shooting on down there and shopping for a pair of kicks? I said I'd love to join him but was counting my pennies till school started up again in the fall. "Well, squash that and meet me at Charivari," he said. "It's like the

New York Dolls mixed with Disco Fever and some shit they wore in *Planet of the Apes.*"

He was preaching to the converted. I'd worshipped at the West Side's outpost of cool since it opened its doors for business on Seventy-second Street. I'd never gone in, of course. It was so de trop, you thought the clerks would cuff you, then call the cops. Even from the curb, I knew to keep on stepping as I ogled the acid-trippy Nik Nik shirts and rubberized jeans by some Versace fellow. You didn't *have* to be a pimp to do your shopping there, but it was helpful to have a stable of girls support your habit of Fiorucci tees at forty dollars per.

Angel got there late, wearing a pair of high-waist flares, a rolled-sleeve tux shirt open to the bottom button, and a Snidely Whiplash knotted silk bandana. Watching as he came, I saw three teenage girls walk by him, then turn and openly check his splendid ass.

"You see what just happened?" I said.

He beamed his high-watt grin and handed a bag across; it bore the name of a shoe store down the block. "Here, it's your birthday. And many happy."

"Huh? But—how'd you know I just had one?"

"I didn't," he said. "It's just an expression. This is for the thing the other night."

I opened the bag and found a boxed pair of dress boots, the Nocona product-care tag still attached. "This is—these are amazing! How much did—"

"A lot less than *here,*" he said. "Now let's see what other flyness the good witch brings you."

A half hour later and a good deal flyer, I emerged from Charivari grinning numbly. In one bag were two pairs of pleated slacks from a promising young designer named Armani; in the other a kaleidoscopic dress shirt by Pucci and two tight-fitting V-necks by Cardin. I barely touched the ground as we walked to Broadway, but Angel had another stop to make. Down we went, by taxi, to a salon in the East Fifties, where I got my first thirty-dollar haircut. I started to tell the stylist how

I usually wore it when Angel interrupted and said to trust him. "That Mott the Hoople do ain't hittin', son. Let Nino do his thing here. You drink wine?"

By nine p.m. we were back at Angel's, after big, greasy plates of *ropa vieja* at the *comidas chinas* joint on West 100th. I was most of the way blotto off a pitcher of Presidente and yammering up a blue streak from the coke we'd done with Nino. Several times I asked about the bill for all this outlay, which I'd ballparked north of five hundred bucks. Angel kept tut-tutting, saying we'd talk about that later, but I'd already decided I wasn't giving the clothes back and was up for any hustle he pitched me. Selling coke on campus? Hell, where was the harm—it got girls out of their pants and made them chatty. East German steroids? Sign me up, Franz: *every* man should have arms as carved as ours.

There were more Presidentes in the living room, then Angel slipped away to make some calls. Parliament-Funkadelic was on the platter, thumping my chest with fatback beats and bend-your-spine-like-grapevine Bootsy bass parts. After a minute I couldn't help it and got up to dance, eyes shut and feet sliding across the parquet floor, breaking in my stiff-soled Noconas. Two songs in, I was doing jazz-hand expressions and some business with my neck you see on chicken farms, all the while trying to put my butt cheeks in motion, ideally at one and the same time. "Giiii-ve up the funk...gotta have that funk," I croaked, and may well have gone on to mime the saxophone parts when I suddenly became aware I wasn't alone. From the hall Spiro and Tommy were watching in horror. I lunged to kill the volume. "Wh-when did you—"

"Where the hell is Angel?" jeered Tommy.

"Uh, I think he's—"

"Hey, Angel, goddamnit!" Tommy stomped his foot loudly. "This is *bull*shit. I'm not training some fuckin' frat boy!"

He dropped his gym bag, storming down the hall.

"Wow," I said dully. "I don't think he likes me."

Spiro trained his gaze on my boots. "How much money you pay?"

"What, for these?"

"I got the same, but brown," he said. "What they run you, two hundred?"

"Um, actually, I couldn't say," I said.

"Why not?"

"Well...because Angel bought 'em."

His huge jaw dropped, and then *he* clomped off. "Angel, what the fuck! I wanna speak you!"

I heard a door open on a quarrel in progress and then just as quickly slam shut. Standing in the garish, half-lit room, my brain catalyzing the last cocaine traces, I listened to the caterwaul of cop-car sirens and suddenly felt alien and endangered. The sleek new boots, which began to chafe; the experience of getting stoned on a Thursday night; the quadraphonic weirdness of being a white kid with prospects in the wall-to-wall malheurs of the Amsterdam Houses — it all came clattering down with a thud and hit me at the base of the skull. I wanted to take off but couldn't think how; wanted to lie with Kate or make amends with Dad or race back to school and take a summer class, do something — *anything* — to grow myself up and set a firm course for the next decade. But none of those options, generative though they were, would put me in the middle of the hulks and self-proclaimers and feed me what I wanted: the whole megillah. When you've snuck your first taste of life's cream frosting, nothing less than all of it will fill your belly and allow you to finally push off from the table.

Angel came back after several minutes, his smooth face sewn up tight. "Tom's a fag," he muttered, slugging his beer. "All he ever does is throw shade."

He paced the room with snapping strides, pivoting like a panther in a cage. "You know he tried to be a cop but missed four times? Kept flunking the damn written test!"

"He—no, he didn't mention it, no."

"Who ever failed the *cop* test?" he said. "I thought if your name was Flanagan, you were in."

"Well, yeah, they do tend to hire the, um, Irish."

"And Spiro — he's *another* fuckin' mental magician. Ten years after he steps off the boat, he *still* sounds like he got here last Tuesday."

I stared at the floor. "Am I causing problems? If so, I could always leave and call you lat—"

He glared. "Do you *wanna* leave?"

"Well...no. Not really."

"Then good. 'Cause you're the *answer,* not the problem."

He spun on his heel and bolted out of the room, returning with the others in tow. They slumped on his love seat, legs crossed and jaws clenched, evincing a sudden interest in their footwear. "Say it," he told them. "Say it or split and don't come back."

Tommy curled his top lip. "S'fugwah."

"Say *what?*"

More glowering from him. "Fine. I'm *sorry.*"

"Damn straight you're sorry. Now tell him why."

Had Tommy come with the gun he was named for, we'd all have been riddled with holes. "Sorry for not being a *team player,*" he snickered. "Whatever the fuck *that* means now."

"It means," said Angel, through a patient sneer, "that you're *supposed* to try'n act like a leader. I ain't got time to be holding your hand. You want to make more money, punch the clock."

Tommy sneered, then went silent.

"Spiro," Angel said, "how much you earn last week?"

Spiro, in his own sulk, barely shrugged.

"If I'm right, it was eight bills, counting tips. That ain't bad for doin' nothing."

"Boolshit, I hustle," Spiro retorted. "You think iss easy, getting grope by Jewish grandmas?"

"*Shit,* yeah, compared to what you been did before. And how's a grandma grope *you,* you scary monster?"

"Hah, you don't know!" Tommy joined the fray. "Those old Hebe broads don't care! And their daughters are *worse* once they get a buzz on. Squeeze your sack like the onion rolls at Zabar's."

Angel hissed a laugh. "Well, say, 'Hands off the merchandise, ladies.'"

"But you *can't;* they think they *own* you for the night. They paid their little money, and they're getting their buck's worth."

Angel turned to me. "What do *you* think? Could you work a bridal shower and not come back bitching about *It's so hard*?"

I looked from face to face, thoroughly stumped. "What, you mean like cater it? Yeah, I guess so."

The three of them eyed each other.

"You didn't *tell* him?" said Tommy. He let out a whoop and punched the couch.

"Tell me what?" I asked Angel. The other two traded fives, making hay of the word *cater*.

"I wanted *them* to do it, tell you how much dough they make, but obviously—hey, *shut the fuck up, Tommy!*"

This last rang out with such sonic violence that the room seemed to stand on its end. Angel aimed his finger at Tommy's head. Tommy glared back at him, then looked down.

"See, I was gonna have *them* do it, but I guess they're just bitches who can't handle a little competition," said Angel. "What they *would've* told you, if they weren't both *bitches,* is they're clockin' thirty thousand working four nights a week, if you could even call that shit work. They would also have told you, if they weren't both *bitches,* that they get more ass than they know what to do with, though neither of 'em knows how to pull a woman and can't even talk to their own moms. And the other thing they'd tell you is they've got all day to train and *still* go audition for parts they'll never get, because—again, as we just saw—they're both *bitches*."

Although this speech conveyed nothing of the job or its discontents, it had the effect of rousing Tommy from his pout. He jerked himself upright, to the edge of the couch, where, half on and half off it, he was poised to lunge. A stare-down ensued. I edged toward the wall, looking for something blunt—a lamp base, a pitcher—to brandish if all hell broke loose. Angel was up already, his feet planted beneath him, his right hand clenched behind his back. "Whaddya got, Tommy? You got somethin' for me? You come up off that sofa, it's do-or-die, slick."

Tommy was breathing fast, his chest rising and falling. The veins in his forearms jumped. It seemed clear he wouldn't stand, but wouldn't stand down either, having worked himself up to this pitch. Whatever it was between them had surely brewed for months, and neither he nor Angel could casually back down, not with all that animus on the line.

"I'll do it," I said. "Whatever you're asking. No problem. I can start tomorrow."

Angel let his fist drop. "You *see* what I'm sayin'? Paulie's with whatever, sight unseen."

"I'm just hoping to make money for school. Assuming there's enough to go around."

"Oh, there's enough cake for *everyone* here. Am I right or am I right, Tom?"

"Only because you *fire* the ones I bring you."

"I do?" said Angel. "Like who?"

"Like that guinea dude, Leo, with the abs. I wasted a week teaching him how to dance, and then you canned him for stripping to the *Godfather* theme!"

"No, I *canned* him for being dumb," Angel said. "He stole that chain from the woman hosting the party and tried to stash the bastard in his G-string."

"That was bad," Spiro concurred. "Leo make us look wrong. Plus, and then he have the small dick."

"Fine. What about the other one, the kid I brung from Jersey. Nothing wrong with *his* dick, as I remember."

"Nah, but I didn't like his country ass."

"Because?"

"The cat was straight redneck, saying Elvis danced better than James Brown! He's lucky I didn't *frag* his monkey ass."

"And so what? Money comes in one shade."

"Not in *my* house. You wanna brag on Elvis, go work in Georgia."

He cleared his throat gruffly to change the subject and bade us help him open up some floor space. By now, of course, I'd twigged what the hustle was and was trying to both conceive it and to keep from laughing at the thought of taking part. Women who'd spend money—certified U.S. tender—to see *me* shake *my* ass? In what cosmos, pray, and who were these sad specimens who had to rent a man merely to look at? The other way around made a certain dippy sense—men so solitary and touch deprived that any female flesh, no matter its imperfections, was a comfort and affirmation to behold. Pensioners, truckers, the perennially enisled—I'd spent enough time among their lonely number to slip into the peep shows on Forty-deuce, then skulk out more morose than when I entered. But the *objects* of that ardor? Why would *they* have to pay, almost a decade after the Summer of Love unleashed them?

"So, Paulie," said Angel, after we'd moved the couch and he'd cued another album on the stack, "what we do at these parties ain't really about dancing, or even, when you think of it, taking clothes off. It's more what I like to call *illusionating,* making these females think we crave their body. Even if they're fat and have a snaggletooth, or rock those scratchy wigs the Jew broads wear."

"What, the *Lubavitchers?*" I gaped. "You're kidding, right? You strip for Orthodox women in Borough Park?"

"Why wouldn't we?" said Tommy. "They're major freaky-deekies, especially the ones married with eight kids."

"Arghh!" I cried. "I'd rather chug borscht. There's no way I'm stripping for *them.*"

"Think again," said Angel. "They pay good money—and trust me, they're gonna love them some *you.*"

He bent over the turntable and advanced the needle, landing on a slow jam by the Isleys. "Now check this," he said. "Imagine a girl on the couch there, sitting with a handful of dollars."

To the lushly libidinous synthesizer moan, he began to unbutton the shirt he'd just fastened and slowly, adroitly, swiveled his hips so that nothing above the belt buckle budged. His crotch and thighs shimmied like dune grass. "Watch my *eyes*," he said, "that's the thing to learn now. The swerve, you'll have to get down later. Notice how I stare, keep my eyes locked in: they're always on the eyes of the girl who's paying."

Off came the shirt with a sinuous flick, drawing notice to what was bared, not discarded. "See?" he said. "I'm just *taaa-king* my time. She knows what she's gonna get when I'm finally naked."

And there went the pants, an artful stop-and-start, teasing them down his granite thighs while he turned to present his ass. Here was another shocker: a black man in a G-string. The taut taper of rayon split his smooth-shaved buttocks and barely bundled in his genitalia. I started to giggle, then stopped myself short and covered it up with a cough. He sent a look backward but was deep in the sway, caught in his own lascivious spell. He spun again slowly, his arms behind his head, making his abdomen rise and fall like the New Year's globe at midnight. At the bottom of its drop, he swung his groin hard; his dick and balls jumped inside their pouch.

"Wow," I cried. "That was unbelievable! If *I* had any singles now, I'd throw them."

Tommy shot a glare. "That would be *gay.*"

"I'm just saying—"

"And we don't make *jokes* about it either," he snapped. "Ballet dancing's queer; this is *art.*"

"No, I—I get that," I said. "I didn't before, but now I really see...what all goes in it."

"Good," said Angel, "then I'll shoot on out. Tommy can take it from here."

"What, you're leaving?" I quailed. "I—I—I was hoping *you'd* show me."

"Just listen to what he says," he said, dressing. "Tommy can teach his ass off—at least the dancing."

"And—but—I mean, when would I start? Should I be out tomorrow shopping for a G-string?"

Tommy gave a snort. "Nah, borrow *mine.*"

Angel zipped his matador flares and beckoned me to walk him to the door. I followed him out, casting a glance behind me. Tommy and Spiro conferred in head-down whispers.

"Look, don't worry," said Angel, sotto voce, as he slung his leather flight bag over a shoulder. "The costumes, the schedule—I got that all covered. You just do your part and learn the ropes. I'm counting on you to pick this up. I got plans for you, and dancing's just the start."

"You sure?" I said. "I don't really see it."

He flashed his fierce smile. "I know you don't; you're a star that ain't caught his own shine yet. The best thing for now, though, is up your dosage. What kind of stack are you on?"

A shudder went through me. "It's that obvious?"

"White boy, *please.* I can spot a juicer at sixty yards. Plus, I scoped the bruises on your ass."

"Oh," I said. "Right. You saw me naked."

With a gulp, I told him what and how often. His brows came down with a thud. "That's *it?*"

"Well, yeah, that's a lot. For *me.*"

"Go home—and I mean *tonight*—and do a double of Deca, and tomorrow I'll front you a cycle of test cyp."

"Really?" I said. "You're sure that's safe?"

With a last frown to hold me, he was out the door and gone. I edged back down the hall to my instructors.

"There he is," said Tommy, "the great white dope. Go ahead and strip so we see what's what."

Nine

The Horah! The Horah!

July 1976

THE THIRD-FLOOR MEN'S ROOM of the Vanderbilt Y was an unhappy place to work through a moral quandary, with its chipped-tooth tile and stink-bomb fetor reminiscent of an Ozark swamp. But there—three stalls down, one foot on the toilet—I stood poised, as it were, over my conscience. I had a needle in one hand, my butt cheek in the other, and a wave of dread working its way north from my chest to my pinched epiglottis. I'm not one for fainting, but the walls were starting to spin, an eddy of ripe graffiti in foot-tall Spanglish.

Angel, in the next stall, had no such qualms. Noisily unbuckling his lumbar belt, he chirped, "The big boys get the toys," as he blithely self-administered an ampule of Deca-Durabolin. He was a great one for Deca and pushed it strongly on the malleable young men he hired, touting its merits as the "cleanest and meanest" helper in the hormone pharmacy. Even at high doses—a thousand migs a week for guys hoping for twenty-pound gains—you got little or none of the androgenic blowback that the heavier steroids threw off—the squishy-soft pecs known as "bitch tits" by juicers from high-dose Anadrol stacks; the acne, baldness, and blood pressure spikes from the prolonged use of Dianabol. Provided you were canny enough to titer your cycles — going up and down in 200-mig steps over eight- or twelve-week stints, then giving yourself a month or so off and switching to test cypionate-and–something — you could go on taking it indefinitely without fear of your liver springing a leak. Or thus spake Angel, the oracle of Deca. "Ain't tryin' to be the biggest one out here," he'd say. "Just tryin' to be big for the longest."

In my case, however, there was no such caution; Angel wanted me harder in a hurry. I had nice lines from the navel up, but below it I had made the blunder of slacking my quads. He put me on a monster course of lunges and hack squats, upped my calorie load with a mid-night meal, and prescribed a two-week blowout of "catch-up juice" to maximize my protein burn. Comprising daily bumps of Deca and test cyp and twenty-mil tabs of Anadrol, the cocktail did its dirty work, turning me into a rabid thing. Ravenous and speedy, I'd sleep four fitful hours, then bound out of bed at six a.m. like a tiger smelling a wart-hog in the brush. I'd run a fast mile to the Four Brothers Diner, wolf a five-egg omelet clotted with bacon, then do pull-ups and push-ups in Riverside Park before waking up Kate around eight. She lent herself drowsily to my pawing exertions, then asked me, after a week, to give her a break. "It's great that I turn you on, but I'm getting blisters," she caviled. "And what's with all these bruises on your ass?"

But the jump-off, as Angel called it, brought swift returns. In a fort-night, I'd added ten pounds of mass and at 197 was within hailing dis-tance of that most mythical of numbers, 200. Some of this, he warned me, was water weight that would melt off when I cut the Anadrol, and despite the new ripple in my lower quads, I had "far, far to go" in sym-metry. Still, he said he was pleased with my progress: I was "serious as cancer," his highest praise.

And so here I was now, needle in hand in the filth-daubed confines of the john, poised for a second blast of Deca *that day* to steel me for my debut three hours later. The suggestion, of course, was Angel's: he said the bump would calm me, smooth the case of nerves I was sure to have. "It's hard, poppin' your cherry. I was scared out of my mind dancing for fifty *chicas* on Fordham Road," he told me. "They were feeling on my hips, goin' 'Feed me, *papi*,' and sticking singles in my G-string with their teeth. I wished *I'd* had somebody teach me game back then, but the other dudes were, *Fuck you. Sink or swim.*"

I got the point, of course: I was to be grateful for his care. The drinks and coke he comped me when we cruised for girls, shooting the vapids of East Side bars and cave-dark discos in the Village; the pep talks he gave me at predawn diners over plates of walnut pancakes and waffle fries; and the check-in phone calls on nights we didn't hang, making sure I was "taking care of biz" — the attention was flattering, even addictive. But none of that made me any less nervous about my second shot of Deca that day. I was, as Kate noted, sporting lurid bruises on the flesh between hip and spine and having a tough go finding places to shoot that didn't burn *before* I plunged in the needle.

The greater cause for worry, though, was my mood of late, a loop-the-loop of sentiment and short-fuse fury. I belly-laughed at things that had left me stone-faced before, blurted out "I love you" during a scalp massage from Kate, and blew my stack without warning or cause, then walked away, rattled and confused. The teens that pushed in front of me boarding the M5 bus, whom I chased down the rear steps two blocks later; the couple across the hall who woke Kate up with their crash-bang fights at three a.m. and who had to phone the landlord for a new front door after I caved theirs in with a kick — the steroid bump turned me into the goon I now resembled, seized by emotions I could only convey through big, teary hugs and property damage.

"It's too quiet in there. This ain't a prayer booth," said Angel. "Just handle your bee-eye and be out."

"I'm trying," I said. "But my *ass* is on fire. Where am I supposed to shoot this anymore?"

He chuckled, zipping his pants. "That's test cyp for you. You want me to find you a spot?"

"Uh, thanks; I think I'll handle it myself. But meanwhile, what do I do about these bruises?"

"No problem," he said. "I got concealer for that. A little makeup and you'll have the butt of a newborn babe."

"Really? What happens when I sweat?"

A snuffling laugh. "You're nervous is all. Stop freaking; you're gonna *kill* 'em out there."

"Yeah, about that," I said. "You *are* going to show me the end-move, right? Because I asked before and you kept saying later, and here it is going on five o'clock and—"

He tapped my door suavely as he strutted by, the rings on his fingers playing staccato. "I told you: don't worry, man; I got you covered. Just do me a favor and fire that Deca. You want to be extra sharp there for your close-up."

I heard him go out and the door close behind him. The thought of the business ahead that night unmoored me. I reached for the wall to brace myself and gagged when my palm turned moist. An ooze the color of steamed kale daubed the pipe, sweating the tiles behind it. I knelt, with the needle still in hand, groping for toilet paper. There was none, of course, and I slapped the roller, enraged. It spun on its pegs, so I slapped it again for smarting off to me. Earlier that week I'd given a good, swift kick to the Castro Convertible that wouldn't fold, then hopped around the room in starburst pain while my big toe turned bright colors. I had no prior history of violence against furniture and could fairly be said to have enjoyed cordial relations with inanimate objects in general. But lately I'd begun wondering if there wasn't something afoot with the appliances in my life, a tacit agreement between toasters and blenders to thwart my every move. The hair dryer that quit on me before a club crawl; the iron that singed my Armani flares, basting a nasty arrow near the crotch: it didn't take the mind of a Magritte or Dalí to think that they begrudged me—yes, *household appliances*—my vastly improved new sex life.

I stared at the needle. It stared right back, its tiny, leering eye wet with love. *Fuck it,* I said, and pointed it at my ass, when the door of the stall creaked open. An old man in swim trunks stood before me, holding a battered cane. He stopped and gawked at my naked rear. His mouth worked in slow, dry circles.

"B-tvelve?" he said in a Yiddish brogue, eyeing the syringe.

"I-I'm sorry, what?"

"It's a B-tvelve shot, for make you exercise?" He formed a sort of muscle with his arm.

"Oh, a B-*twelve* shot. Yeah, that's right. I do it before I work out."

He pointed proudly to his gnarled biceps. "Tuna fish," he said with a toothless smile. "I make from scratch tvice a day."

"That's nice." I nodded at the open door, but he wouldn't take the hint. "So I'm gonna finish up here, okay?"

"Sure," he said, not budging an inch, except to broaden his grin. As I turned to slam the door, he caught sight of my erection. It was a hard thing to miss, being a hot shade of purple, which will happen when you're hard for three days.

"Boy, that B-tvelve's something." He whistled. "For this, you need a *prescription?*"

WE GOT TO THE GIG AFTER NINE that night, an hour-plus late and in ill humor. Angel, who loathed maps and leaving the city limits, got hopelessly lost taking the Meadowbrook south, went east instead of west on Sunrise Highway, and drove us past Babylon before he turned around and inched his way back toward Long Beach. "*Putos gringos!*" he yelled, more Dominican by the mile. "Put a fucking sign up we can read!"

He rarely served as chauffeur on the dancing jobs, but this one was important on several fronts, not least that he was mounting a beachhead in the burbs. He laid out his vision as I sat up front with him on the crushed-velvet bench seat of his Toronado. "In a year or two — watch — I'll have Nassau locked down, and you'll be running a crew of college strippers. I'm telling you, Paulie, it's all about the body. Muscle is takin' over. It's the next cocaine."

I nodded and said nothing, my stomach doing cartwheels off the *last* cocaine. I was jumpy below the jawline and scattered above it, my butt crack puckered by the strap of the thong I'd donned for the first time that evening. Fighting off fear-stabs about the job ahead — *What if the client's house was fraught with mold and I suddenly found myself short of breath, or if someone I knew was there, a girl from one of my classes or my aunt in Hempstead?* — I turned my mind's eye back on whence we'd come. I saw Kate hunched over a torts textbook at the all-but-empty diner, stirring cold coffee with the cap of her Bic on another summer night given to work. I saw my father in his study, drumming the desk with two fingers, blocked by a review that resisted being written and the implacable woman in the next room. I saw Ivan and his friends on the moonlit grass overlooking Wollman Rink, camped on a blanket, gobbling blotter acid, at a Hot Tuna concert in the park. I saw them as a bird sees his brood below, of them but away, caught in gusts. No malice, no rapture, only the propulsion of air and the fact of being aloft. That alone held power that I couldn't — or wouldn't — relinquish. Flying high was all now, come what might.

Meanwhile, in the backseat, Tommy wouldn't shut up, a one-man talk show, no guest needed. A self-called "mutt" whose father had fought in Korea and whose brother had come home missing most of a leg from a hang-mine explosion in Quang Tri, Tommy had had his political awakening when Nixon was granted a pardon and flew home to San Clemente "with almost a million fucking dollars of *our money.*" "Here, ya crooked bitch, you lost Laos and Cambodia — here's a million bucks and an attaboy!" he railed. "Have a nice time there in sunny California while the rest of us are sweating out World War Three. Ya know the Russians moved their nukes in during the 'seventy-three war? Dropped 'em in the desert and aimed 'em right at Tel Aviv, saying 'We want the West Bank back!' And what does Israel do, does it say, '*Fuck* that, you can have it'? Nooo, 'cause they got *Nixon* to back their play, and so off *they* go, throwing Stingers across the Suez. I read where the Knesset built Kissinger a house there, and every time he gave 'em another batch of missiles, they added another wing onto his house. You can look that shit up. I think I saw it in *Hustler*, which is more than just a tittie mag now—"

"Tom, *squash it,* man, I'm tryin' to drive!" said Angel. "Can anyone read that sign there? We need the Wantagh Parkway."

I bent forward to look. It said Robert Moses Causeway.

"I mean, *I* can't figure it out, but maybe Paulie can. *He's* the smart guy going to college," said Tommy. "How—and no offense here—do the Jews keep doing it, make the president of America their bottom bitch? Can you help me on this one? D'ya have an uncle somewhere who knows the high rabbi at the World Bank? Me, I got no ins; I'm just a schmuck from Bell Boulevard. But you, you got a father wired for sound, being a big-time publisher and hanging out with James Michener—"

"Tommy, I swear, I'll drop your ass here. What is *wrong* with you, that you can't stop for five minutes?"

THE HOUSE IN LONG BEACH was three in from the water, fronting a sandy strip of Cape Cods pushed together on plots too small to permit a lawn. Sitting there, in the bluestone drive where several cars were parked, Angel ran the game plan for the third time in an hour. We were to do our thing and leave, he said—two hours maximum, start to finish. He'd be waiting out front at eleven p.m. sharp, which allowed for no side jobs in the upstairs den or picking up spare coin in the master bath. Above all, we weren't to wander off the grounds for a one-on-one moon dance down the beach. The man of the house, he said, was "a person who knew people," and we didn't want to be there, holding our dicks, if he got back early from his trip.

"And where *you* gonna be while we're making you rich?" asked Tommy from the seat behind him.

"Don't worry," said Angel, patting his courier bag. "I gotta see a man about a dog in Queens, but I'll be on the button, so you be, too."

He didn't get out and walk us to the door but caught my wrist as I went past his window. "Let me see," he said, doing a fast inspection, eyeing me in my work boots and Dickies. Flashing his gleamy grin, he said, "Get ready to be *paid,* man. You're my new sensation, starting today."

I thanked him for the encouragement and headed away, but he had me by the wrist and pulled me closer. "You *did* do that thing at the gym, though, right? I forgot to ask you before."

"What thing?"

His smile, by way of answer, took an edge.

"What, the Deca?" I said. "Well, yeah, I...I found a spot. Right beside the tailbone, middle in."

"Yo, Paulie, let's *go,* man," Tommy groused.

Angel went on staring. "You sure?"

"Yeah, after you left, I did that vial up and got a nice boost from it. Like you said."

His stare narrowed to a sword's point. "No, you didn't."

I glanced at him, then down at my feet. He released me with an angry snap of the hand. "I asked you twice to hit that, and you dogged me out. Are you on the fuckin' team or just out for you?"

"No, no, I'm totally on the team. A hundred percent. I—I just didn't get a chance to—"

"Then *listen* when I try to tell you a thing! I happen to have some *knowledge* you can use. It's very few people that I kick game to. Like they say, it's to be sold, not told."

I turned over pebbles with the toe of my boot, building a little mound beside his tire. "You're right," I said. "I'm sorry I lied. It's just...I'd already done a bump today and—"

"*Confidence,*" he said, and let it linger a moment. "It's all about the confidence of the lion. You do that second hit, you're the king of the fuckin' jungle. Walk in any door and they say, *There's Simba.*"

He dropped the car in gear and backed up shrilly, spraying my shins with pebbles as he spun.

THERE WERE TWENTY WOMEN, minimum, in the big room on our left when we passed through on our way down to the basement. Most, as I learned later, had been drinking since seven, and Teresa, whose bridal shower and house this was, needed to throw the bolt on the cellar door to prevent their following us down. We could hear them through the ceiling, though, stamping their feet and chanting "We want men!" in giggly chorus.

"That's what you get for being late," said Teresa, who was both sozzled and furious. A tall brunette with a metallic tan and the full efflorescence of *Nass-ore* County in every contentious vowel, she had her arms folded as she read us the riot act on the sanctity of Her Night. "This is the one and only toym I plan on getting married, and yuh not walkin' in heah to savatawge me on the week of my joyous occasion. To *troy* to make this up, you're gonna work an extra owuh, and tough to whoevuh you're sposedta go to next. And anothuh thing: I want you to be extra-special noyce to all my valued friends. They work hahd fuh their money and spent a lot to make me happy, so get up there, chop-chop, and make me happy!"

Tommy tried to argue, citing the outbound traffic, but Teresa, who said she dealt with liars all day as a sportswear buyer for Gimbels, wouldn't grant a word in edgewise. So up we went, not lions but lambs, trooping in in our thoroughly moot disguises. (Our cover as Con Ed men had been fatally breached when the woman who let us in yelled, "We got beef!")

The guests, whose number seemed to have swelled since our arrival, were grouped in a sort of horseshoe in the living room. Some sat, some stood, some danced in place, knocking over gift boxes and their cargo of rayon teddies. They were women in their thirties with a certain shimmer: elaborate hair and makeup, nails done to a mirror finish, and great care paid to their shoes and purses, the totems of careers in the garment trade. I'd met girls on campus who could have been their sisters, and knew at a glance we were in trouble. Besides being raised by compulsive mothers who wouldn't give their offspring an inch, they'd been taught by their fathers to be tough as nails in their personal dealings with men. The dictum handed down — *Don't get taken advantage of* — had turned them into accountants of feelings.

There were open bottles of wine on the white credenza, others sitting empty on the coffee table, and at least two joints going around the room, neither of which were doing us any favors. A thicket of hands came at us as we entered the room, sampling our rumps like fabric. I looked at Tommy, who swerved matador-style, trying to save his honor with fake cheer. "Easy there, ladies! You'll get plenty of chances later. *Whoa,* baby, the show hasn't even *started.*"

We huddled by the bench of the grand piano. "Holy shit," he said. "This is out of control. How do we—"

"There's no *space,*" hissed Spiro. "I got no room to dance. I fall on one of these chicks, they go after my father. Sue him for his diner *and* his house."

"Man, *later* for that. Just guard your fuckin' nuts—this is survival mode."

Agitated before, I was panicked now, my heartbeat kicking the bass-drum opener of Zeppelin's "D'yer Mak'er." My breathing galloped, short sips of air that didn't seem to make it to my lungs. Tommy was talking fast, but I—dizzy and damp-palmed, panting hard—barely made him out. He had an eight-track in his hand, the Isleys' "The Heat Is On," and was shouting at the woman in charge of the music to *something-something* play the *something-something.* But there was a record on already that the girls were wild to hear, and when he handed her our set list, she stuffed it in her pocket and shout-sang in unison with the thirty or so women the words of the tune being played. *"These boots are made for walking, and that's just what they'll do, one of these days these boots are gonna WALK ALL OVER YOU!"*

Tommy turned to Teresa for guidance. "What am I, your choreogra-phuh?" she cried. "*Shtrip!* Take those pants off, damn it!"

Bumblingly, then, with no fanfare or stagecraft, we began doffing socks and boots. We were bunched, like Custer's men, in a cul-de-sac, our backs against the piano bench, our left and right flanks blocked by women. Spiro asked them nicely to sit down, please, but only a handful obliged. Others saw an opening and pressed in closer, the scent of their posh perfume and cigarette smoke commingling with the musk of supermarket wine to create, if you will, a confetti for the nose, a bouquet to the enhanced male form. I grabbed Tommy's arm to stay upright.

"*What?*" he said, looking frenzied himself. "I thought your people had *class.*"

"Would you *stop?*" I croaked. "I-I'm really freaking out here. I need to go to the john and be—"

"You do and I'll beat your ass!" he seethed. "Don't you try pulling that tonight!"

He turned to face the crowd, mounted a crooked grin, and picked his way to the center of the room. Spiro bent toward me and, in an act of mercy, gave my arm a squeeze. "I don't like Scotch, but we drinking *hard* stuff when we done. Meantime, do what I do." I staggered behind him, feeling a bit less stricken.

Tommy got the crowd to hush and the woman minding the music to turn it down. "Ladies, I know we're late and you kinda started without us, but we're gonna stay till each of you gets their...*doors blown.*" He gave the two words a pelvic tilt and dropped his work-suit zipper to his waist. "I personally see loads of you I wanna throw a private show, including, of course, the gorgeous Tina herself—"

"It's *Teresa,*" snapped the bride-to-be.

"As how can I forget?" He avoided her gaze, taking his zipper down to bare his thong. "But ladies, we need your help to make this a great show. We need you to all take five steps back and form a big V. Or a C. Whatever."

The women took three steps back, formed a polyhedron, and started a rhythmic clap. Tommy reeled us in and called an audible. "These chicks don't want to hear *schvartzes* from Teaneck sing about 'Fight the Power,'" he said. "Just follow my lead for three or four numbers, and then, when their panties're moist, we'll give 'em the finale."

I heard my heart again. "*What* finale? You told me to—"

He pulled away gruffly, said something to Spiro, and asked the friend in charge to start the record. "Um, the first song's not real with-it," she said. "You've got Nancy doing 'As Tears Go By.'"

"Nope," he said. "No good. What's after that?"

"Um, let's see…Oh, 'Day Tripper'! Now, *that* she really gets down on."

"Perfect!" he said, with a note of evil. "Nancy Sinatra rocks out!"

And on it came, with high hat and horns: Frank's daughter burying the Beatles in a Vegas grave. To polyester chords and the *blat!* of a trombone, Tommy tugged his zipper the rest of the way down and let the work suit shimmy to the floor. In a stars-and-stripes thong, he did a medley of sixties dances, milling his arms in front of him to the Frug. "*She's a big teaser,*" he mouthed, tossing his head. "*She took me half the way there, now.*"

Spiro fell in with him, and I slid to Tommy's left, my soft tissue as taut as guy wire. After weeks of practice with a funk-soul groove, I was way off-kilter with Nancy's oompah cover and got so bollixed trying to find the beat that I clean forgot to strip as I went along. Several guests pointed this out to Tommy, who danced up on me and made a joke of nudging my zipper down. I was aghast, but he'd hit on something: the women yelled as the bit wore on. He went and stood behind me while he peeled my work suit off, adding a gay-sex hump gag just for laughs. This *killed* with the crowd, as did the G-string Angel had made me: a big blue Star of David on a bone white field.

"That's right!" barked Tommy over "It Ain't Me Babe." "Paulie's Jewish, ladies—and *verrry* single!"

I'd all but stopped dancing now, stump-legged with shame, but the women seemed not to care. They bunny-hopped in place, blowing kisses and throwing money. Tommy spun me around, bellowing, "Shake it for the shekels! Show 'em you put the *he* back in *He-brew*!"

Wooden and unwilling, I twitched a circle with my ass.

"More!" cried Tommy, whipping his arms. "Do it like I showed you—move it faster!"

A chant sprang up now. "Faster! Faster!"

"Put the pedal to the *shtetl*!" one girl hollered.

I glanced over my shoulder. The place was bedlam, a dense throng

143

of shul-going daughters and sisters shouting like the sidemen at a fight. Several were barely upright, staggering against their friends. Others tossed their heads back or clinked cocktail glasses, spilling wine coolers on the expensive rug that, like everything else in sight, was snowflake white. There were late-arriving guests in the narrow hall, a couple of them shrieking "*oohwuh-ooh*"; two teenage girls hopping up and down; and somewhere in the back a woman standing apart, looking as if she might begin to cry. The song, in all its bebop kitsch, ended with a sax salute. Tommy pointed at the floor around me. It was littered with crumpled cash.

"And now," he cried as I bent to scoop, "who here knows the words to 'Hava Nagilah'?"

I heard nervous laughter, then somebody started singing. By the second bar, everyone was at it. "The grand finale!" said Tommy, linking hands with me and Spiro. "I didn't show you 'cause I knew you would know it."

"But I—I don't—"

"Sure you do!" he shouted. "You were *born* knowing how. Do the funky horah, Paulie Pesach!"

And away he led me, hand in hand, as we flew a fast circle, kicking high. Left foot, right foot, jerked this way then that by the crush of women who joined our little band. Around we went, now faster and wider, arms and feet tangling and women shouting Hebrew as they goosed me and Spiro going by. *Uru achim b'lev sameach, uru achim b'lev sameach...* Having nowhere else to put them, I'd tucked the wad of damp singles in the half-inch strap of my thong and could feel as well as see them working their way loose with each new jostle and bump. I freed a hand and grabbed them, then was seized by new dancers and yanked into a circle within the circle. We spun double speed in reverse direction, howling and laughing at the blur of features whipping dizzily past our heads. There was a hand on my ass, grasping the knot of sheer fabric, and a woman drunk with laughter droning "*Love!*" as loud as life, and I suddenly stopped caring about the tumult in my lungs and the insult done my pride by the butt-dance-for-dollars, and opened my hand to let the money go. It flew up and seemed to flap a moment, suspended by the stiff, centripetal breeze. Then, one by one, the bills lost their wings and wafted down like ticker tape greeting a train. We danced and danced on a carpet of cash, we children of an unremitting God, who gazed down, hard-eyed, scribbling notes.

THE NIGHT STROBED BY, a reel of freeze-frame commerce. The last I saw of Spiro, he was headed outside with his arm around the blonde who'd handled the music. I tried to stay put but was pulled from room to room by groups of slurred-speech women. They yelled questions over each other while they stroked my chest and investigated my smooth-shaved thighs, asking if it was "different having sex with *treyf*" and what my girlfriend thought of my vocation. I told them, as Angel had taught me, that I was seeing no one special, and improvised a riff about stripping my way through law school so that one day I could repay my mother for all her sacrifices. This met with *aahs* from the older women, several of whom slid their business cards between the singles they tucked in my strap.

I danced in the kitchen for Teresa's aunts and was tipped with loose change and a couple of those coin-shaped chocolates you get for Hanukkah. Later, I got roped into the upstairs john for a couple of lines of coke and some sloppy kisses with the zaftig next-door neighbor who attended Hofstra. But in spite of my pie-eyed blunders, the cash kept coming: $112 in tips, not counting the $40 for showing up. That was what I'd cleared all *week* at the Wall Street job and helped mediate some of the creeping guilt I felt on Kate's behalf. I was, after all, earning a living now, as she'd surely understand if the subject arose, though there seemed no urgent need to broach it soon. I'd buy her a lovely gift with the money, or wait till I'd done a month of gigs, then spring for something lavish, like diamond studs. They'd speak to how I felt, express my deep-going affection, even after her crack about me strutting the street like a champion rooster. That was how I walked, and she'd had no right to slag me for it. It made me, frankly, wonder whether she really *got* me, understood how rare a bird I was.

Strangely, there was no sign of Angel at eleven. I looked out the window every five or ten minutes and by midnight began to panic about our ride home. I asked around the house and found Tommy upstairs, "performing" in one of the two guest bedrooms. "Angel *who?*" he chortled, sticking his head out the door. "He's probably getting his helmet buffed somewhere."

"But weren't we supposed to leave before this guy got back? He warned us not to do, um, private shows."

"Yeah, funny, *ha-ha.* How you think I bought my Beemer? Look, we'll grab the last train when I'm done."

"You're sure there is one? I could ask if they have a schedule..."

"Yeah, you do that, then come back in an hour. In fact—"

He shut the door, then opened it. "I was saving this for me, but you earned it, chief. Great job your first time out."

"Oh." I brightened, taking the joint from him. "Well, thanks, man. I was worried that I might have—"

"Nah, you did good, and I'll pass that on to Angel. But grab yourself a girl and do this right. It's mellow gold and makes the sex *outrageous.*"

I thanked him again and padded downstairs, winking as I passed the hall mirror. Angel, it seemed, was prescient: there *was* a nice market for a well-built Jew with a turn of phrase. Spiro had the size and Tommy the swagger, but I brought panache to the beef parade, classing up a low-rent operation. No need to quote Keats or wear horn-rimmed glasses, though those might make a nice prop. All I had to do was open my mouth and let the enchantment unfold.

But something in my reflection made me stop and turn for a probing second look. I spot-checked, as always, my chest and arms, then stepped back to take in the whole. What I saw appalled me: a smirking hulk in a teensy thong with a big Star of David on the front. Suddenly, I was staring through my father's eyes, agog with shame and betrayal. *Is this how you use the gift I gave you? Is this all you really amount to?*

I fled downstairs and hid out, briefly, in the powder room off the foyer. I'd spoken to Dad twice since the ride from school, deflecting his invites to a Yankee game with lies about catering jobs. It was too soon to see him and proclaim détente, behave as though the bad years were just a blip, the prologue to a free-and-clear engagement. He was trying, I knew, to seed the ground, to say (by not saying) that he'd suffered, too; there was more than enough pain to go around. But his gestural language left me cold: I wanted a full admission that he'd done me wrong, had sabotaged my boyhood with a single blow and was committed to making amends. Anything less would be met, for now, with polite but firm demurrals.

But that didn't mean I'd stopped thinking about Dad or felt myself untethered. He was always nearby, the stern gaze behind me, watching and sifting, appraising. No thought went unread, no utterance unheard; he was hardwired in me and wouldn't leave. Also on hand was his daunting example, the one by which I judged all others. He'd fashioned magic from his ragged start as the son of a brutish father, leaving home early to birth himself in the navy and then Ann Arbor, a ravenous reader and critic-in-training from the day he arrived on campus. He worked so hard he was known as the Ox, winning the Hopwood in fiction and lit crit before bulling his way through grad school in Chicago. There was no stopping Dad, though he was perennially broke, and bewitched, and burdened by Mom, having wooed her from Bellmar to the Tahoe casino where they blew their tuition on craps. He churned past resistance, some of it self-made, to land a big job in New York, the young but hard-nosed impresario of a new generation of writers—Ozick, Paley, Coover, Barth, to name just the first wave of stars. And here stood his son with a clump of singles and his dick in a rayon sling. I needed a Scotch. In fact, make it a double. I was drinking for two.

A HALF HOUR LATER I was headed upstairs with a schoolteacher friend of the bride-to-be and her plump, eager cousin from Hewlett. I did a two-song snake dance to the radio on the dresser, then nervously accepted an invitation to come lie down with them. As I lit the joint, the plump one, Elissa, peeled her blouse and jean shorts off and wrapped her thigh around mine. Tension developed over how to proceed. The girls were good friends as well as relations, and agreed it would be awkward—"gross" was the term employed—to engage in carnal knowledge of each other. *Say something,* I told myself. *Don't just lie there.* But when I opened my mouth to speak, nothing happened. I was stoned to the point of paraplegia, my arms and legs heavy as phone poles. *Tommy!* I thought-shrieked, then floated away, watching myself from somewhere overhead.

I may have dozed a while; that seems likely, because when I turned to ask Elissa what time it was, I found myself alone on the bed. The room was stationary, but I was moving, spinning slow circles around the ceiling fan, which was shaped like birds of prey. I was cold and hot—a breeze chilling my arms, the sheet damp beneath me from perspiration—as well as famished and nauseous in alternate waves, recoiling from a stench I couldn't place. Hours or minutes passed—I couldn't say which, because the arm my watch was strapped to wouldn't budge.

At some point I decided it would be a fine idea if I at least sat up; that way, gravity would work for, not against, me and enable me to find my clothes. Inch by inch, I rolled off the bed, an act of will joined by such grunting and groaning as to conjure the slaves of Egypt building dams. With my feet on the floor, things improved, and I found I could stand on my own power. I didn't see my work suit or the Red Wing boots, but I did learn the source of the demon smell: a small lagoon of vomit near the bed.

"What the hell is this now—you're still *here?*"

Teresa was standing in the open door. She'd washed off her makeup and removed her blouse, ready to collapse into bed.

"I-I'm just looking for my—"

"For *what?* You stole enough with your dipshit friends—oh no, you didn't, you son of a *bitch!*"

I saw her gaping at the ooze behind me. "Hey, that was there when I woke up."

"You barfed on my brand-new carpet, you prick? That's *wool*, not some cheap-shit weave!" She grabbed a stuffed zebra at the foot of her bed and proceeded to flog me with it. "Get outta heah *now*. Get outta my *goddamn house*! I'll give you such a beatin', you'll..."

She ran to her bureau and searched for something blunter, tossing support hose over her shoulder in search of God knows what. I wanted to explain that I wasn't the perp, that I shared her outrage at the demise of manners, including, I'd a mind to tell her, those of her cousin, who hadn't even bothered to towel me off after making me come on myself. I also meant to add that she'd gotten a deal, paying the going rate for a party of twenty, then packing the house with her friends and neighbors and the girls from the deli up the block. My mouth, however, was on tape delay, and by the time I got a word out, she'd grabbed her belt and swung it with a convincing flick of the wrist. This made no inroads on my speech impairment but did improve the blood flow to my feet. I clomped down the steps, tightly gripping the rail in case my legs gave out, and jostled a woman on the bottom stair who was too tired or drunk to move aside.

There were half a dozen stragglers in the living room, their shoes off and makeup smudged. One looked over and gave a bleary wink. "Hey. You lift weights or something, don't you?"

I reached behind her head for the dark blue work suit. There was no T-shirt, however, or shirt of any kind, and I frantically sank to my hands and knees looking for it underneath the sofa.

"I was thinking of maybe going to a gym myself," she said. "My arms — right here, see? — are starting to get fat. Hadassah arms, we call 'em. What works for that?"

There was nothing under the couch, but my boots were behind a chair, along with a white ribbed tank top. I hadn't worn a tank top but was in no state to carp; the general unwellness that had dogged me all night now ramped itself up to dread. What I yearned for, besides a train to Penn Station, was my feet underneath me and going fast.

"D'ya have a business card, in case somethin' comes up? My girlfriend's getting married and I —"

I was out the door and gone while donning the shirt, heading in the direction of the train station. It had cooled down some, the air sifted by breezes, and the avenue lay out long and straight, bounded on either side by shrubs. It felt great to be going again, my legs strong beneath me, my feet shaking out the lead-sole torpor of what I suspected was PCP. Even my tattered lungs were clear as a bell doing a nine-minute mile, a pace I was proud to have pushed my way past in those early-morning runs in Riverside Park. And gone, at least for now, was any introspection about the panic that sent me barreling down the road. *Something* was going on here that needed attention; anyone who could lat pull more than his weight was supposed to earn a pass from fear. That was the point of those maniac sessions from five to eight each weeknight, work-outs that left me so fatigued that I sometimes overslept my stop on the bus and was rousted by the driver in Harlem.

Three-quarters of a mile down, I heard a noise behind me. It whined as it got closer, a high-rev gulp, the sound of someone shifting into third. My pale heart jumped, taking a dive off its board. I looked around for something to crouch behind. Ten feet ahead, I saw a break in the hedge and, not stopping to size the gap, barreled through it. Short, spiny twigs brushed my face like wire and caught hold of my shirt, ripping it open. I cursed and checked my torso for cuts; the tank top was matted with brambles. A red BMW sprinted by, with Hadassah Arms peering over the wheel. I punched my thigh so hard I saw stars.

By the time I finished combing my clothes for burrs, tore the T-shirt off, and limped the last mile, it was going on two a.m. The station, of course, was shuttered, its platform empty, a tube light blinking on and off. Chilled to the bone, I tried the ticket house, the door of which rebuffed my angry kicks.

Sometime after dawn, a train pulled in. I paid my fare and slipped inside the john. Throwing the bolt behind me, I found a roll of Charmin and wound it out to form a padded seat. There I sat, counting the wad of singles, till we reached the wine-dark tunnels of Manhattan.

Ten

The Ride of the Four Whoresmen

August 1976

OWING TO MY SCHEDULE—I'd danced till one a.m. for a party of legal secretaries in Dyker Heights—we didn't get to Jones Beach much before noon and had to walk forever in the hotfoot sand to find a patch of grit to lay our spread. It was a boiling Sunday in a summer full of them, and *todo el barrio* had caught an earlier train and was all set up for the *quinceañera*. Radio–cassette decks boomed from blankets, treating us to Spanish class at one hundred beats per minute. Teenage *mamis* in full eye makeup congregated at water's edge, careful not to get their toenails wet. Kate made a face as she slipped her shorts off. "Somebody here owes me a week away and *not* to South Jersey," she said. "As little as I see you, it better be nice. Block Island would do, for starters."

"Well, but when?" I said. "Angel's booked me through the month, and then it's back to school the week after."

"And I tell you I don't get it. Who's *here* still in August, that you have so many catering jobs suddenly?"

"It's crazy, huh?" I reached up under her shirt to spread lotion on her back. "Believe me, it's hell wearing that hot tuxedo, but I really need to strike while there's all this work."

I cinched my arms around her waist and clasped her to me to graze her fragrant neck. "We'll get away this fall, do a four-day thing. Maybe fly to Jamaica or someplace. In the meantime... *Mmm*, I love the scent of you here. And there... and—"

"If you loved it, you'd take me to *Bermuda*," she vamped, trying none too hard to pull away. "And no sex here in little San Juan."

"What, I can't give a harmless kiss to the hottest girl on the beach?"

She snickered softly. "You don't have a harmless bone in you. I *thought* you did, but boy, was I ever wrong."

Still, she sagged against me, eyes shut and head back, humming a drowsy tune. We'd fucked at three a.m., when I came in from work, and then again at nine when we awoke. Such was the force of my seething need, though, that here I was again with my billy club. I arched away from her and looked down timidly; the head of my cock poked out of the low-cut Speedo. Before I got things sorted, I glanced around. There were half a dozen people staring at me.

"Fu-uck," I groaned, yanking her to me again for cover.

"What?" she murmured. "Did you forget to bring the—whoa, and what's *this* now?"

"Don't move," I said. "Just stay there till I tell you."

On the blanket across from us, a grade school girl cast a frown at me. "You *nasty*," she said, picking a scab on her elbow.

I mouthed the word *sorry,* then winked at her, trying to buy forgiveness.

"Ucch," she said, and spun on her heel, marching toward the G-rated surf.

"You're scaring me," Kate murmured, oblivious of the girl but not the crazed intruder against her rear. "I'm serious now; I want you to make an appointment. Isn't it time you got that thing of yours looked at?"

Getting it looked at isn't the problem. I hiked her blouse and folded it before me to provide a sort of shield. Modesty reclaimed, I flopped to the sand and lay on my gut for hours.

Sometime after three, the breeze kicked up. It sent newspapers whipping like flattened kites and drove most of our neighbors to the parking lot, dragging their coolers (and *culos*) behind them. The two of us huddled behind our berm of towels, letting hands go wherever they liked as we licked the dried sea from each other. There's magic in being alone before a body of water, all that relentlessness at your feet, the *life-life-life* that churns thousands of miles to land up here, its force spent. While the wind moaned an aria of mild regret, we let ourselves be pulled down into the spell, whispering things we hadn't said all summer — not in the daylight, anyway. Clambering up the dunes, we made watchful love, and Kate wept a little when she came. "I said I wouldn't let myself care," she croaked. "We're children still; this has no shot whatever."

We hitched a ride to Merrick and took the train the rest of the way. Rounding the curve in Queens, she broke a taut silence. "I want to meet your father. And soon."

"Um...not a good idea."

"Fine, then; your mother."

"That's a worse one."

"I don't care. I need some history here. For all I know, you're from a research lab. I mean, *look* at you, Paul: you get bigger by the day. How is that possible at your age?"

I wanted to tell her then; truly, I did, be done with all the shameful withholding. I sensed she'd receive it in the spirit offered and forgive this concoction of muscle and pathos and a preteen's notion of forging ahead. Perhaps she'd even see my chemical stunt as a means to self-creation, breaking open the bars of the cage I grew up in to live as my nature decreed. Ah, but that nature had banked no credit, having lied to her since June. Once she learned the truth about those bruises on my ass, she'd drag from me, in no time flat, what I'd *really* done for Angel all those nights. There was no hope — none — that I could titrate the truth, tell her this but not that. The only one who fell for that was me.

"It's just, our time together is precious, and I don't want to waste it having a meal with my father at Gitlitz deli. Why don't we go to Windows on the World? Play dress-up and drink champagne till one a.m.?"

"Because it's crazy to blow a hundred dollars on dinner. He can come to my place for a third of that, and that's *with* two bottles of decent red."

"Right, but it's not the money; it's the quality of time we—"

"Oh, but it *is* the money!" she said with sudden umbrage. "Ever since you met this Angel, money and what it buys you are all I hear."

I gawked at her. "Come on, I wouldn't do that. I know what kind of budget you're on."

"Maybe you don't hear it, but it's all…the…time. 'Look at my new slip-ons from Charles Jourdan!'"

I squawked in indignation, but Kate was right: I couldn't keep my wallet in my pants. The worst of it was clothing—it *summoned* me, called me from the windows of boutiques. *You've earned it,* said the pair of eel-skin boots, winking through the glass at McCreedy & Schreiber. *No one's had it harder,* said the Ultrasuede jeans on the mannequin at Ted Lapidus. Wherever I went, I saw something hot that filled a hole in my closet and quelled, for a moment, the voice in my head that started each sentence *I need…*

"I…What can I say? I'm flabbergasted. I'd no idea I was being a…"

She said nothing for a while, taking short, slow breaths to hold off pending tears. "I know you were badly raised, but it doesn't *excuse* things—let you come and go like rules don't matter."

"Well, and I agree. I need to learn that."

"Do you?" she said. "Because I'm not sure. It feels like there's this…*thing* in you I can't talk to."

"Thing?" I laughed. "What, an alien probe?"

She stared at the flame-shot dusk. "Not alien," she said. "More like *animal.* This big, angry beast ready to spring."

THAT NIGHT, UNABLE TO fall asleep for the tension we'd left unpacked, I lay glaring holes in Kate's ceiling. The problem wasn't some beast inside me rising up out of its ooze. I could *handle* my temper and the occasional urge to put my fist through a wall. Ditto the adrenaline spikes that hit me on buses or standing in checkout lines, a feeling akin to being electrified, my brain circuits lit up full. Those I could manage by training *harder*, lifting four hours a day instead of three.

No, the problem, I decided, was exactly this: I'd gone from having no life to two of them. I adored being with Kate the couple of times a week we spent the evening together. There was, beyond the sex, a cord of natural kinship, some neural recognition of parallel lives, as if we'd grown up sharing her bedroom in Ohio. We'd both built a worldview from dammed-up rage, loathing the rich for the havoc they wrought and pledging ourselves, in currently unformed fashion, to salving the harm done the poor. We spoke the same language of cynic's ennui and clung to each other the way loners do, filling the space left unpeopled. There's nothing like solitude to glue you together — or rip skin from skin when you part.

However. My second life was just as delicious and filled up space that Kate got nowhere near. Three or four nights a week, usually right after work, I'd connect with Angel and the other guys at a bar on Bleecker Street. Dressed for battle in our rayon armor, our big arms busting out of Nik Nik sleeves and shirts unbuttoned to the waist, we walked rather than drove the five or six blocks to the Flamingo on Houston Street. When we strode through the door there, Angel leading the charge, the whole room swiveled to watch. Even the sound died, or so it seemed as I read the stunned faces we passed. The other men's said, *I've got to compete with* that? The women's said, *There's* other *men here?*

If I was addicted to anything that drug-sick year, it was those loping stares. Wherever we went — the Infinity, 12 West — heads and eyes followed, locking on. Angel ate it up as much as I did, insisting that we cruise the discos GI-style, a band of brothers out on dawn patrol. Rules were drafted, a code of honor inscribed. No fat chicks, no coke fiends, no girls from New Jersey — and no skank exceptions at three a.m. He even coined a name for us — the Four Whoresmen of the

Apocalypse—though tactfully didn't sew it on the pouch of the thongs we wore to work bridal showers.

By then I was pulling a full-time schedule, generally working one or two weeknights plus Friday and Saturday. Typically, I'd earned about five hundred bucks by the time I settled up on Monday, meeting Angel at a diner on Broadway to hand him a fifth of my take. He partnered with a guy who handled the bookings, though it wasn't clear how they divvied the cash or how clients found their way to the office Tad kept above a shop in Chinatown. I'd met him there once and was duly repulsed by his scent of Hai Karate and crispy noodles. A small, brusque Slav with more hair on his knuckles than on the top of his shiny head, Tad lectured me in bursts of plosive speech. He scoffed at Angel's suggestion that I fess to being Jewish, saying, "Women fantasy *h'Italians,* not Hebes." Responding to my canard about saving for law school, he bade me tell clients that I was "studying to *h'act.* Women want you *screw* them, not *sue* them." And if age came up, I was to say I was eighteen: "Women like to rob cradle, too."

Like many of Angel's dealings, those with Tad were chemical, the substance in play being cocaine. They'd met through a lawyer Angel sold to twice a week, and soon enough Tad was a regular, too, picking up an eight ball on Friday night for the poker game he hosted down the shore. This led—again, like so many of Angel's transactions—to a larger enterprise. Tad ran a party store in Brighton Beach and began putting the word out to patrons and friends that he'd branched into "live performers." Angel provided the talent, initially pimping his friends, then cruising the gyms and clubs for fresh meat. In fits and starts, Tad's Entertainment grew, running ads in the pennysavers and taking on female strippers.

But while Angel made his money coming and going—taking a cut from Tad and a rake from his "artists," as he preposterously called us—stripping was just one of his hustles. His core trade, I learned, was pimping *himself,* and that summer, at least, business was booming. One drizzly evening, getting ready to lift, I got a phone call from him. "Take the night off; you can use a break," he said. "I'll buy you a steak and all the beer you can drink, then we'll shoot to a party."

I met him at Gallagher's, the chophouse near the Garden beloved by bookies and other no-necked entrepreneurs. We sat at the bar, a brass and oak beehive abuzz with men shouting calumnies at televised ball games. The bartender, a fastidious, flame-eyed chap, lovingly laid out white cloth mats and, at a nod, brought rounds of flash-broiled scallops. The beer kept coming, faster than I could drink it, whisked away from me with its head still foaming for a pint of superior coldness.

By the time our steaks arrived, I was half-past bombed and perched, with mounting vertigo, on my stool. As Angel sawed through a twenty-ounce slab so rare it seemed to still pump heart blood in the center, he praised me for "picking up game" after my very rocky beginning. "Takes more than a body to work this lick, and you showed you got the skills to pay the bills."

"Well, thanks, man. I had a great mentor."

"That you did, but you're a fast learner. Got guys that been doin' this shit for years and *still* can't keep it in their pants."

"Hmm. Can't guess who you mean by that."

"Yeah, Tommy think he's slick, doing side dates on the job. He'll find out the hard way I don't play."

This was old news and an empty threat. Tommy was entrenched, his best earner. But *something* was up—I saw it in his grin. Angel had his game face on.

"But let's get back to you and your cash potential, which is fittin' to go right through the roof."

"You think so?" I said, feeling my neck stiffen. "School, you know, starts again soon."

"No, I hear that," he said. "I hear it: school is major. None of us'll look this good forever." He loaded his fork with a wedge of yam and a confetti of bacon bits. "But let me ask you this, slick: Where's your head at *now*? Is it books or gettin' laid and paid?"

I glanced in the mirror to avoid his eyes.

"I mean, do you *like* all of this, eating steak and crab and making more on Friday than these fools do all week?"

"No, it's great, I can't thank you enough, but—"

"And those new Bottega boots, which I just now noticed and match up great with that dress shirt. What is this, a blend or straight silk there?"

"Um..." I tried, dully, to recall.

"You've been able to stack some coin, though, right? Where do you put it, in the safe deposit?"

"Well—"

"'Cause I *know* you know better than to dump it in checking. The IRS *loves* to see that."

"Of course not," I said. "I've got it at home. What money, you know, I've managed to keep."

Angel put his fork down and clapped his hands softly, a time-release laugh that ran long. "I knew it," he said. "You're just like me: *Fuck saving bank; there's a sale at Barneys!*"

"Well, so what," I muttered. "When you've never had stuff, sometimes you go a little ape-shit."

He eyed me over his hen-eating grin. "What? Pops bought you the three-speed Schwinn instead of the ten-speed Italia?"

"*No.*" I glared back, drawing a line. "Pops never bought me shit."

"Then what'd he do with his paper?"

"Don't ask me. Talk to his ex-wives."

"Ohhh. It's like *that* with you."

He returned to sawing his underdone meat. I pushed my beer away and tracked the game on the wood-grain Zenith. Behind us, bruisers in sharkskin slacks leaned in for refills or to pay their respects to the men in aprons pouring shots. I heard Angel grunt, debating himself. From the curve of his brow, he was betwixt and between, casing all the angles before he spoke. "Yo, I 'pologize. I didn't know that."

"Please," I said. "Drop it. It's just drama."

"No, seriously, slick. What's up these days? *Everyone's* pops is buggin'."

"Oh? Like who?"

"Well, Spiro's is straight *crazy*. Used to beat him as a kid, though he hasn't fucked with Spiro in a while."

Spiro's father, Panos, was a baker who had plowed his money into an expansion in Sunnyside. He worked like a demon but bet like one, too, and when his losses brought him down, Spiro's mom stepped in, leasing an Astoria diner. The place did all right, spinning off enough cash for her to eventually buy the building that housed it, but Panos detested being under her heel and took it out on his sons. He was hardest on Spiro, a ponderous kid who was sensitive about his size, calling him "donkey."

"What about Tommy?"

"Different, but still . . . His father hasn't talked to him in years. Comes home from work and goes straight to his room, drinking Miller and smoking Luckies till two a.m."

"Huh. And where's the mom?"

"She bailed a long time ago. Moved to Boston when Tommy was little. Can't say I blame her, between the father and Tommy's brother. Now, *that* guy—you wanna talk scary strong? He lost a leg in 'Nam and *still* hands beat-downs out. You say the wrong thing, he'll yoke that fake foot off and whale you over the head till they drag him out."

I thought on that a while through a beery fugue, the scallops I'd eaten dancing a reel in my throat with the rib eye and breaded shrimp. These under-parented men dragging their pasts around from the bench to the leg-press station, crafting a sort of life out of kiln-fired rage and a past-due claim for attention: they—make that *we*—had structural flaws that no amount of sanding would make smooth. We were trying to fashion manhood from a spurned boy's grief and instead had merely primed and epoxied the hurt, built a walking shrine around the cracks. As an engineering fix, that was hopelessly wrong: you don't do big repairs from the outside in.

"And what about you?" I said. "Did *you* get the ten-speed, as long as we're on the subject?"

He cooked up a smile, his stock expression, which always seemed to border on a sneer. That was Angel for you: half merriment, half menace, those brilliant teeth arrayed like cutlery. In the moment before the grin, though, I saw his eyes crease; something unhinged behind his jaw. "Yo, I'm ghetto, if you forgot. *No one* got the ten-speed where I'm from."

"Right, but not really the question."

The grin went bigger as he eyed me sideways, but I sent it right back at him. This caused him to laugh and wave for more beers. I was still staring when he turned around. "Well, *look* at you, man; all big and bad. Gettin' in my biz like that."

I said nothing, letting the silence soak. It was a ploy I'd stolen from him.

"Look, man, all's I'll say is, I got somethin' for Pops if I ever see that faggot again. But trust me, I *won't*. He bailed back to the islands, and he knows I got a bullet for that ass."

"How's he know that if you haven't seen him?"

The grin shriveled. "I thought I told you before, man: too many questions."

I faced away and glanced at the game, prepared to wait all night. Angel wanted the check, though he rarely skipped dessert; his metabolism, like mine, was an atom smasher. In lieu of the bill, though, two brandies were put before us. "From the ladies over there," said the barman.

We turned in their direction: two blondes in their thirties, one pretty in an unenameled, upstate way; the other stocky, wearing lots of mascara and that most fatal of unforced errors, red lipstick. It was ever thus: the hot one wanted Angel, tilting her head in a way that left no doubt.

"Do we have to?" I groused. "Where is it written that we can't just drink up and go?"

"*Bro*-ham, where's your manners? We got an hour before the party, maybe two before it really jumps off. Besides," he said, raising a glass to the women, with his high-beam smile on full, "this is my *job,* and work is good."

An hour or so later, I was on the Herculon couch of a cramped one-bedroom in Kips Bay. Angel was in the bedroom with the lissome Janine and the only bottle of white wine in the house, while I, reduced to pink Champale and a bowl of macadamia nuts, suffered Marcia's kisses but not her hand down my pants, despite a lot of breathy persistence.

"You know what's hot about older women?" she whispered. "We can be very...grateful."

I pulled away from her mouth. "You know, these nuts are *amazing.* Where do they come from, I wonder?"

"The supermarket," she said, taking my salty hand and placing it square on her breast. "Ahh, that's *nice*—you can give it a little kiss now. The bra unhooks from the front."

"Yeah, but I have to say, I-I'm terrible with those. I wouldn't even attempt to—oh, boy."

She shrugged off her blouse and unhitched the clasp. A plump, pillowy boob spilled into my palm, wobbling like a soft-boiled egg. "Huh," I said. "Well, that takes care of that."

She clambered onto her knees and brought the breast to my lips. I gave the nipple a flick, then tactfully unmouthed it and grabbed for my pint of Champale. "I-I've gotta be honest: I'm a little distracted. Something you said before in the car."

"Oh?" she said, not bothering to cover up. "Tell me, what'd I say?"

"Well, uh, we were driving past Port Authority, with the bums and the hookers, and you joked about New York becoming Calcutta. And I said to myself, *Wow, she's hard on black people.* To say nothing of the untouchables in India."

"Because it's *true,*" she said. "I've watched this city drown while liberals like Abe Beame let it burn. It's time we had someone call a spade a spade and lock them up in cages that belong there."

"Whoa," I said. "Abe Beame's a *liberal*? What does that make John Lindsay, Pol Pot?"

She yanked her bra on curtly. "If the shoe fits, wear it. And God help us if that hag Bella Abzug wins. I'll be on the first bus back to Utica."

"Then you better start packing, 'cause she *will* get elected, thanks to those spades you just mentioned. One of whom's fucking your friend now, by the way."

I'd have been happy to go on in that vein a while; I met so few Republicans in my line of work. But Marcia tugged her blouse on and pointed to the door. "Leave," she said. "Go. You can wait downstairs."

"Fine," I said, swigging the last of the Champale. "Your wine list leaves a *lot* to be desired."

Angel followed me down in a couple of minutes, pulling his shirttail straight as he strode the lobby. "The fuck did you say to her? She banged on the door, saying a SWAT team was coming and I better bounce."

"Figures," I said. "She was cracker-barrel racist and didn't want you 'soiling' her best friend."

He stared. "She said that?"

"And worse, which I won't repeat."

"Well, *fuck* that bitch, 'cause I soiled her friend good — *and* got paid to do it." He drew a clump of bills from his right front pocket, most of them tens and twenties. "A hundred and forty beans to wax that ass — and plus I got a date to hit it again."

I gaped at him as he counted the cash, thinking perhaps he'd filched it from her purse. "You're telling me she just now paid you for sex. Is that what I hear you saying?"

"Yup. And got a *deal,* if y'ask me."

"I *am* asking," I said. "In fact, I'll ask again: A good-looking blonde with a job at Smith Barney paid you a hundred and forty dollars to have sex?"

"Well, not in so many words."

"Then what *did* she pay you for?"

"Damn — next you'll ask how many times she came."

"Yeah, if you charge per orgasm."

He gaped at me with hands on hips. "Fine then, bet; I'll break it down. It was forty to eat her out, forty for the hump, and sixty for the half a gram of coke. But next time, she's going for the whole ride."

By now the ground was shaking, a slo-mo temblor. "And what — I'm scared to ask — would *that* cost?"

He eyed me, deadpan, but couldn't sustain it and stumbled around the pavement, clapping hands. "You kill me!" he gasped, before a second wave of laughter washed him up against a parked car. "I love you, Paulie! You make me laugh like Redd Foxx, and that's my boy!"

But he couldn't keep the mockery going forever; he had a "job" to get to before the party. Gunning his Toronado up the FDR, he explained for the first time how the "smart ones" prospered in the muscle-for-money game. "You start out working for your little piece of change, happy to clock your four, five bills a week, which gets you better clothes and pays the bills. But by and by you notice, if you're not coked up, that there's a jackpot waiting at most gigs. It's the girl who's starin' a little too hard and tries to get you alone in the kitchen, or the one whose friends are all ready to bail but yet she's hanging back, hoping to chat. She's never the flyest one and not the richest, neither, but she knows it's gonna cost without even asking."

"Really? Who brings it up? Her or you?"

The big smile. "She does. Every time."

It may have been the coke, in some seismic combination with the clams, beer, nuts, and Champale, but bombs were going off in my head. I felt, on the one hand, grossly obtuse for not having seen this weeks sooner: the choke-roll of cash Angel was never without, knotted up double, the big bills outward, fastened by an inch-wide rubber band; the crazed hours he kept, hanging out till four a.m., then rising at the crack of noon. Of *course* he sold ass: what else was it for, all those thousands of reps in filthy gyms? As beautiful as he was, he wasn't waiting to be discovered on the street by a *Vogue* photographer, or kidding himself in an acting class taught by someone who'd once guested on *CHiPs*. No, he'd pushed it all in on the hand he was dealt and, by all indications, had cashed in big.

On the other hand, his hustle of needy women hit me where it hurt—in the imagination. In ways I hadn't fathomed, I'd sunk a lot in Angel, come down with a case of comic-book awe. With his superhero build and ray-gun cool, he was right off the pages of *Fantastic Four*, all my boyhood half gods rolled in one. But inducing ugly ducklings to pay for sex and selling them coke besides? Which issue of *Spider-Man* was *that* scam in, and had he, with nary a *POW!* exchanged, crossed the line from icon to small-time hood?

We jumped off the FDR at Ninety-sixth and slung back around to a white-glove building off Madison in the upper Eighties. There was nowhere to park, but not to worry; that was why Angel had brought *me*. Stopping at a hydrant, he handed over the keys and said the seat back went down. "There's a *Penthouse* in here somewhere—check the floor behind you—or better yet, sleep before the party."

"How long you gonna be?" I groaned. "It's eleven already. What time does this damn thing start?"

"Oh, it started *last* night," he said. "But trust me, rest up: you're gonna rock out with your cock out when we get there."

THOUGH THEY'D BEEN COOLING THEIR HEELS since eleven p.m. at a fern bar/disco on Second Avenue, Tommy and Spiro were in excellent spirits when we strolled in sometime after twelve. "Boyzos, check it out: we met this casting agent, and she's bringing me in to read for *Guiding Light!*" said Tommy. "And also, get this, they're—"

"No, *I* tell them!" Spiro bounded off his stool. "They finally getting ready to doing a Superman movie, and she think I have a shot when they see the script!"

"Well, that's beautiful," said Angel, submitting to Spiro's hug. "What part you gonna go for? Lois Lane?"

"Hey, fuck you, I'm *flying*," crowed Spiro, doing a two-step folk dance called the *syrto*. "She say I have the look and the size for real. Only thing I don't, I need more speech."

"Well, if it gets you into speech class, I'm all for it. Drinks on me, and I'm having Courvoisier."

He peeled off a fifty and went to the john. Tommy grabbed my arm and gave a squeeze. "So I heard he dropped the bomb on you tonight."

I falsified a laugh, trying not to look stricken. "I'm just the tool of all tools, huh?"

"Nah," he scoffed. "That's some wild shit to hear. Though when you really stop and think of it, why *not*, right?"

"Um—I don't follow."

"I'm just saying. Women have charged for sex since Eve, so why not turn it around?"

"Well, I'm not sure whoring goes all the way back to Eden, but—"

"It doesn't?" he said. "What happened with the apple? Satan put the classic pimp move on her, got her to show some tit and drive Adam crazy."

"Actually, they were naked already."

He turned to Spiro. "Hey, wasn't Satan the first to mack a girl?"

The big man affected a puzzled frown. It was another thing he'd have to work on in speech class if he hoped to play the impassive man of steel. "Well," he granted, "he *do* have snakeskin shoes, but—"

"Exactly," said Tommy. "He played her like a flute, and women have been whoring ever since."

Angel came back from the john ebullient, the base of a nostril tinged with cocaine dust. His eyes, so green they seemed to make their own light, darkened like jade when he took a bump—got big and verdant, leaking color. He wrapped an arm around me and raised his snifter, wearing a grin that skewed his jaw. "Coming 'cross the room, I looked at you three and said, *Those're some stone-ass men there. These other cats in here, they don't stand a chance.* So I wanna give a toast now, and I mean this from my heart: to the tightest fuckin' crew I ever rolled with."

"Hear, hear!" said Spiro.

"The Four Whoresmen!" cried Tommy.

"The Four Whoresmen!" we chanted, flexing arms.

There was a guy walking around taking pictures for a buck. Angel waved him over with his bankroll. "I want you to shoot us and keep going till I say stop. Every roll you got—I'll buy it off you."

"Well, they're Polaroids," said the guy, a cinch-faced Filipino. "It don't just snap, snap, snap."

"Yeah, whatever," said Angel. "This is *history* here. We're the baddest ma-fuckers since T. rex."

OROTUND LOU DIGIAIMO LIKED TO answer his own door at the monthly East Side orgy he threw. It was his way, he said, of "reading the menu," scanning all comers for "fresh delicacies to whet and surprise the palate." In a voice that rolled like machine-shopped thunder from his quite considerable gut, he welcomed us in with a proclamation and kissed us hard on the mouth. "The hordes are here!" he cried, tilting his head back. "Guard the Sabine women with your lives!"

We entered a hall that went east and west and terminated in room-size closets. Two twee houseboys, barely out of their teens and imperious in their pale androgyny, met us with handsome brass-necked hangers and ordered us, archly, to strip. While we sat on benches, zipping off our boots, Angel and Lou walked away to chat, conferring in hushed tones beneath a huge Franz Kline of swooshing blacks and blues. It was a moment before I registered the painting as real, not a poster-board print from a museum shop, and the shock of recognition pulled me out of my drunk and over to the wall, half-naked. Marveling at the author-ity of those fan-brush lines and the way they conjured up terror and awe and the might of brute machines, I had my first ripple of shame in months, connecting with the kid I'd been in high school. On many an afternoon, I had sat in MoMA studying Kline's virile strokes, finding in them something beyond the two dimensions of my cartoon inner life.

He'd been the first painter to evoke in me an adult means of seeing, tendering myself to a set of eyes that looked at big things and didn't blink. That boy-man might have gone places one day if he'd trusted his taste and held the path. Instead he was standing here, five years later, in tube socks and a tiger-striped thong.

"If you stare hard enough, with just the right focus, a naked girl appears, holding a parrot."

Lou was over my shoulder, squinting in jest. His eyebrows arrowed like thatched roofs.

"I once wrote a story about Kline and de Kooning getting soused at the Cedar Tavern and throwing punches," I said. "It was stupid, of course; if they were going to punch anyone, it would've been Motherwell."

"What's *this* then?" he boomed, taking a stagy step back. "A Minniti who can speak of masters?"

"There a problem?" said Angel, hustling over. "Paulie, what'd you say to the man?"

"*Minniti*—that's good," I said, grinning at Lou. "I take it you've been to the Borghese."

"Oh pish, sir, many times," he said. "But I'd like to go there with *you*. In fact, I'd like to take the grand tour."

"The fuck's a *man-eaty*?" Angel demanded. "Someone talk in English, please."

"Minniti," I said, "was Caravaggio's model—the kid in a lot of those paintings."

"And also his lover and rival," said Lou. "To the extent that Caravaggio *loved*."

"Aha," said Angel, watching us both warily. "And who or what's a *car-voucher-o*?"

"Angel," said Lou, feasting his eyes on me, "you and the colossi can head in now. I'll be along with your young man here after we catch up on the last four centuries."

The apartment—a wraparound, suede-walled hulk that incorporated the two flats next to it—was configured like a hopscotch box.

Commanding a high floor, it was carved into wings by halls that ran along the sides of the building. Two shorter halls bisected the place, which culminated in an eye-popping, sheet-glass parlor with floor-to-ceiling views of the river. Off the long halls were a number of small rooms connected by inner doors. Some of these spaces were furnished baroquely; others held just a bed with a fitted sheet. Behind most of the doors, though, small knots of people were embroiled in complex play. "I like a free exchange of ideas," said Lou, as we looked in on a vignette in progress. A middle-aged white man wearing a stovepipe hat was down on all fours, muttering darkly. Behind him, a woman in a torn chemise pounded away with a strap-on. "Say it *louder*," she demanded, throwing her hips at him. "You freed the *who*, you son of a bitch?"

Lou drew me on with a hand on my glute. "What the hell was that?" I said.

"The presidential suite," he said, deadpan.

In a second room, a woman wearing a splendid mink was ringed by men who, with varying degrees of vigor, tried to come on her coat. "This about cruelty to animals?" I asked.

"Her husband's a furrier who dumped her for one of his customers."

On we went, stopping here and there to stand in a doorway and watch. Although the sex on display was Brechtian in flavor and covered most of the known varieties, there was, after the novelty of skin wore off, a kind of willed roteness in what we saw, as if these well-to-do men and their wives and consorts were playing a round of nudist charades. It was one more privilege in a life of same, like hunting the Serengeti or skiing Gstaad. The cast was attractive, excluding the odd potbelly or coke-whittled blonde in thigh-highs, a lalapalooza of middle-aged lawyers and currency traders letting their hair down and pale dongs dangle, while the women skewed younger, in their early to late thirties, awkward in peekaboo bras. Owing to the layout, it was hard to get a line on how many people were there. I counted at least fifty before I ran into Tommy, who was holding court in the parlor. "Paulie!" he cried, hugging me clear off the floor. His blue-gray eyes were the size of saucers, courtesy of the blow he'd helped himself to from a dish going by on a tray. I patted my hip for the amber vial I kept in my Jordache pocket. Tommy laughed, pointing out that I was pantless. "Besides," he croaked, "you don't bring coke to Lou's parties. That's like bringing sand to the desert."

Our host, who'd gone to fetch flutes of champagne, winked at me across the room. "What do I do?" I whispered to Tommy. "This fucker's glued to me and won't let go."

"What do you *do*?" Tommy snickered as a tall brunette slipped an arm through his and tongued an ear. "You take his check, is what you do. That 'fucker,' in case you missed it, is pigpen rich."

"Yeah, but I—oh *Christ*. Here he comes."

Beaming as he navigated the rosewood floor, his red kimono open to flaunt a Buddha belly and the first nipple piercing I'd ever seen, Lou gestured in the direction of a copper door, its salmon fascia hammered and buffed smooth. Meekly, I went, thinking glass-shard thoughts about acts heretofore remote. Figures flew by me—*$200! $5,000!*—as well as numbers with no bearing whatsoever, like Mickey Mantle's stat line in 1956, the year he bagged the Yanks' last Triple Crown. I thought: Here's what it's all been building to, the three-hour workouts and the nights at Angel's heel, tossing myself gladly on the pile. It wasn't about sex or attention from strangers or forensic proof that I mattered. It was smaller and grimmer and hopelessly sad, a surrender to the mean and patient self-loathing that had always been down there, waiting.

The copper door opened to a loft-size space whose sweet spot was a mammoth bed. The right-hand wall housed a glassed-in closet where dark suits hung in rows. On the left-hand wall was an open bath with no door on the shower or toilet. Facing this floated an L-shaped couch in something like palomino. It was there he guided me with a hand on my spine, dimming lights as we went. "What do you say?" he said, curling up beside me. "You think you could make do in this room?"

I edged away slightly from the breath on my cheek. "A family of five could make do here."

"Or a family of two," he said. The hand was on my knee now. "Not that I'm proposing, you understand."

When he reached my inner thigh I headed him off, returning the hand to his lap. "Angel mentioned you were a lawyer?" I said.

He laughed. "Why? You need something notarized?"

"No," I said, sitting up and moving away. "Just that you're assuming facts not in evidence."

A coarser laugh. "Oh, I see *something* in evidence there."

I looked down at my crotch. "It's been like that since noon, and I fucked my girlfriend all morning."

"Ah." He nodded. "Lucky her."

"I mean no offense, of course."

"None taken," he said. "I sleep with women, too, though I can forgive you for being skeptical."

There was no good answer to this, so I twirled my hand like the worldly rake I wasn't.

"I don't believe in self-denial," he continued. "Caesar, Lord Byron, D. H. Lawrence—omnivores all, and history looks kindly. The great ones eat what they please."

Again he moved in, his mouth coming at mine. I ducked and he sailed past me, falling over my shoulder and landing, face-first, on the cushion.

"All right, look," I said, "I'm flattered. But liking Franz Kline doesn't make me bisexual."

He struggled to right himself and catch his breath. He'd sprung a light sweat in the act. "And this," he gasped, "the muscle and shaved legs—*this* doesn't make you bisexual?"

"No," I said curtly. "It doesn't."

"And the tiger-striped G-string, which I must say I'm charmed by: *that* doesn't indicate a broadness of mind and a certain...flexibility on your part?"

"No more than Angel's does. It's a tool of the trade."

"Ah," he said. "Right. Our old friend Angel."

I knew then: the tone, the self-amused smile. I knew, and the act of knowing made my head swim.

"Well," he said, slinging up to his feet. "I wish you great luck in your trade."

"Thank you," I said. "No hard feelings?"

"I think you've cornered the *market* on hard there," he said, and made a last grasp for my groin. I caught his wrist and, without meaning to, gave it an angry throttle. He yelped in pain and sank to the couch, clutching his wounded paw. "Damn it, that *hurt*, you. It was *totally* uncalled for. Aren't you at least going to say *sorry*?"

I glared at him, then stalked to the door. "Wait," he said. "Come back a minute."

I went halfway and held my ground, resisting his gesture to come sit. "Look. Angel brings a lot of young men here, and between the naked women and cocaine—"

"And your money, of course. Don't forget that."

"Yes," he said. "My money. Though sometimes not."

Reacting to my frown, he reached for his glass and took a sip of champagne. "Have you tried this?" he asked. "It's the 'seventy Grande Dame—you don't want to know what I pay a case."

"What's your point?"

He shrugged. "Sometimes being rich means *not* needing to spend. Just *having* money will get you what you want."

"That's great. But not this time."

"Another night, then. That's the beauty of money. One can afford to be patient."

I WASTED NO TIME GETTING a glass of champagne and finding the guy with the coke dish. Instead of the usual lift into gabby cheer, though, the deliriant lit the fuse of my rage and shot it out of a silo. On a heartless bender, I fucked for hours, unable to climax or care enough even to make cursory chatter. Angel shook me awake at eleven a.m., asking what had happened with Lou. "Who's Lou?" I said, then dimly remembered. "Is he angry about the wrist?"

"No idea," he said. "I haven't seen him in hours. I was moreso worried about you."

"Yeah, *thanks* for the heads-up. The man dove for my joint."

"You're welcome," he said. "And it wouldn't have made a diff. If Lou likes you, it's Katy bar the door."

Tommy was two rooms down, asleep with his mouth open and a woman drooling onto his thigh. We eased him out from under so as not to wake her, then conducted a futile search for Spiro. In the front hall, squinting against the recessed lights, we dressed as gingerly as burn-ward patients and showed ourselves out in silence. Downstairs, we couldn't think where we'd parked the car and loitered on Lexington in a world of pain, neither willing nor able to go look. It was a brilliant morning, the sun dancing off chrome and turning windows into laser shows, and as I shaded my eyes with not one but two palms, a woman walked by with her child. The boy, perhaps seven, stopped short and turned back, staring while his mother tugged his hand. He had the soft chin and bulbous eyes of a mildly impaired kid with Down's, and as he stood there gaping, he began to cry—first gently, then with gathering force.

"It's all right," said Tommy. "Everything's fine here. Go with your mommy. She's got *candy*."

The boy wouldn't budge or be consoled. His sobs keened like worn tires squealing.

"Seriously, it's cool. We're just a little hungover, and that noise ain't helping much."

The woman bent down, trying to pick him up, but he arched his spine so that his head lolled back, and wailed at the top of his lungs.

"*Jesus*," hissed Angel under his breath. "How long do I have to hear this shit?"

He glanced at me, either for help or explanation, but my eyes were pooling tears. "*Whoa*, what's with you?"

I pulled away from him, walking fast. He yelled for me to stop but didn't follow. At the corner I broke left, heading west on instinct as the water poured off me in spouts. I walked a long block before the cloudburst eased, leaving me dazed and barely able to see the cars that were blowing by on Park. As I staggered the median, a van running a light skidded past me and screeched to a halt. The driver cranked his window down, spewing curses. I broke into a run, gunning for him. In a panic he hit the gas and swamped his engine as traffic braked hard behind him. He did manage to get his window rolled up, or I would have pulled him through the opening by his head and shoulders and beaten him bloody on the manicured marge that separated the north and south lanes. Finally, he got in gear and lunged away as I bashed the driver's door. I chased him half a block, then came to my senses when I heard a siren wailing over my shoulder.

On the corner, crouched behind a panel truck, I watched an ambulance thread the intersection. I heaved a breath out and tracked its flashers till they blurred with the greens and ambers downtown.

Eleven

Mothers Are the Inventors of Necessity

Two weeks later

I LEANED ON THE BUZZER a good ten seconds, squeezing till my forefinger bent.

"You sure this is the place?" Kate fanned herself dully on the steps of the limestone walk-up.

I pulled the slip out to check the address. "Where *that one's* involved, I'm sure of nothing."

"Maybe it's our fault. Have we come the wrong night?"

I sent a glare downhill. "Don't start, Kate."

She turned away, letting a long breath go with the puff of a mottled cheek. We'd been sparring since I picked her up at six, bickering about whether to bring wine or cake, then sitting in brown silence over a couple of Millers at an old-man's bar on Broadway. "You don't want to be here, fine, we'll go. I don't need to watch you sulk."

I rang again sourly, then tried the knob, shaking the door on its hinges. A tenant on the first floor opened her window. "Buzzer's busted," she said. "Hold your water a minute."

"*This,*" I said to Kate as we waited for the woman to belt her floral housecoat and let us in. "*This* is why I haven't called all summer. You can't put a price on mental health."

She frowned. "No, but I can ballpark it."

My mother's latest sublet was up three flights in the bay-front building off Riverside Drive. In the years since I'd left her for, first, my father's apartment, then on-campus housing at Stony Brook, she'd been living out of boxes on the Upper West Side, camping six months here and nine months there in the homes of teachers traveling on sabbatical. She'd never earned more than a subsistence income as a translator of Russian writers, and even with the alimony she continued to draw eleven years after splitting with Dad, she was hopelessly behindhand to Visa, Con Ed, and the nice-guy pharmacist at Apthorp Pharmacy. Over the years, she'd acquired a small orbit of patrons — the manager at Fairway who let her run tabs; the Ukrainian waiters at Gitlitz deli, who endlessly filled her cup with coffee and forgot to charge for the bowl of borscht or the fat slice of baba au rhum. Her gaunt-cheeked beauty was in marked decline, ground away by years of circle-the-drain worry and three packs a day of Pall Malls, but she still had a pensive, fin de siècle charm, the *siècle* in question being the nineteenth. If Chekhov had lived longer, he might have been her father, so firmly was she fixed in the world he peopled with life's emphatic swooners.

I was greeted at the door of her third-floor walk-up with an awkward, too-long hug. Mom was always a little shorter than I remembered, the huge eyes and cheekbones conveying the impression of both a bigger and a more spectral presence. The once-proud mane of pitch-black hair that had monopolized the light at lit-crit parties was suddenly gray and alarmingly clipped in a lifeless, chin-length bob. Gone, too, was the baked-bean suntan she'd get reading Gogol in the park each summer, sloughed off in favor of a shut-in's pallor and her aesthete's scorn for makeup. She was wearing a silk blouse, though, and costume pearls, and was clearly putting forth an effort.

"My *God*," she said, stepping back but laying hold. "What's become of my son!"

175

"He's huge," said Kate, by way of greeting. "I need a student loan to feed him dinner."

I grabbed her by the belt loop and reeled her in. "Mom, this is Kate," I said proudly.

Mom nodded with her brows but went on staring, sizing me with frank alarm. "But where did it *come* from, these crazy muscles? I saw you six months ago!"

I felt flustered and goony in my own skin. "Actually, it was nine, but—"

"I'm stunned," she said, then said it again, this time in disappointment. I stood there, submitting to her inspection. "Kate, meet my mom," I finally said.

"Hi," said Kate, with her warmest smile. She handed over the bottle of wine.

"Aha." Mom read the label. "Any good?"

Kate glanced at me. "Erm, I hope so."

Mom raised her gaze, scanning us, not the bottle. "And you don't find all this the least bit...offputting?"

Again Kate looked to me for help. "I—I don't really..."

"I mean, these biceps and the rolled-up sleeves—you don't think it's all finally *much*?"

"Oh," said Kate, looking me over in earnest. "Well, now that someone asked me—yes, I do!"

Mom took her elbow and led her inside. "She's a smart one," she said to me over her shoulder.

By RECENT STANDARDS, the sublet was plush: a sizable living room with wide bay windows and two walls terraced with books; an alcove study nesting an L-shaped desk and a portal looking onto the park; and behind it a john that passed into a small bedroom painted a shade of farmhouse red. But going by the desk, I saw it piled with her usual efflux: the dog-eared texts propped open on spines, tabs of yellow paper poking out; ashtrays crammed with filterless butts smoked down to the bitter end; and the bits and scraps of envelope backs on which she was forever giving herself orders. One glance at those scribbles and it all came back—the nights lying awake as a nine-year-old boy while she sobbed and paced in the next room; the off-her-meds schemes for a windfall payday that would free her permanently from debt. Eleven years later, nothing seemed to have changed with her, while I swooped in like a prototype, sleek and smooth as the future. It was grossly unfair, an act of pitched cruelty. I was the life she'd never managed to have.

"I've got a great meal going, my Swedish chicken, and want to hear all about you," she said. "But first off, a favor: You see this little table? I need your manly skills to put it together."

She was standing over a contraption of two-by-four remnants, on top of which perched a marble disk. "I'm sorry, but it looks like...lumber," I said.

"It is," she said brightly. "I found it on the street and bought myself a hammer and some nails. A lot of the best furniture started as junk, until someone came along and jazzed it up."

Some of the best furniture, I thought, *started as junk and made its way safely to the dump.* "Which manly skills? When have I ever been handy?"

"Oh, come now; no modesty. Don't you remember the lovely planters you made me in arts and crafts class?"

I thought a moment, recalling no such objects. There was a functionless cube of Popsicle sticks from my first year at sleepaway camp and, a couple of summers later, a slumping vase just wide enough to house a tulip. Could those, in the mythopoeic forge she called memory, have been raised to a craft, if not art?

I bent to inspect the table's joinery. Sure enough, the thing keeled over. "You didn't *glue* it?" I groaned. "How 'm I supposed to get this back assembled?"

"You'll figure it out. And turn the knotty sides out, so they show. That's what gives it its oomph."

She headed to the kitchen, a tiny galley from which ominous odors escaped. I looked at Kate in supplication. She was having a hard time stanching a smile.

"You enjoy this?" I said. "You find it amusing?"

"I'm sorry," said Kate, "but I'd really like to see that lovely planter."

I glowered at the table with ticking shame and nudged the pile with my toe. Going to one knee, I started to sort the scraps, muttering the sort of byplay that would never pass muster on home renovation shows. I had the parts aligned—knots *in,* for spite—when a splinter from a rough end lanced my thumb. "*Suck!*" I hissed, cradling the finger as if it had been sheared by a slicer.

"Hold still, I see it." Kate plucked at the nub. "Here, move a little, you're blocking the light."

"Fuck me, it *hurts,*" I moaned.

"Please, Paul, you lift giant weights and call it fun. All I need is one more good—*goddamnit.*"

"Let me do it," I snapped. "Who knows where that wood's been? For all I know, she fished it out of the Hudson."

I sucked at the thumb, clearing droplets of blood, then bit the wound open a little. "Go ask her for a tweezers and a bottle of—no, wait. Don't."

"Why not? They'll dig it right out."

"Because the *last* thing I need is to wind her up. Trust me, you've no idea."

At last I got my eyeteeth onto the sliver and pulled it out with a grunt. Kate shook her head in damp alarm. "Christ," she said, "I'm starting to see your point."

There were more pained memories at the dinner table. Mom's "Swedish chicken" suffered from Stockholm syndrome, curled up stiffly in a fetal ball as if cooked by means of electrodes. Its mistreatment at her hands recalled other suppers (her "pork chops Oahu" were broiled to lava, then doused with a can of Dole pineapple) and led me to wonder whether there was malice aforethought whenever she entered the kitchen. Even the steamed sweet peas were leached of taste, reduced to olive drab squibs of rubber, like someone's tiny galoshes. "How long since you had a meal like this?" she crowed.

I loudly dropped my fork. "A while."

"He eats out a lot," Kate put in quickly, working through a mouthful of mush potatoes. "He waits on tables till one a.m. and *then* goes somewhere and has dinner."

"Well, you must be raking in the tips," said Mom. "Especially with the female diners."

I checked Kate with a sidelong glance, but she smiled and went on chewing. "It's catering work, Mom. I get paid by check."

"Still," she said, with a knowing glint. "Arms like those can't hurt."

She mercifully changed the subject to her own adventures as a waitress in a Tahoe casino. She'd gone there after college, "your father tagging behind me," to make money for graduate school, then tossed it all away playing craps. "That was me, you know: a penny earned's a penny squandered. To this day, if I'm down to my last ten bucks, I'll blow it on cab fare and starve all week instead of scrimping on rice and beans."

She laughed at her plucky contempt for fate, expecting me to laugh along. But I had bitter memories of hoarding snack cakes in the drawers of my captain's bed, bought with money I'd earned stocking produce at the Gristedes on 72nd. If anything evoked the misery of those years, it was our tottering fridge with the frost-blown freezer and a lonely twelve-ounce carton of baking soda. In some way I couldn't unpack, it summed up that time fully: the poverty and despond, and my wraithlike gauntness, a global evocation of failure.

"Anyway," she said, "those were kooky years, when we lived on our wits and spaghetti. Do you remember that pathetic wretch of a car, the one that never started? Your father would take the battery and lug it upstairs so it would *maybe* turn over the next morning."

"That's great," said Kate, who seemed to savor Mom's gambols through her hyperbolic past. "My folks had a van that barely went, an old VW that would shift its own gears once you got it going faster than forty."

"Oh, well, a *VW*! Fancy, schmancy," Mom bantered. "The most we ever spent buying a car was two-fifty, and I *still* say we got rooked."

And so it went for a couple of hours, Mom on her sprightliest best behavior, turning the joke on herself. When you caught her in one of these moods, it was best to feed her, and I loaded up her plate with selective prompts from the good and bad old days. There was the time Ivan and I, ages three and four, wanted to give her a birthday gift and, having no money, decided to wash the windows as a token of filial love. We awoke around dawn, filled a bucket with water, and climbed onto the sill of our barracks apartment. Alas, the only cleaning agent we knew to use was the cake of Dial hand soap from the john, and by the time we finished scraping that yellow bar across the room-wide expanse of glass, the suds were so thick that we couldn't see the sun on a splendid autumn morning. "You boys were very sweet when you weren't killing each other or sneaking change out of my wallet," she cackled. "Of course, I was sneaking money from your *father's* wallet, but I took twenties, not nickels."

Things went so well that I caught a kick under the table when Mom got up to use the john. "Why all the scare talk? She's *great*," said Kate. "I was expecting Lady Macbeth."

"Yeah, well, wait," I muttered. "The bloody-hands scene is coming, and the three weird sisters are right behind."

"Oh, stop already. She's a sweet, harmless woman who happens to be half your size."

We cleared away the dishes and put decaf up—instant, the only kind Mom drank. "So," I asked her, slicing the coffee cake, "what're you working on these days?"

"Ah," she said with a dolorous smile that hinted at worlds of trouble, "we don't want to talk about *that* tonight. Let's talk about anything else. Specifically, what's with this sudden transformation of yours? I liked you looking just the way you were."

"Thanks, but I'll take this version—by a mile."

"But why? You're a smart, sensitive guy, as anyone could tell at a glance. *Now*—how to say this?—you sort of look like one of those galumphs in the back of a comic book."

I could feel my ears redden. "That's a compliment, Mom. I worshipped Charles Atlas as a kid."

"And the guy who went to college to get a master's degree and devote himself to helping troubled kids—what's become of *him* since all this happened?"

A heat lamp started in my chest. "What does getting stronger have to do with that? I'd have thought you'd be pleased with my progress."

"Well, but is it progress or demolition? You look like you've taken the old you and tossed it out wholesale. All the things that bugged you, as well as the things I happened to treasure—the shy, heartful kid with an ear for words and for what other people were thinking and feeling—you've put that on the street, or so it looks."

"No, I haven't. I'm the same guy, but tougher. Why does that make me less sensitive?"

"Because look at you," she said. "Look at how you're sitting. You look like you're going to hop across and slug me!"

I glanced at my hand, which was balled up tight and connected to an arm flexed for battle. "Please, Mom, no *shrying*. I'm just a little exhausted. I-I've been working loony hours, and school's starting again soon, and there's a lot to, frankly, deal with before I leave."

I looked to Kate for corroboration, but she, too, was staring at my biceps. I let the arm dangle, shaking till it softened, but it locked up again of its own accord. Alarmed, I stood and twirled it in circles to fatigue the slow-twitch fibers. Now my *left* arm spasmed, bunching like a fist. It was as if someone was pulling a wire through my shoulder, yanking my neck and elbow toward each other.

"You all right, babe?" Kate fretted. "You're dripping suddenly. You want me to get a cool rag?"

"It's this heat," cried Mom. "I've begged them to change the Freon, but the thieving sons of bitches won't respond."

"Kate, grab my arm and squeeze. No, harder, till it stops pulsing."

"I don't like this," said Mom, out of her seat and pacing. "I'm going to call an ambulance in a minute."

"Mom, just sit; it's a nothing cramp. Between the smog and dehydration, my muscles tighten."

"Because you've beefed yourself up eating God knows what, and now you have these—fits. Or mini-seizures."

The heat in my head outran the heat around it. Dendrites were wilting in their glial soup, calling out for chemical coolant, or an ice pack and some quiet time alone. Now, as in boyhood, I had no barrier against Mom. She could jack my nervous system at a glance. "Excuse me, where's the bathroom here?"

In her narrow john, a six-by-six sepulchre with a picture of Dostoyevsky gazing down, I ran the cold water and soaked my face before fishing the little vial from my pocket. Cocaine was always a coin-toss: it could put me back together or cue the crackpot lurking in my adrenals. So, too, with booze: I turned jolly and fond, or cowered under a slingshot paranoia. As altered states went, I had no Ohio. It was either Key West or Fairbanks.

BUT LUCK, FOR ONCE, AVAILED: the two bumps cooled me, brought down the scorcher in my skull. I sat on the tub wall, savoring the freeze and the sweet, numb ellipsis of silence. On the wicker shelf that held Fyodor's likeness stood a lithe little figure of a horse, painted red and gold, its ears pricked. I remembered it from the days on Central Park West, a talisman of the pre-lapsed Mom, her moods merely part of the story then. She'd had, in her beauty, a kind of girlish glee, a head-thrown pleasure in her comic powers. I'd seen it at the parties my parents gave for visiting writers—the great, capering stories she told of Chicago; the impressions she did of Bellow and Roth, to the delight of Ralph Ellison and Tom Rogers. I fell for her those nights and many others besides. She had the kind of charm that wiped the slate clean, made you set aside what went before. Nowhere was her whimsy more on view than in the subversive bedtime stories she told her sons. Riffing on our room-wide sprawl of stuffed toys, she recast Pooh as a bumbling thief who mugged rich biddies in the park, then fenced the stuff to Piglet and Roo, who kept Eeyore around as muscle. We lapped it all up, bouncing plot points off her and vamping lengthy rap sheets for Owl and Tigger. When that got stale, she spun her own fable, inventing an aging royal by the name of Queen Esther, whose moat and castle were crankily patroled by Moshe the Kosher crocodile. Moshe, less a servant than de facto spouse, grumbled about having to eat Gentile intruders and was always bitching about the Bronxville neighbors, who never lit enough Sabbath candles. We'd get three or four nights of these ribald romps—Moshe sneaking out to the pools in East Harlem to expand his fleishig palate to Puerto Ricans—before the tide turned and an epic mood shift took Mom to bed for two days. The house would fall silent and shadow glutted, and we'd have to endure Dad's earnest stories about two young brothers named Michael and Joseph. We gave him a hearing, but our ears pricked up at the sound of her tisking footsteps in the hall.

The spasm subsided while I sat reflecting. I stood up and inspected the horse, its balsa belly stamped Made in Russia. For all her investment in that fervent tongue, she'd traveled just once to Kiev and Moscow, and had come away homesick for them both. The streets there were thronged with people like her, the voluble faces and overwhelmed hearts, laughter never far from fulsome tears. Though raised in Pennsylvania, she shared their fervor, the red-hot pique at brute suppression and "the foot on your neck," her pet trope. It made me sadder still to think her an exile, trapped by the hard-luck hazard of birth in a country that didn't prize her gifts. Even under Brezhnev, she'd have made out better than she had in this culture of bland careerists—lived a life of emotional sweep and earned the weathered grimace she now wore. I soaked my face again, this time to rinse off tears, and made my way back to the table.

"Much better," I said. "I just needed to cool off. Sometimes when I eat a lot, I—"

"But what's this now?" Mom cried. "Is that blood on your pants? Now I'm finally calling nine-one-one."

I glanced at my jeans, one leg of which was spattered, copper splotches ornamenting the thigh. "Fuckshit*fuck*!" I yelled, the heat in my head spiking. I grabbed the thigh and pulped it: no pain. Nothing.

"Let me see," said Kate, pushing my hands away. She was on her knees probing, feeling the quad's circumference. An earnest sprig of sweat adorned her lip. "Whatever it is, it's dry," she announced. "Did you spill, I don't know, Mercurochrome or something?"

"*No*," I said, both annoyed and aroused. The side of her head glanced against my groin.

"Well, what could it be? It wasn't there when we got here, and there was no red sauce on the meal..."

I couldn't help notice the skein of flesh exposed as she knelt looking. From the top of her snug denims to the hem of her peach blouse, that luscious lower back, with its lickable sheen and lone, peekaboo strap of a string bikini, sent a wave rolling past my eyes. I stood there, dizzy, letting the tide go out, and counted down the minutes till we left.

"Well, I'm calling," Mom declared. "You need to be looked at. I'm invoking a parent's right to put my foot down."

"You do and we're leaving," I warned. "I'm perfectly fine. Besides, I've no insurance during the summer."

"I don't care! I'm still your mother, and someone has to be the sane adult here."

"And that's *you*?" I blurted. "That'll be a first."

I winced even as the words came out. Mom gaped as if punched, her eyes welling. She was so much the target of her own arraignments that any outside blow, any statement of the facts, was enough to start a long slide on the couch. I'd spent my whole boyhood ducking fights, turtling up against her provocations. Any counterpunch was taken for bullying, the ten-year-old boy as oppressor.

"Look, I'm sorry," I said. "The heat and so on. Here, I'll show you: nothing's wrong."

I pulled down my jeans to bare the thigh. It was, to my credit, free of
blood. Not so the smaller limb waving above it, naked and engorged,
pointing proudly.

"Baby, what the hell!" Kate jumped between us. "Turn around and
put that thing away!"

"I-I'm speechless!" cried Mom, her eyes big as turnips. "I find this so
disturbing, I—I—I can't speak!"

"We should go," said Kate, fussing with my buckle. "Lynn, I'm very
sorry, please don't—wait!"

She grabbed my right hand and held it up. The lanced thumb—source
of my stain and woe—had started again to bleed. "I told you to get
a Band-Aid, but you don't listen. All this nonsense could've been
avoided."

"And why—on top of everything—no underwear?" said Mom.
"I'm giving you the name of my shrink."

"Yes, please," said Kate. "*I'll* take it if he doesn't."

Both women stared at me and shook their heads. "Fine!" I snarled,
and stamped my foot. At the other end of the room, the table collapsed. It lay on its side in an orderly heap, awaiting its earliest pickup
by Sanitation.

"She's done me good and can help you, too—get to the bottom of
all this anger."

"I'm not *angry*," I said, through jaws winched tight.

"Come on," said Kate, gently guiding my mother off. "I'll help you
go look for that therapist's number."

AT THE END OF EVERY SUMMER since he'd started hustling, Angel threw
himself a blowout party. The locations varied, but the occasion didn't: it
was to celebrate his Not-Dead Day. "I'm twenty-nine this Sunday and
still dippin' and dappin', and a lot of the heads I ran with can't say that,"
he said. "They pitched the wrong product or went the wrong route, and
now they're not here to see thirty. I plan on seein' *eighty* and having a
gang of kids, but I'm smart enough to know that shit ain't promised."

This year he was staging the day-night debauch at a house Tad was renting down the shore. It was a major endeavor to move heaven and earth to the shake-shingled house in Barnegat Beach, and Angel had sent a team ahead, including his mother, to oversee the multi-culti prep. There was to be lobster and a salsa band, mingling Angel's past as a polyglot kid with his champagne aspirations. For his family, friends, and clients, it was a can't-miss bash. For his crew, it was mandatory attendance. Accordingly, he'd booked us ten a.m. cars and left orders not to party the night before. "It won't kill you to stay home and watch TV or something. Or be like Paulie and read a *book*."

As Spiro was heading down there with a guy from Queens, I decided to bunk at Tommy's place and catch a ride with him. He lived in an ash gray tenement in Yorkville, the halls of which reeked of pickled meat and the chronically matted fur of unclean pets. I walked upstairs, leery of the pocket elevator, and tripped on a milk crate underfoot. "Oops," said Tommy from his open door. "I keep telling the super to toss that thing out."

"This building has a super?"

"Supposedly. My old man."

The apartment he shared with his father and brother was bigger than I'd have guessed from the foyer—a shotgun flat with pockmarked walls and fireplaces painted to obsolescence. Tommy's room, the third one down the long hall, was crammed with sleek veneers. The king-size headboard had melamine curves in which you actually saw your own shadow. There was a console that looked to be burled mahogany but was in fact treated steel, and a glossy bar with neon tubes that blinked *Cherchez la femme*. "I'm all about art deco," he said. "When I build my house, it'll look like the Prince de Galles."

"Ah," I said. "When were you in Paris?"

"I wasn't," he said. "I saw it in a movie once."

He launched into a speech about why he lived here still, when all his friends from childhood were up and out. "It's like they left but *didn't*. Got married and had kids but wound up doing the same thing as their dads. Whereas me, when I leave, I'm burning my boats. Going where no Irish has gone before."

I shouldn't have asked but did. "Hetero porn?"

"*No,*" he said, indignant. "A comedy club."

"Oh," I said. "Comedy. There's a thought."

"It's more than a thought; it's *happening,* man. People are dying for a laugh. You give 'em a cold beer and a funny bastard onstage, they'll pay out the ass to forget they're fucked."

"But a nightclub, Tommy—that's major money, and you need a liquor license. You going to have a partner who knows the ropes?"

"Don't need one," he said. "I've got *women* behind me, and one of 'em's wired like you won't believe."

"Ah. Well, godspeed. I'm sure you'll kill."

We stayed up half the night, getting high and telling tales, and I found I liked him better by the hour. He had, as Angel said, been hurt by his mom's departure, going a little crazy when she left. At ten he broke bad with all his teachers, and by twelve he was setting fires in Bowery alleys and tossing lit M-80s at the drunks. In a rare act of prudence, his father sent him upstate to live with an uncle in Utica, and when he wasn't running away or picking fistfights with farm boys, Tommy was in the basement with a purloined *Playboy,* dropping his loads in the double sink.

Then, the summer he turned fourteen, he snuck into a fair, the kind with freak-show acts. "I'm laughing at these hicks, thinking I've seen better on Ninth Avenue, when I came across the strongman booth," he said. "He had decent enough size for that day and age, but he's wearing the big mustache and leather whatsit from Oktoberfest, so I yell, 'Show us what you got, Hansel-and-Gretel!' So he calls for volunteers to help him out, and about six of us trot up there and spread ourselves out on this wooden-bench doohickey on stilts, and he kneels down beneath it and pushes us up till he's standing bolt upright, pressing our weight. Well, fuck me if I'm lying, but there were no hidden wires, and, believe me, I checked when I got off. And the craziest thing is, there's *girls* scoping him out, like *What* else *can he do with those muscles?* Well, that was all she wrote, man: case open and closed. I joined the Y next day and started eating."

In the mania that developed, he spent the hours he wasn't lifting at the reading room of the library, scouring every dime mag and cheap gazette that cross-referenced words like *size* and *power*. It was there he taught himself the rules of "big nutrition" and sopped up the short, sweet history of muscle, beginning with the Victorian giants. They were, in more or less cascading order: mountainous Louis Cyr, the Canadian Atlas, who in his too-brief life lifted Clydesdale horses and pushed railcars up steep sidings; Eugen Sandow, the pumped-up Prussian, who, having sculpted his body to the scale dimensions of Michelangelo's *David,* came to America and earned a fast fortune stripping for women at Carnegie Hall; and Bernarr Macfadden, the Hugh Hefner of biceps, an orphan who built himself a rippling chest, then hawked it so brilliantly in books and zines that he founded his own township in New Jersey.

By the time Tommy fetched down sheets from the closet and made up the couch for me, we'd mooned over layouts of postwar monsters like Reg Park, Bill Pearl, and Joe Gold, and dreamed ourselves present at the big bang moment when Muscle Beach erupted in LA. "*Those* were the days," he said, gazing in his beer. "What I wouldn't've given to be Harold Zinkin doing benches in the cage with Armand Tanny and whoring around with stars like William Holden and the rest of the Hollywood hulks. Zinkin, by the way, only invented the Universal and now owns half of Fresno, from what I hear."

I lapped it all up from him, this lineage of strongmen who passed the scepter from era to era. Each decade they got bigger, Steve Reeves inspiring Dave Draper and Sergio Oliva, who begat Lou Ferrigno and Tom Platzer. There was something chaste about their quest for size, the Arthurian notion that muscle mass was the path to pomp and honor. They were overgrown boys after the grail of adventure, latter-day knights in skin-armor suits clambering onto the stage. But then came Schwarzenegger and his chemical Huns, and you could see it in their eyes: *We're here to pillage.* There was so much violence in Arnold's gaze, a dark-world impulse to rend and tear, as if he knew he'd go on to play Conan one day and was deep in character prep. I'd always been awed by his comic-book quads and set-in-sandstone shoulders, but now, in the context of his earnest forebears, he seemed to me diminished, the huckster unmasked.

"What'll happen when he's fifty—does anybody know?" I asked. "And what's going to happen to *us?*"

I looked at Tommy, expecting a smirk. Instead he stood up, gathered the magazines curtly, and stuffed them into the drawer of his bedside table.

"I mean, do you think about it at all, what we'll feel like at fifty, with all this shit in our system?"

He stared in the mirror of his deco bar, shooting a double biceps. "It's fine," he said flatly. "Besides, I'm quitting in two years, and the arrhythmia, or whatever you call it, will go away then."

"Arrhythmia? What's that?" I said, alarmed.

"It's where your heart speeds up for no reason. It lasts for five seconds, then goes away."

"That doesn't sound like nothing. You see a doctor?"

"Nah," he said. "I saw one about my knees. He said I had arthritis, but just a touch."

"Wait—you have *arthritis* at twenty-eight?"

"Yeah, you'll get it, too. It's what happens."

He turned off the light with no further word. For an hour both of us lay there, he on his bed, me on mine, listening to the drumbeat of our major organs. Finally, around two, I heard him snore and got up to search my pockets for a lude. That, too, happens, though no one bothers to tell you when you shoot your first load of test. Anyone stacking steroids over a period of months will find himself—infallibly— adding something to the cocktail that begins and ends his day. Androgens rev your central nervous system, drive you even when you're dead exhausted. On a medium-size stack of test and Ganabol, I'd get so amped after a night of dancing that I'd toss and turn till dawn before I dozed.

Then the guys hipped me to methaqualone, their fine new friend from Rorer. Developed in the fifties by an Indian chemist to treat malaria in Southeast Asia, quaaludes proved worthless in every regard but one: a tablet engendered pastel, nodding bliss. No panic was so pitched or problem dire that it couldn't be talked off the ledge by ludes, at least for eight blotto hours. When you hurtled through space in a quaalude hole, you lost all cares and half your IQ and stumbled around groggily from room to room, saying, "Anyone seen my Robin Trower album?" In discos like 12 West, we'd watch kids slide down a wall, motionless, beneath the big speakers. Maybe the price tag fooled them: a quaalude cost three bucks. At that rate, who *wouldn't* take two?

The third wheel of the drug-trike was what you took to wake up and bat away the haze of your quaalude stupor. For Angel, it was blow and a cup of the strong Cuban from one of the Spanish diners on Amsterdam Avenue. Tommy liked black beauties, the herbal speed promoted in the pages of *Oui* and *Penthouse*. Me, I took white crosses, though they weren't a great choice. So sensitive was I to Benzedrine's stim that a ten-mil tab sent my pulse rate skying for a good half hour after I dropped one, and occasionally triggered the kind of cluster-fuck headache that made me think I'd burst a cerebral artery. I did what I could to hedge my risk, taking speed only on mornings after I worked and never more than three days running. It was pretty much the same devil's bargain with coke: I snorted only on nights I danced because it made me less self-conscious getting naked. Still, more and more, I found myself tensing when I looked in the weight-room mirror. There were shadows under my eyes that weren't there before, and a fishbowl blurriness to my cheeks and chin, as if I couldn't quite get them in focus. *This is over,* I'd tell myself, bridling. *Once school starts, you're cleaning up.* Innocent that I was, I even believed it, having no inkling of the hell to come.

ALL THESE YEARS LATER, what I recall about that day was the conviction that the ride was over. Even before Nikki got to the party and threw it into a polyethnic panic, I knew in my bones that our good thing had ended and that, from that point, it was *sauve qui peut*. One look at Angel's face told the tale: the puppeteer was suddenly someone's puppet.

He was pacing in front of the fieldstone porch when we pulled up to the drive off Ocean Avenue. There were people milling behind him in the tuneful shade, chatting over plates of eggs and empanadas as a deejay somewhere spun the Fania All-Stars. On a pale, blowy morning, the sun struggling through a wad of cotton clouds, there was Angel in a gold guayabera, staring through the windshield of our LTD. When he saw it was only us, he stamped out his Kool and stormed past the car to eye the street. Tommy tipped the driver, who started away, honking to hail Angel as he went by. Angel turned and, instead of waving thanks, brought his fist down on the Ford's trunk. The driver stopped short, squawking in protest, then hastily hit the gas and charged off.

"Whoa, what?" said Tommy. "Did he say something to you? You want, I'll track him down when we get home."

"Just go in," said Angel. "There's food and all that there. I gotta go upstairs and make a call."

Again he stalked past us and the gifts we toted, including the Canali shirt and tie I'd bought at Barneys. "What was *that* about?" I said.

"No clue," said Tommy. "He's been acting ass all week. Maybe he needs to slack up off that blow."

Inside they'd set up church tables end to end and dressed them with paper versions of the Dominican flag. There were huge chafing dishes of chorizo and huevos and salsafied platters of shredded beef; pitchers of Red Stripe and flavored wine and candy-colored bowls of planter's punch; and tubs of sliced mangoes, baked apples, and caramel-gooey shoestring yams. In my low-grade stupor I'd not eaten all morning, and I heaped my plate with gorgeously varied tastes. Tommy, right beside me, went fork for fork in a race to two thousand calories, the two of us laughing and roughing each other as we headed back for second and third helpings. Someone said *Go easy,* but I was stoned on sugar and went on lapping up the flan. A hand skimmed mine in a puff of sandalwood, and a luscious woman took the spoon from me. "Stop, you're going to be sick. Come sit a while."

She was a shade lighter than Angel and several years older, but you couldn't mistake those eyes—green flecked with gray, flashing gemstone depth and the sparkle of something left out in the sun. She was tall, like her brother, and had some of his bearing, that regal air of commandeering the room. In a thigh-high skirt that hugged her like cling wrap and white pumps to match her sleeveless blouse, she seemed to glow in the dusk of the underlit room, a soft effulgence coming off her skin.

"I'm Paul," I said, extending a hand. "A friend of Angel's from the gym."

"I know who you are." She took the hand, holding it an extra beat. "He's mad for you, you know—Paul this and Paul that. He told me you inspired him."

"He *what?*"

"It's true," she said, laughing. "The classy way you talk and the books you're always reading—it's 'cause of you he's going back to school."

"He's—wow, that's fantastic. Um, when did he tell you this?"

"Oh, he'll do it if he says it. It took years, but we finally taught him to keep his word."

I broke into a grin. "He didn't mention which school..."

"Well, it's not this semester. He has to find his old transcript. But next year for sure. He wants to take up art."

Though she could have named botany or nuclear medicine and been no less plausible, I gave a start at his major. "How *is* he, by the way? We saw him when we got here, but he seemed a little...distracted."

"You got that, too, huh? Probably 'cause of his girlfriend. She supposably missed her ride and caught the train."

Now I couldn't help it and burst out laughing at her sweet, irreparable blindness. "I'm sorry, I didn't catch your name."

"Oh, how rude of me. It's Ines." She offered her hand in penance. "You got me all flustered here."

"Ines," I said, noting the warmth of her palm and the way her pinkie faintly stroked my wrist. "I'm probably wrong to say this, but I think he's fibbing. Angel with a *girlfriend*? Never happen."

"Oh, please, honey, trust me: I know how he is. I told him, put a *turnstile* on that bed. But this time he tells me, 'I think I've met my wife.' I said, 'I'm glad, but she'd best not be no club girl.'"

She explained that what Angel needed was a good Caribbean woman, someone raised right by God-fearing folks who'd shoot him if he ever played her out. Since boyhood, he'd gotten away with murder because he didn't have a father to correct him. "We *all* let him slide, but couldn't nothing hold him down 'cause he's too slick," she said. "The Housing cops would knock, he'd get notes home from school—and he'd just smile that smile and it was problem solved."

By now I was getting antsy about the knee that nuzzled mine and the hand that wasn't eager to let me go. There were people coming in to fill their plates, a couple of whom glanced in our direction. The last thing I needed, given Angel's mood, was to have him hear I was dogging his older sister. But I was eager to hear more about his wild-style boyhood and suggested we head outside and get a drink. There was a large, square deck over half the fenced-in yard, where twenty or thirty guests were talking and dancing on one of those rented jazz floors that snap together. I saw Spiro on the railing with a tallish blonde, his spit curl flattened by the breeze. We waved to each other before he saw me with Ines and his brows bunched together in a frown. He mouthed something stern, to which I mouthed *Don't worry*, extending an arm for Ines down the stairs.

We sat on camp chairs in the balky sun that came and went all day. Much of the lawn was monopolized by a compressed-air castle for the kids, and as we talked, one or another of them came bounding up for a hug or a nip of her sangria. They called her Spanish love names and clung to her knee in a way I couldn't imagine with my aunt, a give-and-take sampler of the family's gift: the power to seduce and be seduced. I asked whose boys they were, and she pointed across the yard to two women sitting by themselves. "The sisters," she said, giving a cursory wave that was

193

just as dully returned. "I love them and all, but they don't love me back."

I offered condolence by saying something bland about tensions with my brothers. "You see that so much now, with fathers taking off and moms trying to cope on their own. The children pick sides, even if they don't know it, and sooner or later it's a food fight."

"Yes," she said. "*Yes*. That's how it goes down. Men are s'posed to stay but yet can't be bothered."

"And you hope the kids outgrow it," I added, thinking of Ivan, "but sometimes it takes years to get past that stuff."

Again she touched my arm. "You're smart for your age. What're you, twenty-three, that you know so much?"

"Something like that," I said. "Meanwhile, you're what, twenty-six?"

"Oh, you're too much!" she said, squeezing my hand. "I wish I could take you home now in my purse!"

"Me, too," I said, springing a rabid boner that I hastily tarped with my paper plate. "But the men here would probably riot if you left."

The look she sent me—brazen, devouring—made my headlights flicker. I actually saw stars, little smudge pots of brown that pop-pop-popped, then turned to ash. "You're not like the other guys he runs with," she said. "I mean, they're nice, some of them, but—"

"No, they're not."

She laughed, taken aback, and touched my arm. "Well, *you* are, and don't try saying that you're not."

"Fine," I said. "On that, my lips are sealed."

We changed tack, for safety's sake, to our workweek lives. She talked about the salon that Angel had helped her to open and that was now on the verge of expansion, and I about the reading I was doing to get ready for the year at school. We were both, of course, lying. I'd barely touched a book, and the salon, according to Angel, was a money pit, burning through the cash he kept advancing. Whatever her skills, she'd fail as a stylist. Her gift was for men, not women. Every sense tingled when her gaze was on you; you could *hear* her caress before she touched you. All I could think of, fight it though I did, was those hands taking a walk up my inner thighs while she talked to me in tuneful, muzzy Spanglish.

"Anyhow," she said, pulling me out of my haze. "Do you got a pen and something to write on?"

Her number: ah, well. "Sorry, I don't."

"Then stay and don't move. I'm gonna find a piece of paper and come back."

I watched her walk off, feeling reprieved and dazed and helplessly under her spell. I'd met a lot of women that maelstrom summer, but none had quite prepared me for this one. Even in sunlight, where the watery glare exposed her for forty, not thirty, her gaze seemed to split me down the middle. The power of that look, a meld of need and know-how, was all in the narrowcasting. It said, *I choose you and not him or him,* and sent word that some rare ravishment awaited. So effectively was I snowed that it didn't hit me till later to ask why, exactly, me and not them. And there, in a nutshell, was the skill she shared with Angel — a knack for suspending disbelief.

She'd been gone for ten minutes when I started to worry and went to look for her. She wasn't on the deck or in the eat-in kitchen, where Spiro and Tad were talking Euro soccer. Nor did I find her in the living room, though I stopped for another helping of the orange flan. Tommy called me over to introduce Nancy, a petite but buxom girl from Angel's block. "Damn," she said, "you play football, too? I was so excited to meet a New York Jet!"

I looked at Tommy, who could scarcely contain it. "Actually, I'm on the Globetrotters," I said.

"Ah, see, now y'all went too far," she said. "I know for a *fact* that they play overseas."

"Have either of you seen Angel's sister?" I asked.

"Which one, Gladys or Tania?" she said. "They're both around here somewhere."

"Um, no, the other one. Ines."

The two of them swapped glances. "You mean his mom?"

"Wha-at? No, the woman in the white blouse?"

"I'm telling you, that's his *mom*. Did you hit on her?"

Tommy's grin fell a foot when he saw my expression. "No, you fucking didn't! Oh, my Christ."

"She said she was his sister, and—and looked younger than the others—"

He grabbed me by the arm and herded me toward the corner. "What'd I say in the car? Stay *away* from her. Didn't I say she's crazy as fuck?"

"Yeah, but I—"

"Why do you think *he's* like that? She ran game on him, too. Trust me, I know things that'd fry your ears."

"Really?" I gawked. "Did they ever—did he—"

He hustled me farther from an eavesdropping couple. "Did *you?*"

"Of course not," I fumed. "How high do you think I am? Only a psycho would hoag her at a party."

"Or a suicide."

"Tommy, I *swear* to you: nothing happened. We might've held hands, but that's it."

"Anyone see that?"

I flashed on Angel's sisters and their truculent stares. "Maybe, but it was nothing. Playful stuff."

"Dude, sharks don't play; they chase blood."

"Well, what the hell do I do? I-I've gotta tell him."

Tommy grabbed my arm. "We'll tell him together."

THE PARTY, ONCE A languid, slow-grow thing, had metastasized in the last hour. There were so many people on the cedar deck, I could hear its crossbeams grumble under the strain. Dark-skinned Latinos in sharp-pressed slacks were fast-stepping the samba to a five-piece band, twirling their partners in four-four time. Elaborately made-up white girls wearing too-tall heels clapped or danced and did their race no honor by yelling exhortations in Spanglish. There were big guys from gyms I'd never been to with Angel, ex-con types with barn-door shoulders he'd met at iron dungeons in the outer boroughs. The sun had broken through, the breeze had drawn down, and the scent of perspiration and cut-price cologne was laying a salty shimmer on the day. It was a hard-drinking bunch—there were cups on every surface—and in an hour or so, couples would start skulking upstairs, looking for somewhere private to screw.

I, meanwhile, wanted to go lie in the dunes. My stomach had started churning, hurling bolts of nausea off the turnbuckle of my groin. I had to find Angel and say my piece to him, but no less pressing, I had to *go be sick*, lock the door behind me in some basement john and let the fur fly for half an hour. I was walking behind Tommy as he forded the crowd but lost him in a thicket of mambo kings. It took the rest of my strength to totter downstairs, crawl through the slats of the deck's foundation, and vomit a liner of hot brown mess in the general direction of the gravel.

Hands on knees, I watched the joists shudder. But instead of backing out, I frog-marched deeper, like an animal digging a hole in which to die. In the cool brown dark, I spied a rise to sit on and unbuttoned my sweat-soaked shirt. It was a relief being out of its Orlon squeeze, and with each vile emission I felt lighter and freer, partly absolved of my sins. I had rooked Kate out of another Sunday together, feeding her some howler about a wedding in Elmont that would run well into the night, and in a twofer crime, I had also blown off Ivan, who was leaving for Ann Arbor in the morning. In a development I might have seen coming if I hadn't ignored him all summer, my brother was suddenly quitting New York City to start life over in the Midwest. This was good, on its face—he'd spend a year auditing courses with the poet Joseph Brodsky, then apply as a resident to the University of Michigan—and I was relieved and heartened that he was taking himself seriously after his walkabout in psychedelics. But I was also upbraided: Ivan had risen from his idylls to pluck the birthright of bookish aspirations, while I had spent the summer doffing a fake cop suit to the strains of "Do the Hustle." I could talk all I wanted about the value of otherness, but there was nothing literary in *any* of this—unless by literary you meant Jackie Suzanne.

It took a fair while to empty my gut and concoct a plan of escape. I would tiptoe upstairs, then try the side door, which let out onto the drive. If I encountered Angel there, well, so be it; I'd cop to the indelicacy with his mom. If not, I'd walk until I spotted a cab, take it to a train station two towns over, and disappear permanently from view. In forty-eight hours I'd be back at school, melting into the fairground of suntanned faces and monolithic, blue-jeaned flatness. There I'd fold away the man-whore jeans, scrub the concealer off my mottled ass, and seek instruction and forgiveness in the fourth-floor stacks, reading Restoration drama till one a.m.

Up the low staircase, past the carnival on the deck, I slipped into a bathroom off the den. There, taking a moment to rinse my teeth with a fingerful of Crest and Listerine, I peeked to check that the coast was clear. There were rooms on either side of the hall I slunk down, and in them couples on pullout couches or sprawled across single beds. I was going too fast to see their faces, but in the last of the little rooms, something stopped my gaze as I reached for the knob of the side door. I turned for a look and locked eyes with Angel, who was standing nose to nose with his mother.

"What's doing?" I cocked up a pallid smile. "Amazing party you've got going."

"Yeah," he said. "Thanks for coming out."

He was flushed a deep crimson, and I saw, with ticking weirdness, that his face had been freshly slapped. His right hand was raised to respond in kind, but Ines had her chin up, uncowed. My gaze, however, went to the woman beside them, a tall, pale beauty with jet-black hair and eyes of an absurdly evolved frankness. Even before she spoke, I felt a tug of recognition, as if the two of us had come from a distant orb and were being held here by a race of brawny satyrs.

"I—I wanted to wish you, um...Is everything okay here?"

"Yeah, we're just talkin'." He lowered his hand. "Go out there and I'll find you in a minute."

"I mean, it's your party and no one's seen you."

"Nah, man, everything's cool. We're wrapping up."

"The hell we are. This shrew *hit* you." The air rang a moment, as from a bullet's report. "She smacks you in the face for bringing a white girl here? She needs to be hauled off in cuffs."

Ines lunged for her, but Angel interceded, seizing his mother roughly by the arms.

"Fuck you, bitch—don't tell me how to act! I'll treat my son any way I want!"

"Because that's what moms do, right? Dress like hookers and beat their kids up for having a life?"

Ines boiled in Angel's grasp, a look of white mayhem in her eye. "Enough," said Angel. "You're makin' it worse. Go out and walk around with Paulie."

"Let off me!" shrieked Ines. "She don't know who she fucked with! She cut her own throat, the skank *puta*—"

"Nik, *go*," Angel pleaded, tightening his grip. "I swear I'll be out in a few."

It was the first time I'd ever heard him beg for something. I eyed her with an interest close to awe.

"What's *your* mom like?" Nikki asked me, not budging. "Does she commit battery when you bring home girls?"

"Uh, no," I said, ducking Angel's glare. "It's more like, you know, a silent scream."

"Wow," she said. "You're telling me you've read Brecht?"

"Well, only *Mother Courage*, but I plan to—"

"Then great," she sniffed. "Let's go where it's the *twentieth century*."

I felt four eyes on the back of my neck as Nikki waltzed me out and down the hall. She had an arm around my waist, steering firmly, though I had her by eighty pounds. Tall and boy-breasted in a Furstenberg wrap, the scent of something sweetly acidic coming off her, she guided us past the gawkers in the living room, including Tommy mouthing *What the fuck?* Out we went to the veranda in front, away from the hurly-burly on the deck, where a deejay had taken over and was spinning the Trammps at a volume sure to summon the fire department.

There was one last beer in a tub of melting ice, and we passed it back and forth as we perched, alone, on the chipped-paint railing. Nikki asked about Angel and how I'd come to know him, then thought and said, no, wait, don't tell her: "The less I hear about him, the better I sleep." But something in her eyes seemed to commission me, and I gave an abridged version of my work for Angel, leaving him out of the tawdry parts. She listened with degrees of humor and horror, stopping me here and there to interject comments or to ask if I'd been tested for gonorrhea. I lied and said I had, then resumed my merry spiel about running away to join the sex circus. And then, on a hunch, I dropped my father's name, adding, for good measure, Roth and Bellow. Her eyes opened a fraction of an inch wider. "Wait," she said. "From that, you're doing *this*?"

"Well, yeah," I said. "I need *something* to write when I start my dissertation this fall."

"Really? You're writing a thesis on stripping?"

"Um, no. I mean, not exclusively. More a coming-of-age thing. A what did they used to call it? A bildungsroman. Or, with me, I guess, a *body*bildungsroman."

"A bodybildungsroman." She grinned, chucking my knee. "You realize I've read *Werther* in the original?"

"I didn't," I said, chucking her knee back. Blind to both the hilarity of "Werther in the original" and the insanity of cruising Angel's girl, I hesitated a moment, then thrust my mouth forward in a banzai mission to kiss her. Shocked as she was—I heard a muffled grunt—she submitted for a gracious, close-lipped second before tactfully pulling away and patting my cheek.

"That's sweet," she said, "but maybe we should—"

"I know," I said, shame-swept. "I'm an ass."

"Well," she said lightly, "a charming ass."

"Sorry, sorry, sorry. I completely—"

"Forget it—it's past now. Done and gone. And as for the *ass* thing, you'll outgrow it."

"Really?" I said. "That happens?"

But suddenly she was elsewhere, out to sea on a sharp, interior draft.

"Yeah, you don't believe it either."

She looked up, damp-eyed. "Hmm?"

"You think people don't change," I said. "We are what we are and rots of ruck."

She slid off the railing with a sour hop and snapped the cap back on the bottle. "Look, I'm twenty-five, I do too much coke, and I'm dating a guy who pimps men. I wouldn't put much stock in what I say."

She took me by the elbow and, like an orderly minding a patient, nudged me very firmly toward the door.

Twelve

My Nature Abhors a Vacuum

THE APARTMENT WAS HOT AND, but for me, empty, drop-clothed in dust and shadows. Ivan was gone, off to Ann Arbor, where, a Gauloise dangling from the side of his mouth, he'd soon play Genet to the farm-stand bards in his Three Great Poets class. David had left soon after, eager for grad school after two loveless months driving a cab. And a couple of nights earlier, I'd parted tensely with Kate, who was bound for Asheville to join her mother at the cabin they'd rented till Labor Day. After dithering for weeks, she'd asked me to fly down with her for three days. It'd only be the four of us, her sister included, and we'd be able, she and I, to duck out after lunch for long, slow hikes up the Swannanoa hills and naked, late-day swims in its glassy creeks. We'd slaved all summer and were owed, she said, though I, in my mounting chemical misprision, took that to mean that *she* was owed. She was, of course (and *how*), but I didn't want a bill; I was already feeling overdrawn.

Worse, I twigged why she'd waited to ask: she wasn't sure which version of me would show. "Half the time, you're the Paul I met in June—awkward and boyish but genuinely sweet and really trying to figure it all out. The other half—Christ, I don't know *who* that is. It's like, if I listen close, I almost hear you ticking."

Nothing made me lose patience faster than being told that I lacked patience. "Well, why invite me if you're afraid I'll blow? Wouldn't that just prove your mom right?"

Her mother, the principal of the middle school Kate had gone to, was a clearinghouse of snap appraisals. Alice loved her daughters with a holy rigor but had set high standards and wasted no tact telling them when they fell short. About the best she'd said of Kate's previous boyfriends was that the last one, Martin, was "harmless enough," a guy who'd one day "make a good uncle." The rest weren't "fit to play in her ballpark," a phrase that made me think of them standing outside, selling hot dogs and Yankee pennants.

"I'm not scared you'll blow—at least I hope I'm not. I just worry what comes out of your mouth."

The heat in my chest banked on. "How so?"

She gave back my querulous stare. "Don't you *listen* to what you say now? Some of it's just...mean. Mean, and gratuitously so."

"Give me an example."

We were sitting in her kitchen after a stilted meal, the conversation a series of fits and starts. Typically, we raced each other to bed while we figured out the night's next move—a Resnais at the Thalia; the West End for beers—but sex was off the cheese cart now. "Tonight—again—you took shots at my roommate, who, whatever her faults, has been nice to you and doesn't need to hear that she's fat."

"She *didn't* hear it, Kate. Not from me. I just said those bratwursts are total death food."

"As if she doesn't know it, Paul; we do have mirrors. She eats because she's lonely and bored."

"And didn't I offer to work her out, put her on a program at the Y? One month there and—why the face?"

"Because you talk about the gym like some new religion. It's anything *but,* judging by you."

"Well, hey, you should've met me a year ago. You'd have taken one gander and kept on going."

"Yeah, maybe I would've. Or maybe I'd have thought, *There's a shy, sweet guy who really needs to trust himself a little.*" She saw my grimace and cast her eyes down. "All right, fine, look. Maybe I wouldn't."

"Damn right you wouldn't. And how's my tone different than when we met in June?"

"Do you really not hear it? Because it isn't subtle. Ever since you started hanging out with Angel, there's this... *hardness* in the way you see the world. And it's more than just copping a vibe from him. You're angry and jumpy and short with people, and I don't get it but it scares me."

By now the inner heat was on the move; it pressed against my Adam's apple. I came out of my slouch and stretched my arms up, a trick from the asthma days to clear a path. But the thickness shifted and redeployed, gumming up the sides of my throat. "Well, I'm tense, I'll admit that. Something's stressing me lately, though I can't get at what it is."

But this admission served only to bump up the ante; in moments I found it very hard to breathe. "Um, can we go to the living room? I'm feeling a little weirded and just want to... move."

"Yes, of course, baby, sure. Do you want some water? You got very pale there all of a sudden."

"I-I-I'm fine. Just—I'll meet you in the—"

I lurched from the table, dizzy-headed, and went reeling down the long gray hall. It was easier, on my feet, to get a breath, but now I was having trouble with my eyes. The glare of the overhead made them throb. I paced with a hand up, kneading my brow. "Headache," I lied as Kate trailed me in. "This is the third one in a week."

She stood by, stymied, offering aspirin and a neck rub, her own eyes damp with feeling. Their decency shamed me, stuck pins in my tongue. I was false, low and furtive, and she was candor itself, a channel between thought and deed. I was lucky just to know her, and luckier still to occupy a piece of her heart. Which is another way of saying I was more and more crazy for not being crazy in love.

Her living-dining area, a box of beige walls that looked onto the rumps of brown-brick buildings, was chockablock with stolid thrift-store finds in varying stages of redemption. I liked the facing love seats, born again in baize, but the wing chair she hadn't gotten around to fixing stuck its leg out when I trundled by. I barked my shin against it and had all I could do not to pick it up and hurl it against the wall. I was sweating thickly, though the fan in the window sent a chill through my clammy shirt.

"Baby, *talk* to me. What's got you so loopy? Is it all that stuff you're taking to gain weight?"

"What? No, I told you: those are *vitamins*. Nobody's ever freaked from a B-twelve shot."

"And that's all they are? They're not speed or something? Why would they raise such bruises on your ass?"

"Please. I've sworn to you: they're nutritional aids, not drugs."

"Well, *what* then: can you tell me? Do *I* make you crazy? I mean, I've tried to keep it easy and let you be, not call you on the days when I know you're working or hassle you to say where this is going—"

"Baby, I *beg* you. Not now. I—I feel like my brain's going to split."

"I see that," she said, holding a hand out to me. I stopped my frantic ambit and curled beside her. She reached around behind me to stroke my scalp in the way that sent pale moonbeams down my spine. I let my eyelids droop and my shoulders sag, the panic ebbing with progressive waves of shivery, blue-black numbness. I floated there, hearing her drowsy hum, and the urge rose up again to tell her all, to bolt the whole thing out and make an end. The whoring and doping were trussed together with the nausea in my throat, driven by an acid reflux of shame that just wanted sorting, come what might. She would listen with a mixture of sadness and horror, then consult her sense of grievance and kick me out. Or she'd let me have it for the dumb-shit lies and for selling her obdurate kindness short, then allow me to talk myself back in. But come what might, she was owed that much, and so, to be fair, was I.

What brought me up short then, squelching the urge? Those five hard words my plea was sure to trigger: *Quit or else, Paul. Now.*

I can't, Kate. Not yet. Not *nearly* yet.

Instead, I put my head down on her lap and took long, rattling breaths till the terror ebbed. The corners of my eyes leaked, and I told Kate the half-truth that I was crying for Mom. "That's why I avoid her, Kate: I have no shield. I just see her and—and go to pieces for a month."

"I know that now. I'm sorry, I should've listened. I just thought if I went with you, it'd shift the equation and she'd see you as you are, not as you were. Because you *are* a good man, Paul; I know you are. Underneath the size, there's a heartful kid."

"Thank you," I murmured, feeling the fear turn back, lashing its bitter spray against my chest. "Not sure what I've done to earn that praise, but I know it makes me want to act better."

"Then *do*. Come with me; it's the break we need. Three days away in that gorgeous air. We'll climb up Chimney and pick wildflowers, then hike back down and swim in Loon Lake, the deepest, bluest water you've ever seen. Trust me—this tension, it'll wash right out of you, and you'll go back to school feeling five pounds lighter after fucking me till we can't walk."

"Oh, Kate, I'd love that; really, I would. But class starts Tuesday and I haven't got a room yet. Once again, they've screwed my housing up. Plus, there's the paperwork for TAP to get, and I can't play fast and loose with that grant; it's half of what I live on during the year."

She glumly retreated, wondering why I'd waited all summer; her forms had been mailed in months before. I explained, with the facts firmly on my side, that I'd waited because it pained me to look ahead, to think beyond these three short months together. They'd been, I said, the sweetest, most memorable days in a life that sorely lacked such, and the end coming on now made my chest clench and was part of the madhouse in my head. I'd come back in on weekends, I swore, and she could come out to Stony Brook whenever she liked, provided she could stand being bludgeoned awake by some hallmate's bootleg of Twisted Sister.

She looked at me, damp-eyed, then smacked my wrist lightly, using just a thumb and index finger. "That's very nicely said, for a pack of lies. But yes, I'll come see you. Till you get bored."

"I'm *not* lying, Kate—and I'll never get bored. I just *look* at you sometimes and want to…melt."

She held my gaze, then permitted a hug, the two of us rocking side to side. The harder I squeezed, though, the less she gave back, her arms meeting limply at my waist. "C'mon," she murmured. "It's an eight a.m. flight. You've got yourself an hour till I turn you out."

IN THE END, KATE WAS RIGHT: I was far too young to properly put a price on what I had. She was twenty-one going on thirty-two, while I, at twenty-one, was shading thirteen, a boy out of the house and into his groin. Every pretty girl going by me on Broadway seemed another nation worth exploring, a language and climate different in kind from the one I took to bed. I was hungry, too, to *know* girls, to ply them with questions about the lives they'd led in school, to learn what I could, in those postcoital chats, about the world I'd missed out on as a teen. All of it fed me, each detail and sidebar, while the encounters themselves made me marginally less lonely, plugging the space in that black-hole chasm that other people called an imagination.

But this didn't explain, or only partly did, why I opted out of going with Kate. Nor did the chance to join Angel and Nikki at a dance-cruise party in Bay Shore. I hoped to make it out there, weather permitting, after a day trip to school to plead with Housing, but I had no hopes for a sign from Nikki that she was ready to ease me in. The glimpse of her I'd gotten revealed a stratum I hadn't guessed at, an echelon of women so at home with money that it might as well have been their atmosphere. Nikki traveled in lucre; it attached to her, littered her path with polished men whose hair always did it what it was told. No, I knew my place: it was straight back to class, parsing Cavalier poets and keeping my head down.

But before I could go, I had to get off the couch, and for most of two days I'd been bolted to it. Over weeks I'd read *The Magus* in the disjunctive way of someone who had better things to do, picking it up and putting it down, a tourist in its haunted, sun-scorched hills. The night before I parted with Kate, however, I drowsed across the book's great, shattering turn, when a hand burst through the page and shook me. The star-chamber trial of Nicholas Urfe is one of the most jolting in postwar fiction, bringing on a bestiary of hooded judges and Nick's lover hog-tied to a wheel, the unforeseen eruption of sexual violence the book has stealthily built to, scene by scene. The section scared me shitless and drove me straight on to the end; I finished up well past dawn. I slept four hours and, spooked upon rousing, started reading again from the beginning. This time the fear went through my bones.

Perhaps you have to be a male in your twenties to be demolished by a book like Fowles's, the approximate age and undercooked character of his swanning protagonist. If you're forty, or even thirty, Nick's romantic self-deceptions may strike you as both boorish and transparent, the conduct of a handsome, donnish kid who's less noble — and knowing — than he thinks. But I, in the first blush of feral manhood, grew more aligned with him by the page, and as such was a bull's-eye for the book's indictments. The brooding searcher who wanders the world over, lonely and weightless and cast out of home, the victim of his own rare affect — it was all just a scam we practiced on women to ease them out of their pants. Lurking behind our pose was a fierce entitlement and a ruthless brand of self-pity, built on the premise that our love-starved boyhoods entitled us to act as we liked. Running off to Greece — and away from Alison, the truth-dealing toughie who lights his loins but is insufficiently precious to win his mind — Nick blames his callow mistreatment of women on a postwar surfeit of cynicism and a hunger to escape a pre-shrunk life. I, however, had no such outs. I was just trying to fill my gut and to wreak a little hell along the way; to leave my mark, in the form of a bruise, on anyone who'd ever overlooked me. I was lying like I actually had a talent for it, making vile remarks to people who hadn't provoked me, and having sex with women I could barely see in the mine-shaft dark of swingers' clubs. And where had it gotten me, all this tramping around in the name of Life Experience? I was heading back to college with twelve hundred bucks and a trunk full of ugly clothes, to say nothing of a jones for three kinds of drugs and no clear means to afford them. Even Kate, my glory, was writing me off, convinced that her affection was no match for my affliction, which she, the smart cookie, knew good and well was linked to those lumps on my ass.

Midway through my second pass, I put the book down and let the shame sluice through me. A reel of degradations aired inside my skull, quick-cut clips of freak-show laughter and the eyes of boozed-up girls. One recent scene kept looping back, a biblical debacle in Syosset. Tommy and I had done a sweet sixteen gig at a lobster place on the water, then stuck around afterward, got drunk on Galliano, and wound up at the house of the birthday girl. He danced a couple of solos in the living room, sold a gram of coke to two blotto moms, and was smartly on his way by one a.m. But I, too woozy to work for tips, was invited upstairs to sleep it off and woke up with the sun to find myself sandwiched between my hostess and her tenth-grade daughter. *I could be in jail now,* I thought in horror as I watched it over and over, then flashed from that stunt to another fiasco, a wild ride two weeks later. I had traipsed with Spiro on a rainy Thursday to a hot new club in Bayside but had lost him in the mix and attached myself to a tube-topped cocktail server. Colleen was a little old to be serving shots to juniors with fake IDs, but she explained that she only worked in order to see the world and had spent the spring in Chile throwing pots.

We waited in the lot for her roommate, Ed, who bombed up in a Nova with noisy pipes. I gulped before getting in — he was massively stoned and laughed about seeing two of me — but it was either go with them or roam the streets for a cab at three a.m. Colleen, who'd lit a joint, had a yen for waffles, and so we trawled for a diner on Northern Boulevard. I was sitting in the backseat nursing the jay and trying to get the knotted lap belt to latch when a cop car, turret blinking, slid behind us. "*Fuckfuckfuck!*" cried Ed, banging the wheel. A skycap at Kennedy, he'd been bragging up the ease with which he brought in hash from Morocco, pausing here and there to relight the pipe that was sitting on his center console. Beside it basked a chunk of resinous blond on a tar-stained tinfoil square. But neither that nor the baggie of bud in his armrest had him on the point of tears. "There's a half pound of Thai stick under my spare, and if they find it, we're so dead — that's *distribution!*"

I stubbed out the roach and gulped the thing down. It singed my throat and stuck there, like a fly on a strip. I tried to hack it up, but it was wedged in behind my palate.

"Shut it!" hissed Ed, stashing the pipe and hash.

"*You* shut it!" I croaked.

"If we get taken in, I swear I'll —"

"*Both* of you shut it," Colleen ordered, rooting through the bowels of her purse. "Here, smoke these — the clove'll mask the smell. And if they ask to search the car, don't let 'em!"

She passed around a rumpled pack of filterless kreteks. I lit one and launched into spastic coughing. It hadn't much abated when the roofline rattled; two cops with long flashlights glared in. "Get out," barked the one on the driver's side. "The three of you: easy on the curb."

"But don't you want my license and —"

"*Now*, I said! And put those damn things out."

Colleen and I got out without drama. But Ed, so baked he had to stand in stages, knocked the bag of weed from the armrest. It landed, festively, at the lead cop's feet, adorning his shoes with stems. "*Sir,*" said the cop, bending to scoop it up, "does this object belong to you?"

Ed eyed it as if from great distance. "Um . . . Not sure . . . Wait, *that* one?"

The cop passed it to his partner. "You have any idea why we stopped you?"

Ed swayed in his shoes. "Because of the, um, object?"

Still struggling not to cough, I watched the cop's hand as it tightened around the barrel of the flashlight. "I watched you run a red on Two-oh-Fourth. Didn't you see me stopped there at the light?"

"Actually, I . . . If I had've, I'd've definitely stopped."

Bending from the waist to read the cop's badge, Ed keeled into his arms. The cop spun him around, forced him onto the hood, and cuffed his wrists with no great gentleness. The second cop ordered me against the Nova while he walked Colleen off to get her story. I leaned on the trunk with sweaty palms, trying to dial my thoughts down to a shriek. *They'll think we're a pot ring and I'm the guy who breaks legs over a dime of sess. What if they check my ass for tracks? I shot two hundred migs this morning! Wait, I can't be strip-searched, I'm wearing a thong, the one with Captain America on the front!*

At length the lead cop called the other one over; they huddled while Colleen wept on the curb. I held my breath as the first cop approached. He asked where I'd met the driver and was I aware that he had warrants? I said I surely wasn't and babbled out the story of my hour-old acquaintance with the girl. "So you're saying you never seen them before tonight — is that what I hear you saying?"

"Absolutely," I said, with a selling nod, to show I believed myself. "Um — why're you jotting this down? They'll tell you that I didn't."

"Not really." He flipped to an earlier page. "Mr. Baldukas states he met you at six p.m. and alleges you supplied the contents of that bag."

"What? B-but he's lying. Ask anyone; ask my *gym*. I lifted from four to seven at the West Side Y."

"Well, be that as it may; I have no way to check that. You were present in a car with drugs."

I felt my arms stiffen with righteous rage and wanted nothing so much as to bull my way past him and yank Ed out of the cruiser. Shaking him upside down till he told the truth seemed a prudent way to solve the problem, and I was about to ask the cop if I could straighten Ed out when a thin reed of sanity piped up. "You know what — you're right. I could see he was trouble, but like a schmuck, I went anyway."

He went on scribbling. "There someone you can call to post bond?"

I let a long breath go. "Yes. My father."

"Give me his information and I'll make the call." He took down the number I hadn't dialed in weeks and closed his pad with a *thwap*. "Unless you know a reason why I shouldn't."

It took a bleary moment, but I caught his meaning and flashed to the Thai stick in the trunk. Ed had all but dared me to give him up, and the world would only profit if someone that soul-dead was doing eight to twelve at Fishkill. But something stopped my tongue: the rules of the street, which Angel had taken pains to teach me. Rule number one: never hurt the hustle, even if the hustle wasn't yours. That was your debt to the game that fed you, and the debt still held if you left the life and got a straight job and a square girl. The hustle would always be there when you needed it, provided you did the right thing going out.

"Sorry, sir. No, I don't."

He cuffed my hands behind me and left me there to stew while he went and filled out paperwork in the cruiser. I leaned against the Nova, shrinking my profile for the occasional car of gawkers going by. The front of my black dress flares was smudged a dull gray, the sleeves of my black poet's shirt had come unrolled, and I looked, with my migrant tan and hangdog shag, like Zorro pinched for stealing the padre's horses. All I needed to complete the abasement was Dad rolling up in his orange Le Car to post bail for me at the Queens County courthouse.

The second cop put Colleen in the cruiser, motioning me over with a nod. "You need better friends. Look at the pile they got you into."

"I told your partner they're not friends."

He was taller than the other cop and fussily groomed, with barber-smooth skin and the Creamsicle sheen of someone who owned his own sunlamp. "A wrong-place, wrong-time deal, huh?"

"No, he *lied*, I was lifting tonight. I'm asking you, just call my boys — please, sir."

"Keep it down, there's people sleeping. This ain't the ghetto; this is Queens."

"Sorry, sorry, sorry. I'm real tired, too. Look, couldn't you just make a couple calls?"

He crossed his ankles and leaned back on the cruiser. "So how much poundage you bench?"

"How much do I what?"

I spied his arms under the starched short sleeves. The cluster of bunched veins told the story. "Actually, I'm stuck at two-sixty now. You, though, you've gotta be pushing three-twenty."

He passed over the flattery with a frown. "No such thing as sticking points. You take a week off, get your tissues rested, then go back in and blast through it."

"I tried that," I said. "Dropped to two–twenty-five and just did reps for a while."

"Well, there's your problem: you overtrained the fibers. Just stop altogether, then see what happens."

"Stop benching? You're kidding, right? *How?*"

A thin smile escaped him. "How long you training?"

"Less than a year, but I'm serious about it. I'm hoping to enter my first comp soon."

"That's cool," he said. "I had a buddy won Mr. Brooklyn. Couldn't keep it up, though: the chemicals got him."

"I hear you," I chimed. "That's why I train natural, though it's hard when you're going to school and working, too."

"You don't know the half," he said, checking behind him. "Try sitting in a car with a guy who smokes Camels. I'm lucky if I still have lungs when I hit the gym."

Addled though I was, I saw my chance. "Well, the cops in my crew, they break their butts doing squats, then go out and do buy-and-busts."

"Yeah? Which precinct?"

"The one-nine. Lots of coke being dealt—or so they tell me."

"Huh. So you train with undercovers?"

"Yup, and they're all loco, especially Dennis. He hangs skells from rooftops by their ankles."

"Really?" He grinned. "That's some roughneck shit. I always wanted to work in vice."

"Well, you ought to train with us Friday night. It's a hard-core session, but we all go out afterward and eat like we're going to the chair."

"I might take you up on that; I could use the push. Besides"—he bent in—"I wouldn't mind meeting your friends. I was thinking of putting in for a plainclothes bump."

I gave him my number. In a moment he had the cuffs off and was discreetly saying sorry. "We weren't going to run you; the girl there backed you up. My partner was just hoping you'd help us out."

They gave me a lift to the Rockaway station, where Tonelli, the lead cop, made a show of thanking me for "the break." As I stepped from the car, I sent a glance at Colleen, who was wearing a look of lead-pipe despair. Too late, it hit me that I hadn't backed *her* up, and the unmanfulness turned me gray with shame. I'd trained to get laid and to make friends, too, to extract myself—by force—from an empty room and the trancey, amber clutches of TV. But beneath those drives was a deeper imperative: I'd done it to become a *man* by hook or crook. The cast of qualities that a man possesses—patience, adroitness, a sense of his own measure—seemed beyond my reach by other means, and I thought, or hoped, that if they weren't innate, perhaps I could install them from without. If I built a man's body and was taken seriously by people, maybe I'd intuit what they thought they saw and act it till I had the details down. Or maybe there was something about size itself that conferred a rote nobility: the strength to own the street and to share it, too, protecting, not provoking, fellow travelers.

As I LAY ON THE SOFA reviewing my crimes, I felt my chest thicken again. I wanted to jump up and pummel something, smash with both fists till my arms got tired and the surge of self-loathing passed. But there was nothing of mine to break in that sublet flat and no place to run that was less oppressive on a dead-dog August day. I racked my brain for someone to call. Angel? No chance; he'd never understand—and if he did, he'd never forgive me. Tommy? Forget it; he'd tell me to take a lude and go get a hand job downtown. Ivan had left no number, Kate was somewhere hiking, and Nathan hadn't called since mid-July, though in fairness I hadn't called him either. That left the one man it always left. I hastily changed my clothes and raced downstairs.

In those days Publishers' Row was idle in August, the half-mile strip from the Fifties to the Forties vacant but for peddlers and Asian tourists. Even Fifth Avenue, that bell cow of commerce, padded through the month in a torpid sulk, closing its doors to keep the cool air in. I didn't bother calling before I flagged a cab; Dad rarely took *weekends,* let alone months, off. His capacity for labor was a kind of voodoo, vast and talismanic to a child of the sixties, for whom pleasure was the first and last directive. Even on the bus from a day trip of skiing, I'd find him poring over a new Czech marvel (who turned out to be Milan Kundera) or jotting marginalia in the knurled headers of his thrice-read copy of *The Golden Bowl.* He used to tell writers who were stuck on a chapter, "Don't just *do* something—*sit* there," and his own affinity for lead-bottomed labor confounded several spouses as well as sons.

For much of that summer—indeed, much of the seventies—he'd been up to his ears trying to save *American Review* from the legal-tender mercies of its patrons. The pathbreaking quarterly he'd founded in the sixties, to effusive national praise and modest sales, was on its third publisher in less than five years and not earning its keep at Bantam Books. Worse, it wasn't spinning off the clutch of "big" novels that had induced successive houses to field its costs, and the suits at Bantam, like their peers at previous stops, were wondering why they'd hired an editor of my father's heft to edit something other than books. He did edit books, though, and wrote reviews besides, and paid his ex-wives and saw his young sons, all while conducting a backstage search for the next corporate savior of *AR*. I knew that each week was a high-wire act of five a.m. wake-ups and missed dinners.

Dad's assistant (invariably a sleek and serious girl whom he mentored to a big career and didn't bed) was away for the week, like most of the staff, and I knocked on his door to find him asleep. He was seated at the desk, his head slung sideways in the half-nod way he had of napping. I thought of the times he'd taken me to movies and dozed off halfway in, only to rouse as the credits rolled with trenchant things to say about the film. (Even out cold he was smarter than me, a fact it didn't pay to dwell on.) He'd acquired his brown-black tennis tan, though God knew where he found time to play, and was dressed in his sole concession to the seventies, a khaki button-down with epaulets. With the tips of his knit tie neatly tucked between the buttons, he looked like a bomber pilot dozing between runs—handsome, self-starting, an engine of forward motion. I caught myself thinking, for the thousandth time, *How did* this *man father* me?

"Knock, knock."

He roused with a lurch, jerking forward. "Huh?"

"Sorry, I didn't mean to—"

"I was opening my mail and closed my eyes a second. Wait a minute, are we supposed to have lunch?"

"No, I was down here buying books," I said, "and thought I'd pop in and say hello."

"Oh," he said, still woozy. "It's been months."

"I know, and I'm sorry. I've had...quite the little summer. Don't worry, I'm not here to borrow money."

"*Oh*. Well, good." He brightened. "Your brother cleaned me out when he left town."

I grunted condolence. "The price of acid keeps going up, huh?"

"Hey, that's unfair. He's finally buckling down, and I thought it was important to lend support."

Ivan buckling down? I'd seen no hint of it, though perhaps resettled in the Big Ten steppes, he'd seize on his hidden Turgenev. But now, as ever, the faintest ray of hope had boosted his stock with Dad, while I and my bounce-back, dean's-list marks had raised not a ripple in him. "You *look* good," I said. "Playing lots of singles?"

"Some," he said. "Still showing that manly chest?"

"Um, less and less." I buttoned up.

"Good. I'm glad to hear, if not see, it."

We stared at each other. The silence of the office lent weight to the moment's strangeness. "So, anyway, on the whole, it's been a solid summer. I made good money working banquets and weddings and definitely got around a bit after my shifts... On the theory that it helps to get that... out of your system. You don't want to be pushing forty and wish you had."

"I suppose," he said, shrugging. "Doing anything else?"

"Well, lifting, of course. I do a lot of that—though I'm starting to think I need to cut back there."

"Uh-huh."

Another blank pause, then *ba-dum, ba-dum, ba-dum:* the rhythmic, two-tone desk tap from Dad. It was his long-standing (and, by then, unconscious) invocation to speed it up, buster, time was money. There were sleeves to roll up and great men to edit. No portion of his day was unspoken for, at least when it came to loose chat.

"Anyhow, I've been taking a hard look, reflecting on what it means to have all this... *bulk.* It kind of came to a head for me reading *The Magus,* which—have you read it?—really speaks to—"

"Yes, I know the book, Paul. I reviewed it."

Again the drumroll, only louder.

"Right. Well, in satirizing Nick, Fowles nailed for me the way I'd—"

"Hold on a minute. What satire?"

"Well... I mean, look at that last scene, where Alison comes back finally, and he can't even ask her forgiveness."

"Yes, the ending's indistinct, but every word is carved in blood. And

Nick has too much energy and three-ply dimension to be the object of Fowles's scorn."

This derailed me: could I have misread the book twice? "But what about his screwing over women before her? He brags about it freely in the first ten pages, then goes and does it again all over Greece."

Putting on one of his ruminant smiles, he spread his hands wide in implication. "And what is he, twenty-six? He's learning what men learn: that there are no Aphrodites and he's no Apollo."

"So what is Fowles saying, that it's hopeless for us? Go out and find a woman who doesn't loathe you?"

Dad let out a congestive laugh, rattling the walls of his lungs. "Well, if he is, I'm oh-for-two and working on number three." He wadded a napkin from a take-out bag, patting his mouth dry when he'd finished coughing. "But you didn't come by to talk about books. Why don't you get to it, old friend?"

Hunched on the couch across from his desk, I cast a look down at my loafers. They were, of course, Italian and laughably supple, and it struck me that ten months prior, I'd sat in his study cringing at my five-inch heels. "Um... You know what? This isn't a great idea. The chaos in my head, it's just out to *here*."

Reaching for a breath, I felt the mass in my chest; that ache was never more than a thought away. "It's just—I wanted what I wanted. To be *solid* finally—treated like I wasn't totally see-through. But then I came home and it—it went off the rails, and now I don't know how to get it stopped."

I heard his chair squeak upright. "Yes, I'm listening."

But suddenly I couldn't speak for the squall of tears massed on the backs of my eyes. Elation one minute, loathing the next—the three-penny opera never stopped. Or maybe it was the lilt of mercy in his voice, a tone I hadn't heard since boyhood. It was the voice in the steam bath, knowing but tender, assured that *this* hell, whatever its threats, this, too, would be outlasted.

"When I started this winter," I said, blotting tears, "it—it was a shot a week, tops, never more. But I found after a while that if I added a dose, then bit by bit I could make some gains. Nothing crazy, maybe a couple of pounds a week, but enough to where I said, *Let's go one better.* And that was where I screwed things, because that next step was a *bitch,* mixing and matching stuff I'd never heard of before. Before I knew what hit me, it was every day, sometimes even twice when we had a show to —"

"Whoa, whoa, *whoa* — back up a minute. You lost me at 'a shot a week.' Is this about you taking — what're those? — *speedballs?*"

I gaped, braking hard. "I'm sorry. What?"

"Because I need to know so I can get you help. There are kids dropping dead from them right and left."

I let out a snort. "Do you even know what a speedball is?"

"No, but I'm guessing you do."

Through his sealed windows I heard the ovine *bla-at!* of the No. 4 bus misfiring. Other shards of noise — the drone of Con Ed hammers; cab horns squawking their crank complaint — rolled me in a rug of brittle sound. For weeks, it had felt as if I had no casing, nothing to keep the world from pouring in. My ganglia crackled inside their sheaths, my skin was sensitive to every breeze, and even lying down I'd hear my heartbeat rumble, going on jagged runs for a quarter minute. A quaalude helped to tame the worst of the nerves, but more and more often I had to resist taking one as soon as I woke up. The couple of times I did, I found myself walking in a stupor the rest of the day.

"Look, I got off track. I'll start over. There's this guy in my dorm who built himself a body like you can't even imagine. And, long story short, I asked him how he did it and...Well, no, skip that, forget it; jump ahead. There's *another* kid, Kenny, also built but shorter, who showed me how a skinny guy could put on weight without having to eat eight times a day. And that part was *great,* those three, four months, and if I'd had any sense, I'd have stopped right there and — well, not stopped so much as...more like...yeah, no, *stopped*...But that's the thing with 'roids, they — they warp the way you think, where instead of

219

getting back to the rest of your life, you compulsively check the mirror and you're *horrified,* a different weakness everywhere you look. So you add another dose just to shore things up, but your calves won't grow or — or your wrists stay puny, and by the time you see results, you're up to three mikes of test and your heart sounds like it's punching through your chest. But instead of slowing down, you listen to *idiots* and toss a couple of downers in the mix, and that helps a little, along with other stuff, but then you wake up and need to get moving, and after three cups of coffee to wash down a benny, you're—"

Telling this to his carpet, I looked up. His right eye was closed in can't-watch horror, his left one wincing in sadness.

"But the flip side is, you're meeting tons of women and — and dancing till dawn at some club that has no name, just a giant loft that's black from floor to ceiling, and as it gets later, you spot people doing things that're straight from *The Garden of Earthly Delights,* guys stripped to jockstraps and women in even less, some of them—"

"All right, *stop,*" he groaned. "Enough. You've set the scene."

We sat for moments in steamrolled silence, the street noise suddenly remote. His eyes were sunk down into their sockets; watering, they stared past my head. Somewhere up the hall, I heard a vacuum going, the cleaning staff getting an early jump.

"I guess I knew but didn't. Didn't *want* to know," he said. "I thought, whatever you've got yourself into this time, there's fuck-all I can do to stop you doing it."

I said nothing, eyeing my heel. It was drumming so fiercely that my calf seized up. I had to dig a fist in to halt the spasm.

"With Ivan, I get a hearing, or he *pretends* to listen. But with you, I—I just never had much luck. And it hurts me no end because we *had* a connection; those early years, we two were thick as thieves. But still, I should've acted; that's what fathers do. Even if it's moot, they step in."

"Look, it's fine, Dad. Really. You couldn't have known, and even if you had, I'd have probably—"

But he was rattling open the drawer of the file behind him, paging through the dense manila folders. "Here," he said, handing across a note. "From an admirer of yours who's worried. For good reason."

I saw the signature at the bottom. "When did you get this?"

"He submitted a chunk of a novel in progress, which I thanked him for but didn't see much in."

I scanned the letter from my teacher of British lit, skipping over the section that didn't concern me. Jerry, as he'd merrily insisted I call him at our first face-to-face in his office, was a corpulent, jocose, red-cheeked man who'd lived the sixties as hard as he now taught them. He actively cultivated his livelier students, threw wine-drenched parties at the house he shared with his girlfriend/protégée, and, considering his heart woes and Tudor consumptions, was in no shape to be calling the kettle black. But there, in his sloping hand, I read:

Your boy is the goods, Ted: an ear for high and low, and a way of drilling down beneath the words. The day he finds his voice, he'll have a piece to say about our culture of holy crooks. But I want to tip your coat, because there's something afoot; he's not the kid I met back in January. The muscles from nowhere, well, that's his business, but his affect, *it's all over the room. I've had kids come see me, scared he'll erupt. I feel it, too, that* heat *he puts out there... Know a trusty shrink here on the Island?*

"Any of that ring bells? It was sent in May."

I wadded the note in my fist. "How dare he go to you behind my back? When I see him, I'll shove my foot up his ass."

He smartly said nothing, waiting me out. Then: "His point exactly. You're in *knots*."

"And what if I am? You're just now seeing it? Well, hi there, I'm Paul, and I'm your son."

Again he held his fire. "You're twenty-one years old, Paul. How long are you going to go on holding that grudge?"

"Ah, but it's not a grudge. That's—your word—*reductive*. It's way more complex than that."

"And? So what's it gotten you, all this complex anger? When do you say, *It's just* shit *I'm eating, and it makes me weak, not strong*?"

He was right, of course; they were *all* right about me—he, Kate, my teacher; they knew me cold. Held to inspection, no part of me passed muster, felt permanent and intrinsic, the real thing talking. Cart those props away, though, and what did you have—a gaunt boy bent over a comic book, his waking life and dream life one gray muck.

I got to my feet on a gust of indignation, feeling crazed and detached, a cold violence. With no plan in mind, I hulked before him; my upper arms rippled for battle. "*Look* at me, Dad. Do I *look* sick to you? Is this the weak kid you thought you'd raised?"

He slid his chair back and stood up, too, eyeing me in frank alarm. My hands found the lip of his faux-wood desk. Nothing would have been simpler than throwing the thing over and hearing its contents scatter, *crash-boom-bang*.

"What are you going to do, Paul? Show how strong you are? Trust me, I get it: you're big."

"You don't know the *half*," I said, tilting the desk. "I walk down the street now, people *scatter*."

"And that's what you want? To run people off?"

"Why not?" I said. "I *like* scaring people. It's nice being the bad guy for a change."

"Well, it works," he said. "You're scaring me now, like you scared your mother last month. She said you were stacked on drugs, and for once was right."

There seemed no response to an obvious fact but to carry through the idiocy I'd begun. I knelt to grab the desk by its brushed-steel base and heft it overhead before I tossed it. As I came up, though, the room went gray, the light through the blinds a sunburst cherry. I set the desk down and crumpled sideways, toppling onto my father's low-nap carpet. The wave was a soft one, like one of those slow curlers you see in surfing movies. I landed on my side and kept on sinking into the peaceable brown hole that opened, delighted to let gravity have its day, delivered from the thrum of bad intentions.

It was a while before I connected the far-off voice with the face looming over me as Dad's. "Can you sit?" he was saying. "Lean back against the couch. I'm going to call my doctor; he's close by."

Smoke-sparks whirled before my eyes. They rode the air in tangents, then resolved. "I'm okay," I managed, letting my head droop. "Just give me...a minute to..."

Beside me, Dad had a hand on my brow. He said I felt warm and asked if "sterols" were at fault for a healthy kid passing out cold. I mumbled that I didn't know, and he insisted we see his doctor, a first-rate internist at Mount Sinai. "You scared me shitless. I thought, *My God, he's having a stroke.* When I came around the desk, you were *twitching.*"

There was a pleasurable drumbeat in my ears, the contrapuntal rhythm of veins contracting and blood getting where it had to go. I'd not eaten since breakfast, but marked the hunger with a dissociative, dreamlike zeal, thinking how splendid a waffle would taste, griddled to nut-brown crispness. "I'm sorry," I said from high in the clouds. "That wasn't...at you. I was gone somewhere."

"Well, good to hear I haven't lost you entirely, but Christ, this has to stop. What can I do, short of calling the cops, to get you to quit cold turkey?"

"Um..." I turned the thought this way and that but couldn't catch hold of its sense.

"Would a hospital stay help? Maybe a week at St. Luke's to flush this stuff out of your system?"

"Well, but school...," I sleep-talked. "Gotta get out there. I've no place to stay and class starts—"

"Oh, for fuck's sake, Paul, would you *listen* for once! Your health is on the line, if not your life."

I lay back lightly on the Swiss-dot carpet, a paper clip wedged against my crown. "Let me just rest here...fifteen minutes. When I get up, we'll go to your...Whenever..."

And, plunging through wool-topped concrete slabs, I fell headfirst and ass-backward. I had my hand out to feel for the bottom, but all I encountered were warm, dark winds going by me in muzzy gusts. The descent changed speed and, after a while, direction, an updraft turning me counterclockwise to ride the dips and swells. At some point I hovered over glassed-in halls that looked a lot like Bantam's. Drifting here and there, I saw stragglers typing bills, enacting the rote, unmagical chores that moved Irwin Shaw novels and guidebooks to Parma from pallets to the hands of those concerned, and I felt a sharp pang on Dad's behalf as I searched for him door-to-door. He was, of course, right where he always was: hunched over galleys, chin resting on palm, his face silhouetted by drowsy light and the late-day shadows of summer's end. I yearned to call down to him from my orbit, tell him something useful but long omitted, a thing so plain as to be self-evident. The wind, alas, rose as I fussed over words, bumped and bobbed me like the wake of a barge, though nothing—no hair of his—stirred. *Dad,* I cried, but the wind took that, too, gobbling up the noise and nuisance distraction of a young man flapping overhead.

Thirteen

Around Here, We Pronounce That Ohio

Autumn–Winter 1976

WHEN I THINK BACK ON THAT FALL, it is always leaden: the sun held hostage in a subgrade cell, the sky sealed tightly behind it. Those were the months when the fear set in, showing up first as a crack suspicion that someone lurked behind me, plotting harm. I felt him in the crowd as I walked to class, the slightest pressure on the nape of my neck, and likewise felt him patrolling the gym, where I'd picked up some hours working security. No threats overheard, no sight of forms retreating, but I couldn't shake the sense that I was under surveillance by someone crazed enough to wait me out.

In response, I took to sitting in the back of rooms, starting at noises and sudden movements. I locked my carrel in the fourth-floor stacks and rinsed with eyes open in the shower stall, lest the enemy get the drop while I conditioned. A range of things scared me: the chrome stand poles in subways, coat hooks hanging at or near eye level, and busily furnished rooms with no space to move if I suddenly felt the need to flee. I bought Ray-Bans and wore them both indoors and out, gaining at least a layer of polarized armor against objects bearing down with no warning. Still, months passed before I marked the changes, thinking I was merely pressed by a grueling schedule. I'd enrolled in five lit courses with thousands of pages of reading, had taken the field-house job so I could steal an hour to lift, and was dashing home to see Kate twice a month, as well as make my appointment with the shrink. Dr. S. was a means of conciliating Dad, who'd vowed to stop the check on my school tuition unless I got some help. So every second Saturday, I got out of bed early to board the 101 bus across the park and sing the blues of the overburdened student to a golf-mad behaviorist named Shelley. He gave me taped tutorials on breathing techniques, requested I keep a day-log of my anxious thoughts, and fielded Dad's phone calls with upbeat parries, telling him I'd "raised my short game." Whatever his methods — we once devoted an hour to the crisis of being flatulent on a date — he did have a way with aphorisms, most of which derived from the back nine.

If I didn't find him useful in the matter of my paranoia, I did take his tip to seek meaning in work, to which I now turned with zeal. Day after day, I'd quick-march from class to a third-floor seat at the library, setting up shop in one of the windows and flicking the little desk lamp on. Lighting a Lucky (new gravitas: *check*), I'd tilt the chair back, prop my boat shoes up, and get lost for several hours in the Oedipal blood sport of *The Rainbow* or *Sons and Lovers*. All of that thrusting, hothouse life, the demon maleness straining to wrench free — it was catnip to a tense kid wrestling with shadows and mostly pinning himself. I tore my way through Lawrence, then jumped to Conrad, and from there hopped a freighter to Melville. Each of them inflamed my sense of scale, kicked down the doors of my self-obsession to a grander view of the world. Being adult was heavy lifting, and not at the gym. To become one, I'd have to find a bigger stage.

As much as I savored the joys of rabid reading — the vellum whiff off the old bound volumes of Tillyard and F. R. Leavis; the back-of-the-scalp tingle invariably wrung from a masterful rhyme in Hopkins — it was a line of Empson's that opened my eyes to the tortuous job ahead. Writing of Thomas Gray, he named tragedy in five words: "the waste of human powers." In that shattering phrase, I saw my family's story, a tale of blown chances and blunted drives. Mom, who'd taught herself Russian in college and was translating Tolstoy by thirty, had taken a match to her life and career on a spree of postmarital rage. Ivan, the teen acolyte of Ovid and Auden, crafter of palindromes and anagrammed obits (his own read "Vain fool of arts"), was nonetheless so invested in rancor that it became his signature. Years later I described my brother as "soured" to a writer who knew us both fairly well. "No, soured is you," he said, shaking his head. "Ivan is downright *curdled.*"

He was right, of course; we were tonal twins, plucked from an acid bath. But how, after childhoods free of violence and manifest acts of cruelty, had we, like Mom, become churlish mopes who, together or apart, blamed Dad? What crime had he committed, what theft of our rights, to trigger such hot resentment? Had he married unwisely? Yes, and often, but which of our friends' fathers hadn't? Had he used his money hassles as a wedge against us, shutting his door to write the reviews that kept his ex-wives solvent? Ah, but that allowed us to run the streets with our wild-child pals from the park, playing ball, smoking Kools, drinking strawberry wine, and earning snap enrollment in the West Side tribe of White Boys Who Wanted to Be Black. Lastly, was he checked out much of the time, hiding in plain sight at the dinner table as he conjured a long night's work? Certainly, and the cut went deep: I sometimes felt like an irksome neighbor who'd dropped by uninvited, disturbing what little peace he had from the tumult of the week.

Still, if inattention was his worst offense, it hadn't inflicted the lasting harm I took to be my birthright. I began to see that I'd been using Mom's scales to weigh my grievance out, limping around like an insurance fraud to bill him for reparations. It galled me to think I'd carried water for her, been her co-complainant in a loony case that any judge would toss out at first sight. No wonder I was still a child; I was running a child's errand: *Here, be a love and give this hate mail to Dad. Oh, and while you're out, pick me up a jar of Folgers and buy yourself a slice of Ray's for dinner.*

In the full blush of shame, I began to reach out, calling him once a week, sometimes more. At first the conversations were knock-kneed stiff: my week, his week, do-si-do, and hey, how about those Yanks? But slowly, fitfully, we found our way, easing past the shallows into open water. I told him about Kate and the wish to make amends after I'd done her dirt all summer. He talked about the last, bleak days of his marriage and enlisted me to help him move his things to a small one-bedroom on Seventieth Street. It took all weekend just to box his books and schlep the several thousand in the van, but afterward we had a convivial dinner at an Irish joint down the block. There, after the third or fourth round of Pabsts, he unpacked the story of his split with Mom, the first time I'd heard his side. "She tossed me out the night before Christmas Eve, and I wound up on the couch at an old friend's gallery while he was off in Italy till New Year's. Then, when I went back to pack my things, she pulled a knife and demanded I move back in." He caught my expression and let off a laugh. "Do I really have to say it was a *butter* knife, Paul? Your mother is all bark and no bite."

"Oh, *now* you tell me," I said, trying for archness. "For years she threatened to kill herself, saying—mystically—'Not today, but soon.' Finally, Ivan bought her a birthday present: an egg timer, to give us fair warning."

"An egg timer!" He howled. "He really did that?"

"Oh, he used to make haiku of her rants. My favorite one was 'Bedtime Story':

You've ruined my life
You sons of bitches
Monsters, both of you.

Again Dad roared, pounding his palm on the table. "Ivan," he groaned, after he was done laughing. "He really is the soul of understanding."

"Well, but he called her bluff, whereas I was tied in knots. I used to walk home after school some days, sure that I'd find cop cars parked outside and a sheet on the ground beside the stoop."

He grunted, suddenly doleful, the joke in ashes. "You probably don't remember—you were four at the time—but she did climb out on a ledge and try to jump. It was a fourth-floor window of the Chicago library. She said she'd heard a voice that said, 'Fly, Lynn.'"

"Oh, trust me, I knew, Dad; she held back nothing. The bottles of Seconal she'd squirreled away; the two a.m. 'joywalks' in Riverside Park—she'd drop these little bombs at the dinner table, then make me drag the whole thing out of her."

He grunted again, wincing. "And I tell you, I don't get it. The Lynn I courted and wound up marrying was the most vibrant woman I've known. She came to New York on her own at sixteen, put herself through college, and became the darling of the foreign studies program. Where did all that manic vigor go?"

I said I didn't know but saw it less and less often as she closed down the options around her. In nine years she'd translated a single volume of Tolstoy's mountainous letters and slid down a rabbit hole of need and loathing, borrowing from faint acquaintances. By the time I left, she'd burned through all her friends and was barely subsisting on alimony checks and some part-time work from *Current Biography*. "She's still mad I left—I kicked in tips from delivering groceries—but I had to get out of there and run like hell, or she'd have taken me down with her."

He nodded vaguely, then reached across the table and gripped my forearm tight. "I'm so very sorry, Paul. Really, I am. It was a miserable choice to have to make."

"Dad, please, it's old news. Let's not—"

"No, not that I left—anyone would have—but that I didn't take both of you with me."

My jaw must have wobbled, because he nodded fiercely to forestall any doubt. "She'd have fought me, of course. She did about every-thing, and in those days the courts were no help. But that's not the reason, as I'm sure you know. No, you were sick with asthma a lot of the time, and I, as sole provider, had to work. Otherwise, you'd have come with me."

I felt my ears thicken, stopped with air. "I—I always wondered, but never—"

"What, you thought I played favorites, taking Ivan?"

"Um, no...but—"

"Don't you remember us sitting you up and saying he'd live with me for a couple of years, then we'd switch when your lungs were better?"

"You know, not that it matters now, but no, I don't."

"But of *course* it matters, Paul. How could it not? That I'd casually walk out of there and leave you with her...I'd have to be the most unfeeling prick."

I tried to let us both off by changing the subject but found myself suddenly strapped for words. Not words of tact or conciliation, but *any* words, including *and* and *the*. I was looking out the window in a tumid daze, lamenting another grotesque lapse of poise, when the wave of water hit and took me under. Tears—dense clots of them, choking, brackish—poured through my throat and kept refilling. A wind in my head shook the lights, then doused them—a hurricane in a basement, hot and loud. I couldn't see or hear, couldn't catch a ragged breath, and clung, in that wild, unliterary pass, to the scene on the moor in *Lear*. Some *thing*—a ghost self or bolus of grief—wanted out of me in one fell howl and wouldn't stop roaring till every last bit of it had been coughed, wept, and sweated away.

The sound came on again, a progressive din, as though a generator were blinking back to life. "You okay?" said Dad, looking ravaged himself, perspiring through the neck of his button-down. "Just sit there a minute and catch your breath. I'll ask her for some water when she—"

"It's all right," I croaked. "I'll live. Let's just go."

"You sure?" he said. "I'd prefer you hang tight. I'm worried about another fainting spell."

"Really, Dad, I'm fine. Just get the check."

"Well, okay...But could you let go first?"

I looked at my fist, which was wringing the tablecloth like the neck of a holiday goose. "Jesus, this just gets worse."

He pulled the cloth toward him, evening the sides, and bent to retrieve the ashtray I'd knocked over. "Right back," he said. "You sure you don't want water? How about a shot of—eh, bad idea."

He went off haltingly, his feet receding. I knew not to look up for the stares I'd meet, New York being a city where public suffering is grounds for a parade. But the shame drew off and my lungs expanded, as if someone had lanced a growth between my ribs. I took a full breath, letting it out slowly. The feeling warmed the small bones of my nose.

"What happened, man? Your dog die or something?"

I heard frat-boy laughter. *Just ignore them.*

"Must've been your dog—I never saw that before. A grown man crying in a bar."

Mother. Fuck. Er. Never fails. I took another breath and stood up. They were older than college kids but not by much, East Side toffs on a West Side toot after a Giants game or day of two-hand touch. "My dog *did* die," I said to the table. "I had him since I was nine, and now he's dead."

"Oh...sorry," said a guy in Boston College sweats, getting the full load of me and making peace. "I had a dog, too, when I was that age. A shepherd named Rockne, but he got sick."

I could have relented, having won the point; could've fired off a glare and burned it in. But the dog I'd been mourning was me at ten, and that kid needed someone to mark his grave. "So it was funny, losing a pet? You enjoyed putting him down?"

He looked at his friends, the grin gone sideways. "Dude, I didn't know...let me buy you a beer—what were you and that guy drinking?"

"He's just drunk," his friend explained. "He talks a lot when he's trashed."

"And what's *your deal*? You *laugh* a lot when you're trashed?"

The three said nothing, fidgeting in pockets. I picked out a spot on the first guy's sweats, a handhold between the words *Boston* and *College*, where I'd seize him and drag him outside. My breath, a fast hiss, was all I heard.

"What's doing?" said someone, putting a hand on my back. I swiveled, fist cocked above my skull.

"Stop!" said Dad, ducking behind his forearms. "Stop right now, this rampage you're on. Act like the man I thought I raised!"

He took me by the elbow, saying *sorry* over his shoulder. They watched me go in horror and relief.

"The offer stands," the first guy called.

"Yes, sorry for your loss," said the second.

DAD READ ME GOOD AS he drove the van to the Avis on the West Side yards, drawing the line between toughness and thugging, the latter being the franchise of a fool. "You can throw your weight around," he said, "but someone'll call your bluff. Then what, Paul? Do you ask him to drop the knife? Do you start talking fast when he pulls a gun?"

He was right, of course. He was *always* right, whenever he wasn't addressing his own conduct. I lied when he asked if I was high that night and lied again when he asked about steroids. I was still shooting Deca on a maintenance basis and adding a blast of test cyp on the weekend. I had tried—God knows I had—to quit full-stop but barely made it out of day four. I felt weak and gaunt and in vagrant pain, as if one or another joint had its tendons lanced and was rubbing together, bone on bone. Worse was the feeling of being dead inside, a hollowness hard to pin down. I ceased giving a damn whether I ate or slept and was at or near tears over the rancid satire of getting out of bed each day.

With Valium and codeine, I managed the inflammation, bringing it down to a dull ache. But the psychic part was a different beast—a mean, pernicious mood I couldn't drug. *Depression* sums it up but doesn't give its measure, because the pain and fear kept shifting shape. The only constant was my grief and terror at the thought of getting *smaller*, an anguish stoked by trips to the john to stand there, sizing and posing. My chest, that showpiece of stopless labor and fastidious care and feeding—my chest was wasting away right in front of me, and I couldn't do a thing to stop it. My arms, those badges of the man I thought I'd built, had lost their fit and finish, too, and bulked instead of rippled when I flexed. I wanted to cry my eyes out and throw weights at the mirror, break every pane of reflective glass from Suffolk to Ulster County.

Then there were the jitters, the sudden onset of nerves that made it hard to sit for long spells. Hunched over the Riverside edition of *Henry V,* my brain would go on runs of circular thinking about something Kate had said in her last call, and I'd be up to stalk the halls till the twitching in my high calves stopped. I fretted about my health, seeing signs of collapse in a recurring sinus problem, and noted that the foods I'd gobbled in bulk now brought on angry bloat. By the morning of day five, I couldn't take another second and ran to the communal john in my suite to fire off an amp of Deca. Nothing happened, of course: no dance of tipped endorphins in my head. But knowing I'd fed those branch-cells let me stand taller and take a robust breath to meet the day.

There, in the mirror I shared with five strangers, I struck a New Deal on steroids. I'd do only as much as needed to keep my cuts and make my peace with the inevitable loss of size. I'd eat smaller but smarter, dropping the dairy products that congested me after meals, and distill my training to a single hour of furious, no-rest sets. Lastly, I'd shit-can the ludes and bennies as the poison they surely were. Somewhere up the road, I'd have to reckon with 'roids, but for now they were keeping me in the game, my little shot of lidocaine at the half.

If I couldn't tell Dad that I was still using, I certainly didn't cop to what I'd done for money over the course of that madhouse summer, or that a couple of times a month now, I caught the train on Friday and worked a show for Angel to earn some coin. The idea of explaining to this priest of belles lettres that his son got a strangely virulent kick out of shaking his naked tail for girls in Queens, lapping up the sweaty, sex-gun power of ass-to-groin thrusting in close quarters, and seeing the glazed eyes and hearing the soft groans of women who'd gotten off while he slid against them—how do you tender *that* to a man who edits Mailer and hectors Roth to rein himself in? I couldn't even tender it to myself, treating the whole business as a savage joke that only I, in my wisdom, was somehow in on.

Finally, I didn't tell him about the connection with Angel, whose couch I usually crashed on after a gig. As friendships go, it was pretty thin stuff, consisting mainly of my holding his coat while he mowed down women of all flavors. Nor did Angel's late-night calls to my dorm room make me think I'd earned his allegiance. Angel *had* no allegiance—we were all dispensable—although more and more often, he seemed fixed on Nikki, wondering where she went and whom she saw. They'd been doing a lot of coke on the nights they slept together, and he needed to "dead that quick" or he'd have a problem; his brother had gone that route with heroin.

In truth, I couldn't say why I clung to Angel. Yes, I was needy, making very few friends with my sudden turn to High Serious. (There was nothing lonelier than being a lit kid at Stony Brook. Even my adviser pushed the pre-law option.) Nate had buckled down and moved across campus with a sweet-faced logician named Alvin, renouncing marijuana in favor of tennis and a scrupulous reading of Marx. When our schedules permitted, we had lunch at the student union and laughed at the changes we'd made, but we found that we didn't have much to share beyond the lunatic-mother stories. So, too, with Kate: I called her way too often, eager to hear her sensible voice and to riff on Yeats and Pound. But it was hard to wax expansive feeding dime upon dime into the slot of the library pay phone, and after a month I began to feel like I was calling mainly to see if she was home. She'd visited only once. We spent a sodden Friday watching a print of *Rififi* at the student center, then holed up with hoagies and a big bag of Twizzlers as I gobbled her whole for two days. She gamely fronted a smile, but I could see the place oppressed her with its sledgehammer views of mud and cars, and she couldn't have failed to think, *He's going* where *from here?* as she boarded the Sunday train back to Manhattan.

So, yes, I was lonely, and scared as well. I peered around corners as I walked the path from the gym at ten p.m., detecting lurkers in the shadows cast by leafless dogwood trees. As the holidays rolled in, I grew more and more desperate, meeting isolation at every turn. Kate was off to Tahoe to ski with her father, with whom she'd begun making modest strides. I couldn't stay with Dad in his tiny apartment, the thought of hunkering down on a deserted campus filled me with icy dread, and after a hastily booked trip to visit Ivan in Michigan left me snowed in and sullen for days, I called Angel from Ann Arbor and asked if I could hang there through New Year's. He teased it out a moment, though we both knew the answer. "Yeah, sure, glad to have you. You can be my butler."

"Well, thanks, man. Really. And I'll help with the cleaning."

His laughter was—that rarity—warmhearted. "Please, ma-fucker, you'd hurt yourself. You with a mop and bucket? Instant lawsuit."

I showed up in his lobby a couple of days later with a suitcase and a gift-bowed bottle of Mumm. Two snorkel-coated dope boys stood sentry in the doorway; they brazenly eyed me down as I angled by them. The fat one nodded at my hiking boots. "Yo, check them fuckin' *snowshoes*," he cackled.

"Damn, Bigfoot's a fag!" jeered the other.

They traded pounds for glee, or to warm their ungloved hands. Here, if nothing else, I could stop fearing shadows. The threat was straight on, eye to eye.

Upstairs, I was startled by a bear hug from Angel. Sloppy affection wasn't his stock-in-trade. "You're looking good, soldier. Pale, but I got the cure: I'll put you in front of my new sunlamp."

"Say what? You have a sunlamp?"

"Got to, bro-ham. Gotta have that glow. But check *you* out— champagne! Let's go and ice this."

He led me to the kitchen, where a skillet of onions was cooking over a medium flame. Angel loved to cook and was splendid at it, a skill set taught to him by his uncle Tegan before the big man caught a bid for B & E. Many was the night I'd had a post-club meal at Angel's chrome dinette, washing down *tostones* with *café con leche* packing so much sugar it was practically pudding, and picking at warmed-up salt-cod fritters that left a butter mustache on the plate. He owned no cookbooks or copper pots, measured salt and saffron with his eyes and nose, and tested for doneness with a salad fork, pronging the meat back from the bone. He talked when he was drunk about opening a bistro, a semi-fancy place in the Theater District where he'd feed the tourists and host his god, De Niro. "Can you see it, son — me with Vito Corleone! For starters, I'd bring him out a bottle of Dom and the fattest line of yayo he ever saw."

I checked him out as he nursed the onions, powdering fresh bay leaf with his palms. At one in the afternoon, his normally faultless 'fro was a high-low, picked-out mess. He wore a terry robe that was open to glen plaid boxers hiked up around his navel. It was an odd display for someone so proud that he washed and ironed his *curtains* once a month. I knew from recent phone calls that he was out later and later and rarely bothered to rise before noon, but the sight of him unbathed, his smooth face crusted, gave me a secret thrill. Not so the swell of incipient fat where his obliques met the boxer shorts: that was a jolt that set alarm bells jangling, knocking me off my pegs. If wrought-iron *Angel* had begun to soften, what small chance did I ever have of keeping my hard-won hardness?

"Slick, you want a beer while the champagne's cooling? I got Red Stripe and some Greek shit Spiro brought."

"No, I'm good," I said, taking a dinette seat and easing my big boots off. "Hey, who're those knuckleheads pitching for Kenny? They talked a lot of rah-rah downstairs."

"When? Just now?"

I shrugged. "I could've been a cop, for all they knew."

"Why, what'd they say?"

"Eh, don't get aggy. Just saying, he should talk to them."

Angel squared to face me, wiping his hands on his robe. "*Fuck* that. I want to know what they said."

There was something in his eyes I'd never seen before, an off-the-leash rage ready to lunge. I was instantly sorry I'd blabbed. "You know, the usual: fag-this and white-that. Why even concern yourself with—"

" 'Cause it's *me* they're really doggin' when they chirp you out, and I don't let that go."

"But how would they even know that I'm your—"

He hitched his robe closed as he barreled past, the slotted spoon still in his hand. "Watch the onions," he called behind him from the hall. "Don't let me find them shits burnt."

I went to the stove and saw nothing to stir with, looking around in anguish. What new hell had I cut myself in for, booking a four-day stay at Casa Loco? Angel seemed altered, more loosely disposed to the anarchy of his calling. Or maybe he'd always had a fuse this short and I, in my blindness, had missed it. You never know a man till you've seen him hungover, sour-breathed and squinting against the light.

But rummaging in his drawers for a spatula or spoon, I came upon fresh concerns. The first was a cockroach, plump and brazen, scuttling across the flatware at its leisure. Angel hated bugs and waged an all-points war, spraying and baiting and wiping down counters with a nose-burning mix of bleach and lye. The roach was a sign of "slippitude," an Angelism for loss of care. The second thing I found was a twist-tied baggie holding what could only be shake cocaine. Blow left sitting in a kitchen drawer, where anyone could stumble on it? That was slippitude of a higher order, a billboard clue to the fire in his eyes.

Now, no one has demonstrated for clinical fact that steroid use makes you rageful, and till Merck devises a way to ethically test subjects with the high-bore stacks that juicers spike, it will remain an article of popular "fact" that has no basis in science. I have, over my three-plus decades of lifting, met a number of large men who scared me silly with their medieval moods and paranoia—the kind who view life as an arch betrayal of some antique code that they observe and whose worst offenders (gays or Jews) would be "dealt with" in a righteous world. But I have also, in those travels, met an elite group of users who couldn't be less like those donkeys. They are members, for the most part, of the wealth professions, bankers and traders in their thirties and forties for whom steroids, in tandem with a watchful diet and a technocratic

237

approach to training, are the capstones of their self-conception, as intrinsic as good grooming and British lace-ups. They follow strict cycles with lab-grade testosterone they get from their East Side doctors, take a drug vacation every three or six months to let their kidneys rest, and get liver panels done during annual checkups, just to play it safe. They suffer no outbreaks of messianic anger and keep the hard contours of their former jockdom without sprouting egg-size tumors.

It can be argued—and they do, with little prompting—that they're practicing hormone therapy, replacing endogenous testosterone that time, that bandit, leaches as we age. It can also be argued that they're loading the dice for a string of midlife cancers, playing Russian roulette with their major organs and the lesser one dangling between their legs. The fact is, no one knows the downstream yield for most people juicing within limits, though the anecdotal outcomes of severe abuse—the mortality rates of wrestlers and pro bodybuilders of the 1970s; the heartbreaking health woes of female athletes who competed for the Eastern bloc, assailed in adulthood by exotic cancers after being duped, and doped, as children—should suffice to give anyone qualms.

But proof notwithstanding, there are things I know from my own fool's errand in juice. It is, first of all, clownish to buy injectable drugs from someone you meet in a gym. His "pharmaceutical" Deca was very likely decocted in his mother's filthy bathtub in Floral Park and probably contains, besides a tincture of the hormone, such muscle-growing additives as rodent droppings and the lather used to shave her hairy legs. Second, seeking drug tips from steroid "gurus" is like buying stocks from cold-call artists. If these men had credible wares to sell, they wouldn't be working out of storage units in a mixed-use eyesore off Route 80. Third, and most germane to the matter at hand, *cocaine plus steroids equals crazy*. Not goofy ha-ha crazy or Syd-Barrett-on-acid crazy, but crazy as in fight four cops barehanded—a black-diamond run to deep dementia. You're taking your psychic chances with either 'roids or coke, and the latter famously needs no help making smart people lose their minds. But to truck with both is a space walk to bedlam:

each drug boosts the other's power to quash the superego, giving free rein to the kind of impulse that even chemists would call evil. Me, I'd gotten off lightly, freak-outs and all, after a summer of mixing the two, and I was sufficiently scared of cocaine's throw weight to quit when I returned to school. But not so Angel—not by a mile. Angel was on the bull and riding hard.

He was back in ten minutes, his cheeks in high color, as if from a spirited round of squash. "Smells *good* in here," he said, rubbing his hands together. "Now let's get to *cooking*. You like *croquetas*?"

"Um, sure," I said, going for nonchalance. "You get that little problem squared away?"

"Wasn't no problem—least none that I had. *They* had a problem, but I solved it."

I waited a three count. "And?"

"And nothing. Them boys been talked to." Rattling beneath the sink for his cast-iron pan, he gave it a wipe with a rag.

I couldn't drop it. "Well, glad it didn't come to blows."

"None needed," he murmured, giving his back to me. "But don't be surprised if they call you sire."

"I'm sorry, what?"

"Nothing. Go ahead and set the table."

He rubbed the pan with oil and lit a match. Soon the air was thick with charring meat.

WE TORE IT UP THAT WEEKEND, the four of us reunited, gunning the town in Angel's Toronado. Spiro and Tommy were geeked to see me, toasting round after round to our "Whoresmen summer," which both of them seemed wistful for. "I hate to admit it, but I missed you," said Tommy, wrapping an arm around me at the Flamingo. "I used to think you were a dipshit Jew."

"You grew on me, too," I said, hugging him back. "I thought you were a racist Mick."

The next night, Spiro pulled me aside during a show we were doing in Elmont. "You like my little brother!" he cried, leaning from the chest so our G-stringed groins didn't bump.

"I like *who*?" I croaked, straining above the din.

"No, not *like-like* him. I'm saying, like him."

"Oh," I said, baffled. "Yeah, me, too!"

Even Angel was happy, making me swear that I'd come back in to party every weekend. "Ain't no reason you can't come each Friday. You can study at the library on Ninety-third."

"You think?" I said. "How's their postcolonial fiction?"

"Who gives a fuck? Besides, you read too much. Who're you tryin' to fool with all those A's?"

"I'm *saying*," said Tommy, "you're *already* in college. It's not like they can send you back to high school."

Spiro tugged my arm. "Yo, forget them, they stupid. I respect you working hard, man. That takes heart."

"Why, thank you, Spiro. I appreciate that, though what's weird is, I actually *like* the work."

"Then bet keep going, 'cause the body, this don' last. Use your brain: meet a rich professor lady."

I thanked him again, though noted tristfully that rich ladies didn't teach in the SUNY system. "So switch," he exhorted. "My sister goes Iona. I *know* they get the big money there."

"Well, I'll keep that in mind, but I'm focused on grad school — racking up the grades that'll get me in."

"For what, *more* years of this?" Angel groaned. "You really gonna strip your way through law school?"

"Actually, I'm thinking about fiction these days. Maybe the Writers' Workshop out in Iowa."

"*Iowa?*" said Angel, trading scowls with Tommy. "Yo, around here we pronounce that shit *Ohio*."

On New Year's Eve, Lou threw his Whiteout Party, an avalanche of satin and narcotics. The great room was dressed like the slalom at

Kitzbühel, with temporary tiles overlaying the floor, the walls hung with cumulous muslin sheers, and couches and love seats gauzed in fabric that glistened like moonlit snow. Even we were dazzled by the silver burnish of glitter globes hanging overhead, used as we were to Lou's theatrics and his love of playing Loki to the damned. New Year's was the only time he charged his guests, though the jaw-dropping admission, $300 a couple, barely made a dent in his cocaine bill. There were finger bowls of blow on the sideboard when we came in, and more on consoles in the hall and great room, attended by Lou's fey helpers. "Go easy," Angel warned me while we hung up our clothes, changing into the silk pajama bottoms we'd all been asked to bring. "He cuts his shit heavy with methedrine, and too much'll make you *una cabra*."

"Ah. Good to know." I cinched the drawstring tight, exaggerating the swoop of my shrinking lats. "But wait a second. Doesn't he cop from you?"

"Yeah, I sell it speedy, but he goes too far. Kicks in so much crank, you'll hump a corpse."

I spotted him checking my torso with a glance. "What?" I said. "What is it? Something wrong?"

"Nah, nothing, man; forget it. It's New Year's Eve. Just real, real glad you made it here." He waded in for a clumsy hug that went a beat too long. "I'm high, so don't quote me, but I miss you, slick. It ain't the same without you fucking up."

"I miss you, too, Angel. You've been a great friend, and I promise I won't forget that."

"Yo, the pleasure was mine, but good on you to say that. I feel like all I *do* is help young cats earn, but *forget* them ever coming and saying thanks."

I acknowledged that and said I'd like to return the favor; something had been on my mind for several days. His pliable grin seemed to lock in place, hinging on the axis of a sneer. "Help how?" he said. "Quit school and strip full-time?"

Well, no, not that. "I know I'm on the outside looking in, and if I'm wrong, just tell me and I'll shut my mouth, but—"

"Nigger, just say it. The girls are waiting."

"I know, I know; sorry... fuck, let's talk later."

"No, now I *really* got to hear this shit. Don't be scared to tell me; you're my droogie."

I swallowed hard but saw no recourse; lying wouldn't bail me out of this one. "That day in your kitchen? I wasn't trying to snoop, but came across the eight ball in the drawer. And it made me kind of wonder, because you've *never* been careless, someone who'd leave his dope in plain sight..."

"*What?* When was this you're talkin'?"

"The day I flew in? You went down to handle those fools on the door—"

"And what, I was whacked on my own supply? Is that the picture you concluded?"

His stare crisped the atoms between us. "Well, I—I was worried a little, frankly."

He nodded vaguely, his jaw in motion, as if biting off the tail of something small. "Yeah, yo, first of all, that was *baking powder.* I use it for empanadas and my three-milk cake. Second, I want to know where you even get the *ass* to step to me like that."

We were standing close enough that I felt his breath; it smelled of sweet peppers and menthol smoke. "Well, but, as a... as a friend, I had to say something."

He went on staring, those eyes drilling down, throwing heat where they once sent shade. Suddenly, he broke it off and tossed his head, laughing, saying he had me ready to piss the bed. "I wisht you coulda seen your look just now: *Damn, this nigger's flipped. Call backup, Sergeant!*"

I cocked up a smile, taking shallow breaths to gear my heart rate down. Angel dabbed my brow with an imaginary hankie, prolonging a joke he never intended with a mirth he couldn't confect. Coke-crazed or not, he had made himself clear: the truth would have no entrée in our dealings.

"And just so you know, I could stop this second. Go a week straight and not get lifted."

"Well, good, then. Great. I'm sorry I brought it up. Just thought — as a friend — I should probably raise it."

"Heard you twice the first time. And seeing as I'm *your* friend, I feel I should tell you that your body's seriously slipping."

I stopped short. "What?"

"Just sayin' what I see: your chest is slackin'. You need to raise your dosage with a *quickness*."

There was a mirror in the hallway. I went and stood before it. "I think I'm hanging in there, for the time I have to train. It's hard when you're at the library day and night."

He gave me one of his sidelong stares, a marvel of pity and disgust. "Do less reading and a lot more *eating*. Then come talk about my mess."

THE PLAN WAS TO PAY our respects to Lou, drink in the New Year with his midlife satyrs, then buzz downtown to a party at Nikki's, where the real fun was set to launch. When midnight rolled around, though, we couldn't find Angel in any of the bedrooms people "played" in. (I despised that word as a stand-in for sex. It conjured plump lawyers on Twister boards, their saggy dongs drooping like crow-pecked corn.) Someone said they thought he'd stepped out with a woman, but until he came back, we were stuck in dry dock, dancing with East Side wives in white bustiers.

It was well after two when Angel roared in, high off his ass and grinning madly. Tommy hailed him, but he pushed right past us to where the deejay spun. They talked for a moment — shouted, more like it — then the deejay dug into his crate. Off went the Euro-schlock of Silver Convention; on, at max volume, came the stomp-rocket bass line of the just-out "Disco Inferno." It rattled the glass teardrops of the chandelier, knocked over champagne flutes on tables, and thumped the drowsy room with a noise so joyous that even stockbrokers leapt to their feet. Couples flocked together at the center of the floor in a mayhem of arms and legs, but Angel went by them, strutting sure-footed to a clearing by the couch. He began to dance freestyle under a strobe like a gamecock girt for blood—fists balled, teeth gnashing, eyes livid with glee, his bare chest drinking up light. Others stopped to watch, chanting *ooh-wuh, ooh-wuh,* and banging their hands together to keep the beat. Somehow he went faster, a blur of spins, the sweat whipping off him as he whirled. At some point he stopped to catch a gulping breath, but his solo, like the single, was far from done.

Unknotting the silk bottoms, he teased them to his calves before kicking them in the direction of the crowd. Nude now but for a black bikini, he swiveled his groin in slow gyrations that ended in leering stabs. A drunk woman, cajoled by her husband, tottered out to dance with Angel. He took her by the hand and, to the crowd's amusement, twirled and bent her over for his thrusts. With each dry jerk, the cries got louder to *shove it in* and *give it to her good.* Angel cupped his ear, wearing a jackal's grin, soaking up the violence in the air. Exhausted finally, he tumbled with his partner onto the hard white tile of the floor. They lay there, grinning and breathing hard.

The chants continued. Angel rose to his knees, soaking in the noise and brute eros. Then something shifted—a gate slammed behind his eyes—and he hiked up her nightie and thrust inside her. The din turned to gasps. The crowd pushed in, closing space around the pair. I got carried forward, catching glimpses of the woman. Her eyes were shut tight and her mouth contorted as the impact of his hammer strokes shook her. Angel, when stoned, could go and go and go without getting tired or bored and seemed, in fact, to thrive on causing pain with that fat, brown club of a cock. "There's times you just gotta *break* a bitch," he said once. "Beat that pussy till it's chewed and screwed, then send her home in a cab."

Time passed; the song ended, replaced by nothing, the deejay having quit his post to watch. Standing there, hearing the woman's moans, I felt more complicit by the second. I looked for Tommy but didn't see him and, absent a plan, went to find him. He wasn't by either of the linen-topped tables or waiting out the show on one of the couches, but I did spot Spiro across the room, propped against the wall, watching dully. "This is *fucked*," I said when I made my way to him. "He's really going to hurt her if we let him."

He weighed the proposition, his square face blank. "What I'm s'posed to do, pull him off her?"

"Yes! Or help *me* do it."

"Let the husband tell him. How you know she don't like this?"

"Because I *saw* her, man! Listen: can't you tell?"

But we could barely make her out now over the crosscut babble of cheers and lupine laughter. Her cries had the distant, garbled bleat of a woman slowly slipping underwater.

"Well, *fuck* me, then — I'll go and do it myself."

I waded into the crowd on a gust of mission. Knees and elbows banged me as I barreled through, breathing in smoke and stale cologne and the exfoliated scent of sweat. Exhausted by the time I got to the front, I saw Angel on all fours, still at it. His eyes were dull and his jaw hung slack, but his hips kept torquing against her thighs: mechanical, whop-whop thuds. The woman's legs were draped around his neck, and it was a moment before I saw that her head was slumped sideways in inebriated sleep. "Angel," I croaked, grabbing his sweat-slick arm. "That's enough, man. Let's go home."

He flicked me off with a vacant shrug, a reminder of his crazy strength. But other hands grabbed now and pulled him clear, Spiro and Tommy bundling him up in a shushing, straitjacket hug. They got him to his feet, then held on tight as he strained to free himself. He twisted furiously, trying to get his hands loose, then went limp a moment and started up again. I was shouting at him — we were all shouting at him — but he said nothing back, a muteness that scared me as much as his manic rage. He was heaving for air in our three-way grip, and I smelled a sickly sweetness through his pores, as if he'd been dusted in days-old honey. "Amaretto," said Tommy while we dragged him off. "He probably drank a pint of it, plus the coke."

Down the long hall, away from the guests, he finally stopped struggling and went slack. He was barely conscious when we slipped on the bottoms that one of Lou's boy-men fetched, and he slumped like a rug on Spiro's chest as we zipped his half boots up. Tommy left to pull the car around from the building's basement lot, while Angel, propped between us in the outer hall, murmured nonsense phonemes to his coat. We waited forever for the elevator; I was punching buttons for the umpteenth time when Lou stormed out in his silver sash. "This is all you get and not a penny more. Now leave before I call the fucking cops!"

He thrust a wad of twenties in our direction. Neither of us took it; he stuffed the bills in Angel's coat. Several of them fluttered to the floor.

"This is how you do him after all this time?" said Spiro. "You see he don't feel right, don't you?"

"I don't care!" Lou shouted. "I'm done with this crazy spic! Tell him to sell his garbage in Spanish Harlem!"

We stared off after him as he marched away, adjusting his plastic wings with an angry shrug.

"Angel ain't havin' this," Spiro warned. "The price you paid today, it just double!"

Lou twirled his hand in the old salute, then slammed the door so hard it failed to latch.

TOMMY DROVE WITH CAUTION TILL WE reached the West Side, then limped to a hydrant on Tenth. Shivering in a car that wouldn't heat up, we stared out the windows in shattered silence as windblown confetti fishtailed by. Sprawled on the backseat, Angel dozed away, drooling a stringer onto the notched lapel of his full-length leather trench. We'd rummaged his pockets but couldn't find his house keys, and it was either head to Nikki's in his current condition or crash on the futon in Spiro's basement. Or we could simply sit there with the engine on and let the carbon monoxide make the call.

"I thought he'd fuck her for a second, then stop," moped Tommy. "Like, *ta-da*, I'm just playing, ya rich perverts."

An absurdly tall transvestite tottered by in lime boots. She gave us a bleary, last-call grin, then bundled around the corner and disappeared.

"But I guess it got good to him, or she was with it for a while, because—"

"Boolshit, Tom. He *rape* her," Spiro growled.

"Well...? She never told him stop?"

"Yeah, 'cause she's unconscious, man!"

Tommy twirled a hand, conceding the point. Past him, out the windshield, a Lincoln whispered by. It slowed for a pair of hypothermic trannies rubbing their rabbit coats to stay warm. A window whirred down as the car snugged up. Out, absurdly, came a household broom, knocking the wig off one of the girls. Her friend gave chase, throwing a bottle at the car. It landed well short, and she lost a heel.

"Did you see that?" I fumed. "Let's *get* those Jersey fags—shove that fuckin' broomstick up their ass!"

"*You* get 'em," said Tommy, tapping a Kool. "I'm a whore, but I ain't in the union."

He occupied himself with the climate knobs. Presently, a whoosh of heat came on, swamping us in its close, metallic tang. Spiro cracked a window. Tommy snarled at him. For a bad moment, I thought that they might fight.

"So what do we do?" I blurted for distraction.

"About what?"

"About *everything*."

Tommy dropped the car in gear, but sat there with his foot on the brake. "I know what *I'm* doing: I'm finding another booker, 'cause this guy is off his bird."

"Talk, talk, talk, but yet you stay," jeered Spiro. "Where you gonna make this kind of money?"

"Hey, I *got* money. And plus my private clients? I could shoot off solo and not look back."

"And you?" I asked Spiro. "Would you leave Angel after one big fuckup when he's stoned?"

He and Tommy swapped glances. "Well, but it ain't just this. He's make some bad mistakes, sending us to parties two nights early or writing the addresses down wrong. Also, when we call and say we training in Queens, half the time he forget and went to Chelsea."

"If he even bothers to show *there*," said Tommy. "He's the first guy I've seen get fat on coke."

I looked at Angel, his head slung sideways, and began to feel miserable for him. Whoever he really was under the street hauteur and armature of ornate muscle, he'd glanced across the gym the day we met and seen something in me worth culling. It wasn't just my neediness and thin bravado, commodities to turn to his advantage. No, under the bluster he'd glimpsed something fraternal in the way I strutted and bluffed, a cast-off boy who burned like him to be brought back into the tribe. That his tribe lacked honor and the usual male graces was largely beside the point. He'd brought me in, made a place beside him, and for me that went a long way.

Spiro and Tommy groused about who should host us for the night. "It's probably *two* nights if he can't find a locksmith, tomorrow bein' New Year's," said Tommy. "How 'bout you take 'em to your house tonight, then call me if his mom doesn't have a spare."

"No, fuck that, Tom, I cooking tomorrow. We got fifteen people for St. Basil's dinner."

"Bullshit. All you're doing is eating honey rolls and watching Michigan-USC, just like me."

"So you take 'em tonight and I do tomorrow. No one goes to *your* house New Year's Day."

"Guys," I intruded. "We'll be all right. Just drop us off at Nikki's place."

"Yeah, *she'll* have a key," said Tommy, relieved.

"And what if he wake up pissed?" said Spiro. "You really wanna be there by yourself?"

"I'll manage," I said. "It has to be better than listening to this."

NIKKI'S LOFT WAS IN THE far West Village, where life, like the dwellings, was cheap. On Washington Street, a block from the piers, you could breathe the Hudson River in all its tailpipe splendor, that putrefactive organ of silt and slag and unkillable smallmouth bass. A quarter mile north were the rendering plants, and when the wind blew right, the stench of slaughtered cattle complemented the whiff of PCBs. Tractor-trailers jounced along that ghosted stretch from Gansevoort to West Canal, sharing the road with wraiths and hookers of indeterminate sex, while artists, wastrels, and men of leather reclaimed the former sweatshops and thread mills. Here was where you came if your private urges were too Catholic or macabre for Times Square, a place where the dark-world id ran free — till someone chased it down and took its wallet. A dozen years later, I'd return from grad school to write my first feature here, documenting the lives of preteen boys trading sex for a nickel of crack. Of the kids who still haunt me, I recall one saying, "They show us pictures of their sons at home, then ask if they can ride me bareback. I wanna know, do they do it to *them,* too, and if so, how much they gotta pay?"

Nikki, as it happened, was an artist herself, though not in any medium I'd encountered. She assembled things fished from the Dada leavings of vagrants trooping the streets — spangling, painting, gluing, and nailing the castoffs of cast-off people. While she eased Angel out of his rumpled clothes and, with Tommy's help, got him to bed, I walked the hall of her rough-hewn place, going from work to work with a puzzled eye. A torn-toed Nike, its swoosh bangled with beads, was tied to the branch of a pygmy tree whose "bark" was Boone's Farm labels. A catapult fashioned from canes and dildos sported pulleys of red-dyed condoms. It was well after three, and I was tired and achy and wanted to be off my feet, but I kept on touring her carney show of boho-homeless collages. Some of them made me laugh out loud. Others stumped or pissed me off, like a runaway's letter home that was tacked to a board with a pair of hypodermics. She had a mordant eye that went beyond my schoolboy sarcasm, but there was cruelty in the jokes she cracked about poverty and its degradations. People like us, with our streetwise affect, were merely playing at being molls and pimps, while the kids working the Stroll had no such luck. They came from the kind of chaos we could only visit with our day-trip ghetto passes.

Her loft was in various stages of refinement. In the main space, the plank floors were pickled blond and the furniture, if sparse, was Italian. But down the long hall that was her gallery, lead wires dangled from roughed-out boxes in walls of coarse-grained sheathing. It seemed to me loony to buy a place this big if you didn't have time to hang Sheetrock, and loonier still to camp among trannies when you could swing a flat on Irving Place. Here was where you lived when you couldn't decide where to put your brains and talent. Or—just as likely, given the night's debacle—here was where you lived if you had a coke jones and a fast-receding sense of who you were.

There were half a dozen dawdlers on the black-and-white couches in the open living room, art-world jetsam too stoned to take the hint when we'd stumbled through the door carrying Angel. They affected not to see me as I came back in, and I waited before asking if Nikki had left a blanket and a place for me to sleep.

"A blanket," said a stick-thin guy in tortoise glasses. "Why would she do *that*, I wonder?"

"Because I'm very tired and need to lie down. Is there a second bedroom here?"

"A second bedroom?" He licked a hand-rolled Drum. "Is there a second bedroom, Amy?"

"I don't know, Don," said Amy, a pallid woman in garish, cat's-eye makeup. "It seems like something you wouldn't have to ask."

There was coke, a couple of rails' worth, on the coffee table, and empty bottles of cheap champagne and vodka with Cyrillic labels. I waited, inanely, for someone to speak, while a very loud clock on a Lucite credenza *tick-tick-ticked* its indifference. And then, because my eyes hurt and my shoulder whinged, and because I loathed these people and loathed myself and loathed any creature trying to be what he or she was *not*, I went to my knees and flipped the sofa, dumping Don and Amy and a third pretender on their insubstantial asses. Don got up squawking, but not for long. I grabbed him by the belt and dragged him like laundry to the door and heaved him out. A second guy came at me, plumply Germanic, wagging an index finger. I put him against the wall with a hand over his jaw and squeezed for just an instant, then two. There was something so delicious in the terror I caused him that my brain went bat-cave dark. How grand to finally bring that strength to bear, let out all the liquefied fury till I'd emptied the tank and could start fresh. Who could stop me—who could *try* to stop me?—if I felt like maiming a perfect stranger?

"Enough! You're *hurting* him!"

Someone on either side of me was tugging my arms. I turned around, seismic, flailing elbows. Amy stumbled backward, cupping her mouth. I'd clipped her with a wild forearm. The others stood frozen as she opened the hand. There was blood there; not a gusher, but enough.

"I'm sorry," I said, the lights coming on and the sound roaring up in my ears. "I—I didn't mean to do that. Are you going to be okay there?"

"No, you ass! You broke my fucking *tooth*!"

"Um...actually, it's your lip that's bleeding. Here, I'll go get you some ice—"

"Fuck you, we're leaving, you proto-fascist! You're crazy—I hope you know that. You need help!"

By now the German had recovered enough to join the accusing choir. I was a thug, a killer, a Young Republican. There'd be a call to the cops when they got home. I went to the door again, threw it open, and in a firm voice started counting. Amy paused on the threshold to glare, fleshing the cut on her lip.

"One word," I told her. "To the cops or to Nikki, and I'll show you what crazy is."

I double-locked the door, set the couch on its feet, and listened to my heart run wild. Exhaustion, horror, amazement, shame—they were whipping so fast I couldn't keep up, trying to pin down a feeling. A vile thing had capped off a night of crimes: I'd snapped with no cause or warning. It was what I'd been dreading but far, far worse, because I'd pushed around fey men half my size and clocked a woman in glasses. The eyes of the German guy told the tale: I was a selective bully, a chemical coward.

I woke around nine with my shoulders throbbing and my bare feet frozen to stumps. I sat up, rubbing them back to life, when Nikki came in from the kitchen. She was dressed against the chill in a cowl-neck sweater and a snug but pilled pair of navy sweats. Her hair, dyed a candied shade of scarlet since summer, was tied behind her head in a helix knot. She was frail in ways I'd missed when we came in—a red transparency beneath the eyes; an absence of color where it had peaked before—but was still a formidable sight to see on a loveless New Year's Day. Carrying two mugs, she set one before me and folded her legs beneath her on the couch. "It's green tea, matcha. They say it kills cancer, but *they*, of course, lie like dogs."

I took a sip, breathing in the tawny steam. It smelled of stooped labor in some hilltop province where no one looked or dressed like Nikki. "It's very, uh—"

"Tasteless?"

"Well, that, too."

She apologized for making me fend for myself while she'd tended to Angel all night. He'd been up and down with sweats till passing out for good, and she'd maybe gotten a couple hours' sleep herself before getting up to clean her kitchen. "How much coke did he *have* at that stupid party?"

I said I wasn't sure, having lost him in a crowd that must have numbered a couple of hundred people. She pressed a bit, asking why we'd stayed there till two, but I fed her some crock about being blotto myself and hastily changed the subject. "Look, I have to apologize: I was rude to some of your friends. They wanted to stay after you went to bed, but I was dead and just wanted to—"

"Those aren't my friends," she said with a wave. "However you got them out, it's fine by me."

"Oh," I said. "Then I feel better."

She said nothing for a moment, staring into her tea. "No, my *friends,* or what's left of them, had long since split. The ones you ran into were something else, though I'm hard-pressed to think what you'd call them."

"Leeches?"

"More like cows coming home to roost."

"Huh," I said. "Well, if it's any consolation, I roughed them up."

She laughed: a lone, plosive snort.

"Look, I—I know I got off badly with you, pulling that stupid stunt of mine at the party—"

"What?" she said. "That's long forgotten. You were the one good thing that awful day."

I ordered my free hand not to touch her, tucking it beneath me for safekeeping.

"Also, you're the friend who actually cares for Angel and was worried enough to stay here, keeping vigil."

"Well, that, and we lost his keys last night."

"Regardless. I'm glad you're here."

We talked for a while about other things—her room-by-room salvage of this sprawling place, which had belonged to an old drag queen with dozens of cats that had treated it as their litter box. "The stench was enough to blow you back out, but I had a little money I'd actually made myself," she said, "and thought, with work, I could make this sing." She asked about school and sounded intrigued by the monastic turn I'd taken, approving my crank delusions about writing, saying I'd have quite the subject for a book. It was a lively conversation, taking this curve and that, but I sensed in the one or two lulls we had that a subject lurked behind it, pressing in. She seemed to want to tell or ask me something, but I, lacking any hint of skill or tact, couldn't think how to broach it. Finally, it came to me: *Just ask her.*

"No, I'm not holding back," she said. "Why, do I sound like I am?"

Her eyes told a different story. They seemed to send a message from the woman behind them, trapped and blinking hard. As I reached for her arm, though, a door scraped open on poorly mounted hinges. Angel shambled through it, blue-jay naked. He zombie-walked toward us, shading his eyes and holding out his hand for Nikki. She rose to take it and, with nary a nod goodbye, followed him through the door and back to bed.

Fourteen

You Can't Go Ho' Again

Spring, 1977

WE'D BEEN TO A FILM, something with Gielgud in it, and had wound up, in an act of joint self-torture, at that silk-stocking hash house Serendipity. The place was jammed with its pastel mix of East Side swells and tourists, and Kate and I picked at our rococo salads, nursing a mutual horror of the vapid. Things had been strained all evening, as indeed they'd been for months, tonight's snit concerning a blouse I'd bought her that sat in a drawer unworn. It didn't take much, at that stage of the game, to kindle tensions between us, and the setting only underscored the tacit question at the edge of our conversation: *What are we doing here?*

"I was thinking of maybe checking out Boston next weekend. You interested in going with me?" she asked.

Boston was where she'd be moving for law school. She'd also gotten into Brooklyn Law but was schlepping three hundred miles for an equivalent degree. "I'll see," I said. "I can't promise now. Two papers due that following Monday."

"Well, but when do you think you'll know? I could always ask Janis, but would rather go with you, of course."

"It's hard to really know. Could we talk on Wednesday? By then I'll have a better idea."

"Fine. I'll book with Avis, and if you're able, then come. I don't want to call last minute, then find out there's no cars."

It wasn't that we'd stopped caring and were holding on against the prospect of being alone. Kate could walk down Broadway in a butcher's smock and still draw leers from the newsstand guys, while I was back to working Fridays for Angel and fielding my share of bridesmaid passes. No, quite the contrary: we were too invested to let this die without a fight. It was our first affinity, that glimpse of emotional likeness that is readily mistaken for love. You don't part easily when you read each other's thoughts, even when those thoughts start to exclude you. You cling still tighter to this thing you've made together, squeeze until you've wrung its very life out.

Sometime during dinner, I became aware that we were being talked about. A party of raucous couples was getting trashed across the room, and several times I happened to glance that way and caught them eyeing us. I said as much to Kate, but she told me to ignore them; she wasn't in any mood for a scene. "We're going to sit and eat in peace," she said, "then grab the check and forget we were ever here."

"But who are they to throw shade, those community-college burnouts from Ca-*nahh*-sie?" I could feel the pressure build behind my eyes, a thing that happened with dismaying swiftness since I'd doubled my load of test cyp. "I'll mind my own bee-eye till we've finished dinner, but trust me, I'm saying something when we leave."

"Can you really not let a thing go?" she said. "Do you always have to be the wounded fawn?"

I let out a snort audible in the kitchen. "Wounded fawns don't flat-bench three-oh-five."

"Paul," she warned.

"*What?*"

"If you need to throw a fit after I've asked you not to, then call your dad and spend the night with him."

My heels pounded under the table. "Are you really so above this that it rolls right off?"

"No," she said, "but I'm trying to be an adult, and I wish you'd join me in it."

By dessert my blood pressure had returned to peacetime levels, and I made an effort to recoup the evening by agreeing to go join her the following weekend. I hadn't been to Boston—hadn't been anywhere, really—and said I'd spring for a real hotel or a B and B. Between the field-house job and my shows for Angel, I was fairly well fixed for money then and could afford to spoil her a little. In August she'd be off to a college town that pointedly didn't include me, starting down the road with other right thinkers and earnest adults in progress. All I could offer, by way of competition, was some tender moments these next three months, a store by which she'd judge my future rivals.

Brightening, Kate took my hand and kept it, sketching out the weekend she envisioned. We'd sleep in late that Saturday and have brunch on Beacon Hill, then start the day off at Boston Common, where Elizabeth Pain, the model for Hester Prynne, was buried in the King's Chapel grounds. From there we'd hit the Gardner, with its Titians and Veroneses, then walk the pretty mile to the BU campus, where she'd nose around and begin to get her bearings. Finally, we'd hop the T to Copley Square and have a twilight dinner above the park. She loved old cities, with their accretion of life, and her excitement was palpable across the table. I paid in a hurry and led the way out, eager to grab the first cab to her place.

She was a step or two behind me when we passed the table with the bridge-and-tunnel snarks who'd set me off. By sheer dint of will, I looked ahead and kept my balled fists in pockets. We were almost through the archway to the outer room when I heard the words that reduced the night to rubble.

"Fuckin' *whoo-uh*."

I remember turning around and seeing Kate's hand up. "Don't," she said. "I beg you. Just keep going."

But I was already by her on a bullet of rage, the wind howling murder in my head. The one I thought had said it was looking up with a smirk that flipped to panic when I charged. He backed out of his seat, knocking the chair on its side. I kicked it away and started around the table.

"Get over here, faggot. I'll shove my fist down your throat. How dare you talk that shit about my girl?"

The other guys were up now, forming a berm between us. I had one by his polyester shirt. The three girls were yelling over each other at me. In my fury, I didn't hear them till I glanced at Kate; she was staring with tear-stung eyes at the birthday girl.

"What?" she said, advancing a step. "I want to hear what you just said."

Too late, it hit me. I'd seen the girl before, at another kind of party in Mill Basin. "Shut it," I warned her. "Just shut the fuck up. No one's talking to you, and no one needs to."

"No!" said Kate, as I grabbed her hand. "You say what you just said. *I* need to hear it."

The girl glared at me. "*He's* the whore!"

"You didn't know?" said the girl beside her. "He shtripped at her cousin's bridal shower and had sex with two of her neighbors in the upstairs bedroom."

It suddenly got still in the room. "Come on," I entreated, tugging Kate's arm. "Let's leave before the hostess calls the cops."

"When?" Kate asked, not budging.

"Last summer, but I know he still does it. One of my aunt's girlfriends booked a show with him. She said he's good, but the Greek guy's way more hotter."

I FOLLOWED HER DOWN SIXTIETH STREET, calling her name, then settled for staying abreast of her and saying nothing. She was crying softly, little runs of stifled sobs, but when she reached the park, she suddenly let out a scream that scared me to my shoes. "Go away!" she beseeched me, eyes brimming with tears. "I need to be alone now, can't you see that?"

"I'm not leaving you in the state you're in, to be preyed on by who knows what. Get in a cab and talk to me, Kate. It can't end like this—I won't let it!"

Again she wailed a yawp of pain and started downtown, coughing tears. I trailed behind heart-stabbed, punching my thigh with as much avenging force as I could muster. We walked like that for a couple of blocks, Kate reeling past the gated shops, me staggering on a leg I'd just bruised. At the corner of Fifty-seventh, she caught her heel and stumbled into the busy crosswalk. A step van all but clipped her as it made the turn. When I lunged to pull her in, she shrieked for help.

"Kate, *stop* and come home," I begged. "I promise I'll leave you be there, but—"

"Help!" she shouted. "Won't someone please just help me!"

We stood there, frozen in the crosscut headlights, a caterwaul of car horns blaring at us. Two men leapt from the cab of a truck, one of them wielding a wrench. Other voices joined them over the din, yelling at me to let the girl go. I was yelling back when a *bang* unhinged me: a beer can lobbed from a car exploded, soaking the hem of my jeans. I tore after the bastards, chasing as they drove west. They were up the block and gone before I got ten steps, and by the time I had my wits again and circled back, Kate and the truck had vanished, too.

FOR DAYS I CALLED CONSTANTLY, every couple of hours, scourged by the need to be heard. But mostly her phone just rang and rang. The rare times Kate answered, she set the receiver on its side and left me to plead with air. I also, of course, wrote her: typed, single-spaced letters full of longing and tortured self-arraignment. They came back unopened in a manila mailer, with a two-word injunction: "Just stop."

The post-shock fallout was severe. I stopped sleeping nights and dozed in my carrel, an hour or two of fever-panic dreams. Most things put me in tears or near it; my thesis about Milton's treatment of Eve was, in tone and vantage, menopausal. The jitters came back now, though I kept my doses steady. I'd wake from a nap and find my hamstring seizing, the band of muscle beating like a heart.

With no one else to tell, I poured my heart out to Angel, but found him less than Quaker in consolation. His coke sales had cratered since the New Year's debacle, and instead of hustling at clubs and parties, he was staying indoors to keep an eye on Nikki, whose movements he distrusted more and more. "She's got this dude, her so-called *teacher*, who she goes to twice a week, but yet her three-hour *art class* goes from five to ten and she comes back smelling like booty," he railed. "How's she gonna act like I can't even count? I got one-plus-one fists to beat that ass."

I gathered from Tommy that this wasn't loose talk. His last time down there to drop money for Angel, Nikki answered the door with collarbone bruising and scratches at the base of her neck. "I never liked that broad from day one," he said, "and *then* she went and got him sprung on coke. But still, she don't deserve how he does her now. It's a *New York Post* headline waiting to happen."

Spiro was just as bleak about Angel. "Five years I know him, never once he hit a woman—it's not on him to do that, and that's my *word*. But now I see him and who *is* this scary guy that's all the time mad and where's-my-money. He don't party; he don't train but maybe two times a week, and run downstairs to call her every second."

"But shouldn't we *do* something?" I said. "Shouldn't we sit him down and say, *You'll die if you don't stop this*? I mean, if no other reason than our pocket, Spiro. He's made us all a hell of a lot of money."

"Man, we *been* tried. Even his mom try told him, but he's the great Angel; he know better. You best off staying out there, get a beach job this summer. You don't need to be here if you don't need to."

Coming after Kate, I couldn't bear to hear that; my heart was as bruised as week-old fruit. I ached for Nikki, having dreamed of her for months, gauze fantasias of rescue fiction that ended on white sand beaches. I hadn't seen her since February, at Tommy's birthday party, when, for the night at least, she'd pulled herself together in a tight silk sheath and heels, and I'd let myself hope that she'd throw Angel over in a big-push effort to get clean. She herself had teased it, saying she'd been doing a lot of thinking, and asked for my number "in an emergency." But that was so much smoke: she'd acquiesced to taking the cliff dive with him, a spiral beyond my help or understanding.

The second body blow was the crack-up of our crew. Spiro and Tommy had taken a step back after the New Year's outrage at Lou's, and I heard in Angel's tone that he knew it, too, and couldn't bring himself to patch things up. "I did too much, gave 'em all they have—bought Tommy his BMW and Spiro that Boston Whaler. They want to bail now, that's on them."

But I couldn't be so cavalier. No, they didn't read books (or a newspaper without comics), and their idea of world cinema was the midnight screening of *She Wolf of the SS* in Times Square. Nor did they feign even a nodding interest in the life I pursued at school, asking why I didn't cash my two years of college in for a broker-training job on Wall Street. ("Twenty-eight large just to start!" said Tommy. "By thirty, you could have a house in *Islip*.") Still, I thought I'd pierced their narcissism, believed that something so one-sided passed for fellowship. Which is a fancy way of saying I was sprung on steroids and clung to the company of other juicers. They lent the illusion that I had a life, and gave me moral cover to go on using.

Though Angel was, by then, all but living at Nikki's, he and I usually crashed uptown after I'd done a Friday night gig. Occasionally, I wound up working a show *with* him; in a stark sign of ruin, he was dancing himself, claiming he'd run short of capable help to handle the weekend bookings. The first time he joined me, I was so distracted that I barely managed to keep my feet moving, watching him grandstand and ace me out at a post-prom bash in West Orange. He teased the front of his thong down to flash his cock, pulled girls off the couch to do the freak dance with him, and stood them upside down in a sixty-nine, a stunt that never failed to raise the roof. Shameless and cutthroat, he walked away with hundreds, while I limped home with forty in singles and a refurbished sense of my own slightness.

The drive back home was vintage Angel—ebullient and boastful about the girls he'd just *faux*-manced, doing his take on their Jersey diction and see-through coyness about sex. "When I came through the door, it was 'Oh…my…Gawd: Who let *Blacula* in?' Then I grind against 'em, it's 'Wow, his skin is *soffft*—maybe he's just a really tan Italian.' Last, they see my python: 'Wow, he *is* a nigger!…Well, fuck it, just this *once,* if no one tells."

We came through the tunnel and swung up Ninth, where an old friend ran a topless joint. It wasn't much to look at, with a chipped, tin bar and women long past their ductile twenties dancing in dead-eyed boredom. Angel and I sipped our two-dollar Scotches, waiting to collect from one of the girls on a past-due cocaine marker. She was late for her shift, though, and as we sat there talking, Angel's mood darkened by the drink. "This is what I get, selling to stank-ho strippers who can't even feed their own kids," he said. "I need to get back with my East Side mommies, 'cause this shit's over and I ain't dead yet."

We waited another hour, then slunk uptown in a decidedly chastened mood. At a booth in the back of Los Tres Hermanos, he had himself a snort right there at the table while ignoring his pecan waffles, rambling on about the recent past and the people who'd burned his trust. He'd fronted his sister money to open a nail salon, and the next thing he knew, the sister's boyfriend had split with most of the twelve grand, cash. He'd hired a private eye to track down his father after his mother let it slip that he was still alive, and the idiot led him to a used-car dealer off Eastchester Road in the Bronx. "Dude was almost seventy and looked nothin' like me. When I told him why I came, he called the PI himself. Said, 'I'll show you my passport—I was in *Guam* then.'"

"I'm sorry," I said. "I didn't know that mattered, finding your dad."

"It doesn't," he sniffed. "I went there to *cap* him if he didn't step up and help my moms. I've carried her forever, but I ain't got it like I used to. It's time for *somebody else* to man up."

Another revelation—not the fact but the admission—from a guy who gauged his worth by the roll of bills in a rubber band. "You're a hundred percent sure he's not the one?"

"Man, no one's comin' to help. It's all on me."

"Well, whatever I can do, just ask. School's over soon, and then I'm back here."

He studied me a moment. "You don't mean that."

"Of course I do. Where else can I make this money?"

"You're on your way off to somewhere better. This ain't you, and you know it."

"I'm not saying I'd move weight for you. But if you need me to work the weeknight shows, I'm more than happy to."

He stared through again, then looked away. "I hear that, man. Thanks. I'm just down right now. It's all fuckin' up, thanks to me."

I stirred my cold coffee. "You want to talk?"

"Nope. All I do is talk. I need to *work.*"

He shifted in his seat, growing agitated, and pushed the plate away. His eyes kept cutting to the door and back, as if someone long awaited was en route. "You know what's messed up, though? I kinda hoped it *was* him. I'm like, damn, maybe I do have a pops."

Disbelieving my ears—Angel, reflective?—I muttered something intended to keep him talking.

"I mean, I *know* it's fucked-up, the way he left my moms, right when we moved here from Decatur and she was ass-out broke in the middle of winter. I *can't* forgive that, or what happened later, when she sent me back to live with his aunt. But if I saw him now, I'd at least hear him out. See what he'd say to make it right."

"Wow—I never knew you lived down south."

His mood, so mutable, turned dour now. He scowled past my shoulder at thin air. "Broke-down Shreveport, if you call that living. A bunch of simple niggers in shotgun shacks actin' like they never freed the slaves."

"Ah. That's why you came back?"

A scowl said, *Leave it there,* but I pressed ahead. When would such an opening come again? "Do you ever stop to think that's why you took up lifting, or why we still train so hard?"

Down a memory hole, he gave a shrug.

"See, I used to think it was about getting laid, or scaring the schmucks on my hall. But the longer I do it, the more I think it was to get my father's attention. For ten, twelve years, he barely looked at me, but you can bet your ass he's looking now."

"That right?" he said, coming out of his fugue. "What, is he scared of you?"

"No," I said, "more like mystified. Like, *What did I do to create this beast?*"

"Hah!" he cackled. "He ignored his own kid. Now you could squash him like a grape."

"But now that I've got him looking, I don't *need* to squash him. Other people maybe, but not him."

"Not even a smack for those years?"

"I mean, I'm still pissed, but less at him. Now he's just some guy who could've done better."

He gazed at me glumly. "Well, there you go."

"Sorry?"

"You *had* a pops, even when y'all weren't vibing. He lived around the way and paid your rent. Whereas me, the ma-fucker was up and gone and never even sent an Easter card."

"But maybe in some ways that was easier, no? You didn't have to go there Friday nights and get frozen out at dinner, or wait for him to show at your jayvee game when there wasn't a chance in hell he'd actually make it."

His brows came together in scorn. "Son, I'm *high* and I know that makes no sense."

"Well, but—"

"And as far as bulking up, that wasn't me showin' him. That was me trying to survive."

264

"Sorry," I said. "I can imagine how hard it was, being a pretty kid in the projects."

"No," he said, "you can't imagine shit—or know what it's like right now."

"Fine. I'm listening."

"Are you? You sure?"

"Yes," I said. "Intently, in fact."

"Man, you ain't heard a word since the day I met you. *Coño,* where's that white girl with my coffee?"

THOUGH HE SAT IN THE DINER for an hour that night and gave not an inch of ground, he called my dorm room a couple of days later to say he'd "checked himself." "I know I'm out of pocket on the cocaine tip and need to get my head right, here and now. I talked to Nikki and we made a deal: no more parties on weeknights, *period,* and only one gram, maximum, Friday to Sunday. She's even hit a meeting—you heard her father goes, right?—and we're gonna get it together as a team."

"Well, wow," I said, "that's great to hear. The one thing that scares me, though, is that out clause on weekends. I mean, how're you going to hold it to a gram?"

"Oh, easy—I'm back to training, slick. Lifting with the Whoresmen Monday through Friday and back on my j-o, which is makin' dollars."

"Well, but what little I know about coke addiction is that you can't just—"

"Hey, be *glad* for me, Paulie. The old Angel's back, and it's all because of you that I saw the sign."

For several weeks after, he called regularly to brag on the progress of getting "pure." His quads and lats were "blazing" on a regime of five-day workouts, and Nikki now joined him on his morning runs from the Battery to Union Square. "It's a beautiful thing, Paulie: we feel that poison leave our system. But hey, I'll put her on and let her tell you herself—*if* she can stop starin' in the mirror."

"It's not *me* in the mirror—that's projection!" She laughed, taking the receiver from him. "Do you have any idea how hard it is, sharing a one-bath apartment with Narcissus here?"

"Well, better that than the alternative, I guess."

"I know, and I thank you every day. Whatever it was you told him, it really took."

She said she'd found a meeting that she liked on Bleecker and was trying to drag him along. "He still has a beer when he winds down after a show, and I've told him that's a threat to both of us. We need to stop *all* of it, not just choose our spots. But one thing at a time, he says."

I asked her how she felt about him dancing again and whether *that* was a threat to their sobriety. "Well, it doesn't thrill me, but one of us has to work, and right now I'm just finishing up with school. The good news is, he's stopped selling the other thing, and that's a major step in the right direction."

Tommy wasn't sure that Angel *had* stopped dealing, but he confirmed that he showed up, hungry to train, at their iron-dungeon club in the East Village. "It's good to have him back doing dead lifts like a madman, but I take it with a pound of salt," he said. "I know from my brother that there's rules to gettin' sober, and this dude's way too cool for school."

This was in early May when, between finals and papers, I was holed up on campus for several weeks. I continued getting rehab reports via phone, but more and more often it was Nikki making the call, and it wasn't strictly good news she conveyed. "I'm sure he's not using—at least I *think* I'm sure—but he's hanging in the clubs again till three a.m., which he claims he has to do to get more gigs. The more gigs, the more money to start his own business, but in the meantime I'm scared that he's an easy mark for the cocaine lizards in those places."

"Are Tommy and Spiro with him, watching out?" I asked.

"Yeah, but you know Angel—there's no guarding him. If he senses you're playing cop, he'll blow a fuse. Sneak away to do what you don't want."

"Well, what can you do? Is leaving him an option?"

"No. At least…no. Not while he's making an effort. But if I thought he'd picked up again and lied about it, I'd—yeah, I'd think about going."

"You'd *think* about it?"

"Paul, don't hound me. I'm trying to do the decent thing. I was the one that got him into this fix, and the least I can do is see him through it."

"Not if it means going down with him."

"True, but remember that I'm not helpless. I've got a solid family that's been through this with my dad, and the money to get treatment someplace nice. Whereas Angel's family—"

"I know; I've had the pleasure. But I worry about you. I've seen what it's like when he erupts."

She took a calming breath and lit a smoke, her third in fifteen minutes. "I appreciate the thought, but I'll be fine," she said. "You won't get a phone call from the cops."

IN THE END, of course, I didn't. The reverse occurred: silence rang in the final act. I'd moved back home after the spring term finished and was staying with Dad for a couple of cramped weeks when the calls from Angel and Nikki stopped cold. I made nothing of it, figuring they'd lost my father's number, and tried them several times at both apartments. But by Friday of that first week, fearing the worst, I called Tommy for an explanation. He hadn't heard from Angel in days, however, and had done some checking of his own. Through Angel's mom, he'd tracked down a number for Nikki's father in Connecticut. Tommy passed it over, saying that I should make the call; I knew how to "talk to those people better."

Tommy and I were at a bar in Yorkville on a dazzling day, the air rinsed clean by overnight rain and dried by a snap breeze off the Sound. Around us, pensioners nursed eight-ounce Schaefers over copies of the *Racing Form*. The light by which they worked their stubby pencils was the exact color of failure. As I dialed, Tommy ducked his head in to listen. A man picked up on the other end. "Good morning," I said. "Is Nikki there, by chance?"

"No, by chance, she's not," he said. "And it's afternoon, not morning. Is this one of her jobless pals?"

"Um, no, I...go to college. Do you know where I could—"

"And what college would that be? Do they hand out actual grades there, in their wisdom?"

"I-I'm sorry, I don't follow—"

"See, most of my daughter's friends attend the sorts of institutions where they've done away with the drudgery of A's and Bs. No, now these young royals are judged according to mood, or by the alignment of their *chakras*, whatever those are."

"I go to a state school. We're all serfs there."

"What's that now? You surf?"

"No, sir. *Serfs,* as in servants."

"Oh. And what's your connection to my daughter?"

"Look, could you just tell her Paul called? I'd like to leave a number where—"

"Are you connected in any way to that thug she dated?"

Dated—past tense. "I'm the friend who pushed her to get sober."

"Himmph," he said, and the line went silent. I listened for several seconds, awaiting a dial tone, and was about to hang up when a voice in another room came on the extension. "Hey," said Nikki, in a washed-out drone. "Sorry I didn't call...So tired these last days...The drugs they gave me make me sleep a lot."

"What? What drugs? Something happen to you, Nikki?"

A frogged pause. "You haven't talked to Angel? You swear?"

"*No,* he's disappeared, not even his mom knows where. Please, already, tell me what's going on."

She hedged a bit longer, saying in stops and starts that I wasn't to tell anyone we had spoken. Once back on her feet, she'd be leaving town awhile; she needed to turn her focus to getting well. "A retreat in Colorado...Basic but serene…Can stay as long as I need to…In the mountains…"

The pain medication sent her on tangents; it was a while before I got the crux of things. Angel had stumbled in the door one night, reeking of Gilbey's gin and THC. She let him sleep it off but confronted him in the morning. They argued—loudly—and at some point he conceded, resolving to make a meeting that night. He went out in the afternoon, though, and didn't come back till after ten p.m. By then she had packed a bag and was waiting on some friends to come pick her up. Again they quarreled, and this time it turned ugly: Angel grabbed her shoulders and shook her hard, demanding that she "give him his respect." She fell dizzy and toppled backward, hitting the lip of the bureau crosswise. The pain in her right side blacked her out on contact. "I remember then…the car. He was crying to forgive him…Said he loved me and was sorry and…could never hurt me. But in the hospital, I looked over and he was gone."

Tommy, listening in, was flush with rage. "I'll *smash* him," he hissed. "I'll fuckin' smash him! I told you he was dickless and hit women!"

"Who's that?" said Nikki. "Is someone there?"

"Just Tommy," I assured her. "He's as pissed as I am. When we get hold of Angel, it's going to be—"

"*No,*" she croaked, "that's the last thing I want. I said some things that hurt him and…not his fault."

I pressed, but here she clammed up tight, saying that her ribs were just "displaced." "It's soft tissue. I'll be up in five days. Could you hand the phone to Tom now? I need a word."

"In a second," I said, holding on a beat longer. "Nikki, I'm just so…sorry. I feel responsible."

"But why?" she said. "You tried to warn me. *I* was the one who…God, I'm such a dolt."

FOR SEVERAL DAYS, I walked the streets in an anoxic, head-down fog. Nothing endured or had an ounce of honor. Life was reduced to neuronal throbs. The Angels, Nikkis, and Tommys were lone pilots of their flashy vessels, zipping around at high rates of speed and stopping here and there to take on riders. When it suited them, they simply dumped you off and hurtled on to the next bright port of call. That was the code of the Body Shop, where other people were used for parts, swapped in and out like wiper blades. Don't fancy what you have? Trade it in; there's always something hotter on the racks. Same for the self: rebuild it on the fly and toss away the pieces you don't want. The more work you do, the closer you get to being the hot-rod remake of your dreams.

I'd come home hoping for a remake myself, to fix what I'd botched during the spring. Kate was on the list, though I held out little hope. She'd responded to a last, desperate letter of mine with the following on a postcard from Boston:

Very few people are larger than life. You, however, are smaller. Don't write me again or I'll call your father.

The plan had been to go on dancing for cash but get a half-time job at a West Side bookstore so I could meet a pretty girl who read Camus. With Angel in the wind, though, I had to regroup, and grudgingly accepted a grounds-crew job at a posh camp in Massachusetts. I was to report there in June to prep the ball fields and clay courts for hundreds of tetchy non-athletes, and went about the business of buying chinos and work boots like a man checking in for radiation. One day, a week before I left New York, I was woken by a call at the crack of noon. "You still nodding? It's *lunchtime*, chief. Damn, you've all went slack without me there!"

Drugged on sleep, I gave a stalling grunt. I'd lost all hope of hearing from Angel.

"You're pissed at me, right? It's cool if you are," he said. "I did a stupid thing, as I know you know."

"How? You speak to Nikki?"

"Nah, but I heard she talked to *you*. Everything gets back to me, by and by."

"Where've you been?" I said, trying to turn the tables. "Tommy said you'd split to LA."

"Bull*shit*. I'm over at Victor's, 'bout to order paella. But I'll wait for your sleepy ass if you get dressed."

I mounted small resistance, but my heart wasn't in it; I needed to see him again. He'd become one of those people you have to rip yourself from if you want to be free and clear.

I took my time showering and got there late; he was just finishing off his *tostones*. He smiled to himself at my show of defiance. A waiter swooped in to pour water.

"You're lookin' tight, slick. I like those two-tone loafers. Very Trevi Fountain in *Roman Holiday*."

"Um, thanks. You've seen *Roman Holiday*?"

"Hey, we get *Million Dollar Movie* uptown. That signal don't stop at Eighty-sixth Street."

His grin still sparkled, but he was different somehow, careful in his movements and bearing. After a minute I saw he favored his left shoulder, grimacing as he raised a water glass. "Slight accident," he said, tracking my gaze. "Blew a flat in Jerze, but I'm okay."

"You sure?" I said, checking the tilt of his frame. "What happened, were you—"

"*No*, I wasn't high. I was drivin' in the slow lane when the back tire went. Car did a spinout and hit the rail."

"Did you break any bones or—"

"Nah. A separation, but I'm good to go. Never even took the Percocets."

"Oh. I know someone who could use them."

He stared at me with that bullfighter's grin. "Hey, *go ahead*—just get it all out. I admit I did wrong and said so."

I returned his stare, pressing my luck. "She's a woman," I said. "You were *raised* by women. How the hell do you put your...? I don't get it."

He tilted back in his Breuer chair. "And you? That Kathy you were seein' last summer? You always treat her right?"

My stomach landed in my lap. "Her name is Kate, and ... no, I didn't treat her right. But then again, I didn't *hit* her."

"And all them others you fucked or stripped for while you were dating her? How 'bout them, you do the gentleman thing, or lie like a dog and hurt their feelings?"

"Well, again, that's not breaking their ribs. As shitty as I've been — and I dwell on that a lot — I never sent anyone to the hospital."

His eyes broiled up — those neurons again — and he flung himself forward in his seat. But the sudden move made his shoulder flare; he had to bite down till the throb passed. "Bet," he snapped, "I'm worser than you — the nigger who can't hold his temper. But let me tell you: the places I was, that temper fuckin' kept me alive."

I chided him, saying he wasn't in Shreveport now. He smashed the cluttered table with his fist. Cutlery jumped; people spun and stared. It suddenly got silent around us.

I stood to leave, but his eyes were wet. After a moment, I sat down again and waited mutely till the chatter resumed at other tables.

"Did something happen after your father left? You get picked on by the kids in your project?"

Through his half-buttoned shirt, I watched the polished cleft of his pectorals rise and fall. "Before then, but it's not to speak on ... You done with that mess there?"

I glanced at my plate of soggy paella, doused by the water he'd spilled.

"Or was it later, when you went down south?"

He turned away fast, but I saw his cheek flame as he fished the wad from his pocket. "Wait outside for a minute."

We walked uptown for a couple of blocks in dizzy, smog-tipped silence. I stole a peek at his clenched-jaw profile. The past, far from past, was smack before him, planted in his mid-range stare.

"I know you got mad when I said it last time, but I'm ready to listen. If it helps ..."

He let out a laugh or muffled groan, but otherwise made no comment.

I remembered something he'd once said to me when I started seeing Dr. S. "Shrinks are for dudes who can't get head and chicks too square to give it." It was standard Angel: the bulletproof prince looking down from his tall white horse. But judging from his expression, standard Angel was gone, replaced by a spooked and baffled kid who was crouched in a corner, fists balled. I knew that face, having worn it for years, and wanted to stop there, between Broadway and Amsterdam, and give him a bracing hug. Instead I kept walking till we crossed 75th Street and paused in front of a station wagon. I almost fell down when he produced a key and put it in the driver's door. "Go ahead and clown me—I wrecked the Toronado, and now I'm stuck with this old *mierta*."

"I'm not laughing," I said. "I just—wow, you should've warned me. Angel in a—what's this? Ford Torino?"

"Hey, I gotta get from A to B, and my uncle had this dirt bomb sittin' around. Till I'm back in the game, it's what I'm rollin'."

"I just wish I had a car to lend you. Maybe my dad would trade you his Le Car."

He considered it a moment. "What color? Not that orange...?"

"Sorry. And it says 'Le Car' in big black letters."

He laid his forehead on the roof a moment. "Yo, you really want to do a solid?" he said. "For all the times I helped when you were broke?"

I knew, of course, he'd ask. "That depends."

He stared into traffic, trying to harness something fickle: pride or courage, it was hard to say. "Yo, I really, really need you to work a show. This Saturday in Jersey; it's important."

I took a breath and held it. "You ask Tommy?"

"He turned me down flat, like I knew he would. And Spiro I'm still tryin', but..."

"Did they tell you I leave Monday to start a job?"

"Aw, *hell*, no, Paulie! Why do *that*?"

"Because you disappeared, and I need the money."

"Yeah, but I came back and—fuck that job. You and me'll work this town to death."

"I can't," I said. "Someone put their neck out, and the last thing I'd do is leave them hanging."

He ran a hand down his face in consternation. "You really can't do this show and go from there?"

I smiled glumly. "How does one show help you out?"

Again he looked southbound, as if the answer was out there in one of the flanking ads on the Broadway bus. "'Cause it's the only booking I got for the next two weeks."

ANGEL WINCED PAST THE wheel through the windshield's grime, trying to get his bearings in the weekend traffic. Behind us, drivers making the beach-town crawl leaned on their horns five lengths back. It was eight o'clock on one of those June nights when the sand and fog scudding in off the shore concoct a greasy soup for motorists, and Angel and I had been straining for miles to figure out where we were. As usual, we'd left late, overshot our exit, and, after doubling back around on the Garden State Parkway, were now bumbling south on a one-lane road whose salt-smudged markers left us guessing.

A further tax on progress were the little pink pills Angel had gulped for the pain in his shoulder. The bushings on the Torino were badly worn, and it took focus and steady, two-hand force to keep the car from drifting off the road. The longer he drove, though, the worse his tendon whinged. By the time we saw the placard saying Spring Lake Heights, he'd downed four Darvons and had to pull over. He could barely keep his eyelids up.

"Just rest a sec," he murmured. "Gimme ten minutes and I'll be good."

As nothing quite deadens a festive occasion like a stripper too zonked to strip, I had no choice but to let him doze on the shoulder of Route 35 South. We were an hour-plus late for a gig that had started at seven, but I eased my own seat back and shut my eyes. Even in the starched-twill fake cop outfit that was supposed to surprise and reveal, it was pleasant enough to lounge there and relish the sound of surf tamping down the dark shore. I received it as a taste of the coming summer: ten weeks in Massachusetts and its miracle air; a congeries of girls' camps for miles and miles; and a lush dispensation from my inner life, that snake pit of gloom and dread. The beauty of being young is hopping onto a bus and leaving your freight behind you on the curb, embracing the delusion that a three-hour ride will suffice to wipe the slate clean. Soon enough, you learn, of course, that *you're* the freight, a collection of kinked instincts and botched expressions that never quite sync with your surroundings. But two weeks shy of my twenty-second year, I was itching to shove off and start fresh. The oil-spilling Ford; the beat-cop getup—it all reeked of failure and clown-shoe pathos, death via the installment plan. It was finally time for me to go it alone, step from the shadow of oversize men and see what I fetched on the open market. But first, a short nap, just to clear my head of all the rough weather it housed...

"*Fuck!*" cried Angel, waking me bolt upright. "Fuck, fuck, fuck, fuck, *fuck!*"

"What?" I said from a magenta daze. "Wh-where—what *time* is it?"

"It's ten o'fuckin' clock. We slept two hours! How you gonna let me nod off!"

"But I only closed my eyes for a minute..."

Angel started the car and backed out fast, nearly clipping a phone pole with his tail. Away we roared, belching dragon smoke, as he unleashed a screed against "Rip van Winkle Jews." I might have been offended if I wasn't so scared. The Torino shimmied left and right, taking a drunken run at a water tower. We somehow made it alive off the surfside strip, hugged the dog-legged lake that gave the town its name, and bombed toward the ocean past substantial homes with fussily kept lawns and shrubs. At last we heaved up, trailing clouds of grit, at a lion-crested iron gate. The house crouched behind it was a run-on sentence of boxy cedar segments and shingled dormers, gobbling up the kidney-shaped yard with a two-floor addition of tinted glass. The front door was open, and women were coming out. We'd arrived just in time to say goodbye.

Our hostess, a paunchy, sunburned Sicilian, spotted us and instantly started screaming. "No! Don't even set foot on my property. Get back in your car and keep goin'! You're in so much trouble with the bastard who sent you, I laugh and it's not even funny!"

Angel, long used to handling drunks, walked toward the house flashing his badge. "Ma'am, step back, please, and decease from cursing. I have a warrant to search for cuntra-ban."

"Didja hear what I just said? You're fired—beat it! Have a nice drive back to Harlem!"

Her girlfriends, a dozen or so well-fed women with hair like topiary, formed a chorus behind her. They drowned out Angel with enough *spic*s and *nigger*s to roll back civil rights to the prewar South, while he soldiered on gamely, warning the guests he'd "restrain" them all and spank their naughty bottoms. As much as I yearned to see that, there were problems afoot. Lights were coming on in the houses around us, and neighbors were drawn out by the commotion. A man across the street yelled he'd call the cops. A woman on a patio, disturbed and underdressed, said she'd phone her cousins in the White Army and Blue Army. It was easy enough to imagine there actually *being* a White Army, an informal militia of house-proud Italians armed with pruning shears. "Let's go," I hissed. "It's a lost cause. We screwed this one up big-time."

"*Hell* no, I ain't leavin'. I gassed up my car and drove all night to be here, so you can best believe I'm gettin' paid!"

This evoked new peals from the women. Somewhere close by, a dog picked up the tenor, and soon all the hounds were at it, baying back and forth about our fee. Angel and the hostess—Trudy, I heard her called—were nose to nose on the cutout sod, he looming over her, cursing in Spanglish, she gesturing harshly with the fingers of both hands like the capo of a housewife-gangster crew. The women massed around her made comparable gestures, and with the porch lights behind them and the low mist for backdrop, the scene evoked a frieze from an ancient play—the ripping apart of Pentheus in *The Bacchae*.

I was watching with something like pity and terror when I heard the crunch of wheels on gravel. I spun and saw a black Camaro skid-slide to a stop. The driver stepped out, scowling through aviators. In his fist was a three-foot length of pipe.

"Oh, God," moaned Trudy, "what is he doing back? Now, we're all in shit."

"Frank, no!" said the beehived woman behind her. "He's not a real cop, he—he...The girls made me a party, and—and thought it'd be a goof if we had a...stripper."

Frank came abreast of me, breathing through a nose that appeared to be mounted sideways. He was built like a rhino, with ham-hock arms not made in a gym and thighs that strained the crease of his Sansabelt slacks. He cradled the pipe, sizing us up. "Which of you gentlemen's the stripper?"

I looked at Angel, the thug from Spanish Harlem who leg-pressed five-and-a-quarter. Bum wing and all, he had the strength to wrap that pipe like a balloon animal around Frank's head. I spread my feet wide, ready to jump in and help once he'd taken Frank safely to the ground. Instead, Angel stared at him, rooted to the spot. A flight of worry ran across his face.

"I—I guess I'm the stripper," I said. "He just drove."

"You guess you're the stripper? What's that mean?"

"Well, we screwed up the directions and only just got here, so...technically...no one stripped."

But this was neither edifying nor all that responsive to the question put before me. "So whatta you actually do? I seen female strippers, but guys doing that—it's something new, right?"

"Um—not really. It's been around."

"Huh!" he said. "So, what, you dress up like a cop, then take off all your clothes and prance around?"

I looked at Angel but couldn't catch his eye. His gaze was fixed on the back of Frank's waist, trying to make out something under his shirt. It was a very bad moment when I twigged what that meant: my lower legs turned to poured cement. "Well, not dancing per se. It's...adult entertainment. But not *sex,* either. Never sex."

"That right?" He stared over his mirrored shades. "You never slipped one of the ladies a nice *braciole?*"

"Ucchh!" brayed the beehived woman. "I'm skeeved you could even think that! We wouldn't let 'em into the house, these queers, but the moulie says he needs to get paid. On account of the gas he used."

"Oh," said Frank. "How much to fill your tank?"

Angel glanced past him. "We'll just pack it up and be out, chief," he said.

"No, no, no—how much you out of pocket? Ten, fifteen bucks? Here, take twenty."

He produced a bill and flicked it into the air. The note fluttered down to the grassy marge and lay there like a flattened duck. "Go on and take it," he said. "We pay our bills here."

Warily, I bent and scooped it up.

"And now that you got your money, I wanna see a show. Give me twenty dollars of adult entertainment."

I was slow to comprehend. "In front of your neighbors?"

"Why not? You got a crowd; do your fou-fou dance. I ain't paying you something for nothin' here."

Again I eyed Angel, but he gave no sign. "Look, enough of this. Let's just bounce."

Frank whacked my thigh with the pipe. The pain, late in coming, sizzled the leg in *whomp-whomp-whomp* alarm. "Just drop the shirt and pants and do a little sashay. *Then* you and your pal can bounce."

This is madness, I thought. *I'm bigger, faster, stronger. People cross streets to avoid me!* I balled my fists tight. Frank stared back, waiting. *Hit him!* I ordered. *Break his guinea jaw!*

But instead of letting fly with a bang-bang combo, my hands were at my waist, unzipping. The shirt came off freely but not the pants; I had to tug them over my shoes. After a fair bit of labor, which produced no end of mirth, I stood naked to the world but for footwear and thong, the pouch of which read SWAT TEAM in gold letters.

"Stop!" Frank howled, sinking halfway to his knees. "Panties that say SWAT TEAM on 'em...! Where can I get a pair for Antoinette?"

"Frank!" cried his girlfriend, but the rest of her party roared, covering their eyes or pointing in savage fun. I glanced over my shoulder: some of the neighbors were clapping, one man dancing a sort of jig with his shorts hiked far up his ass. Only Angel, who was stricken with a sudden case of lockjaw, had the decency not to buckle in laughter.

"All right, look," said Frank, blotting a small tear. "Just one time up and back, shake for the girls, and then we can all go home."

But I was stone-footed, sensible of nothing except the fierce contusion.

"C'mon, show us what you do, since you drove so far to do it. Here's another twenty to get you going."

The bonus didn't move me, but a shove in the back did. I limped a couple of steps and almost fell.

"Give 'im some rhythm!" Frank yelled, banging his palms together and encouraging the girls to do likewise. Stiffly, I began to shuffle.

"That's all?" he jeered. "Put your *back* into it—you dance like you got a dick up your ass!"

IT WAS DEATHLY QUIET most of the way back, a light rain ticking the glass. There were a couple of quick stops—one for gas, one for smokes—neither of which drew remark. I fidgeted, trying to find a sitting position that dulled the throb in my thigh. The big bag of party ice, melting fast, bled through the towel and soaked my pants.

Suddenly, in view of the city skyline, Angel veered off the right-hand lane and stopped on the shoulder of the Jersey Turnpike. We sat there, listening to the fan-belt whine. The rain, picking up, came in sideways.

"If only he hadn'ta had a piece," he moaned. "I'd'a straight squashed him and made him *eat* that pipe, but couldn't take the chance of him drawing down."

I turned to him, seething. I had seen no bulge, though I hadn't gotten a clean look at his back. But Angel went on, saying the guy was "mob for sure," and even if he'd stomped him, what then? His crew would find out where we lived and hit the town hell-bent for leather. I went on staring, hearing a friendship dissolve. I wanted to be home, wherever *that* was.

"What?" said Angel. "Don't look at *me*. I didn't see you go at him."

"Man, you bitched out, plain and simple. The almighty Angel."

"And if *you* hadn't let me fall asleep for two hours, we'd'a done the show and been out!"

"*Let* you? You were in a coma from all those Darvons."

We stared straight ahead through the sheet of rain. I could hear him breathing in short, sharp throws, as if air was being bled from a valve.

"Yo, I never before told this to no one," he murmured, "but that time down south, there was this cousin..."

I didn't glance over. "Yeah? So what."

"He was fifteen; I was eleven...Big country nigger wasn't even in high school 'cause they kept on leavin' him back."

The out-breaths got louder, damp as steam. He turned so I couldn't see his face. "Used to be always punching my arms so they'd go dead and I couldn't fight back. We'd go to this pond with some older dudes, and he'd make me drink that Mad Dog till I puked."

I waited, willing my own breath silent. A semi going by kicked a wash of water over the hood of the station wagon.

"This one time, coming back from there, he —he..."

By now all I heard was his respiration. A long pause stretched to the breaking point. I turned and saw a look of such abject grief that my heart contorted in shame.

"Nineteen years now—nineteen *years*!—and at night I still think of that. If I find his black ass, I'm'a cut him up slow and feed him, piece by piece, to his dogs."

A sob escaped him, then another and another. It was minutes before he'd choked out the bitter root reaching down inside him. He wiped his face dry with a rag I found and took a couple of waist-deep breaths.

"Look," he said. "Today...All that shit that happened—not a word to anyone, understand?"

"Please, man."

"Not to Tommy or Spiro, your girlfriend, whoever. This shit dies with us."

"As God is my witness."

He dabbed at the last hot trace of tears and threw the rag behind him. "I'd give you *my* word, but we know what that's worth."

With a snort, he threw the car in drive and merged into northbound traffic. It was light all the way to the Lincoln Tunnel, while the rain beat steady, plump gray droplets on a windshield that wouldn't wipe clean.

Epilogue

July 1978

I HAD A KEY TO THE FIELD HOUSE — it was summer; no one cared — and had traipsed across the quad at one a.m. The night was mild, with a ruminant breeze that made me long for other summer nights gone by: the sour-sweet warmth of Kate's drowsy breath, her knee snugged in between mine; the backseat grapple with Christina, the lapsed Catholic, in her lime green Super Beetle, my gawky induction into disco mores and oops-I-forgot-your-name sex. Too wired to sleep or read William Blake, I went through the back and propped the door open, hoping to draw the soft air in. None entered, however, and after each set of benches, I wandered out to the field to cool off.

I'd been sweating for weeks, a viscous sheen that lacquered me in my own clear funk. No less noxious was an off-and-on fever that plumped my tongue and glands. With one summer class and a soft job on campus, I'd set myself up for an easeful stretch after a nerve-gnawed spring semester. Instead, I was spending a couple of nights a week at the skeleton-staffed infirmary, complaining of vagrant pain and chills that stumped the nurses on duty. Strep, they conjectured, but a culture scotched that, and my blood work ruled out mono. They graciously kept testing and seemed to enjoy my late-hour drop-ins, but by and by let on that they thought me a faker, trolling for pills or friendship. Lonesome as I was, I half-agreed.

Looking over a row of recently planted elms, I let my gaze ride the blue-black night, thinking back two summers. That ride home from school in Dad's orange Renault, the sex-bomb kid in a tight Lacoste ready to gobble New York, skin and all— *that* Paul had screwed me but good. Criminally stupid about the price of things and glandular profit and loss, he'd bartered my health for Italian menswear and blow jobs from dental hygienists. Gone, gone, gone was his chest-out swagger and two-day-old erections; now I walked on swollen joints that clicked if I took the stairs, and went weeks without mustering a half-speed hard-on or caring when the next one rose. A distant memory was the blacksmith stomach that burned Ring Dings for taut-armed muscle; now even salads left me gassy and limp, choking back the bile in my throat. And far, far behind me was the manic vigor with which I'd attacked the day; now all I yearned for was a solid nap, dozing in my carrel after lunch. Everything ached and nothing mattered. I'd retreated to the shadows, marking time.

Back in the gym, I logged another set, then cut the weight and threw some light reps up. It was the only way I had then to build a pump, but often the extra effort left me faint, the dust in my brain flung backward. Sure enough, a swoon came on as I was getting to my feet. I caught the stalk of the shoulder press, holding it till the darkness passed. On this night, though, a strange thing happened: my heart started thrashing against its cage. I grabbed at my chest. The thud got louder, off on a high-legged gallop. I sank to my knees and hugged the bench, trying very hard not to take it down with me as I fought against the pull of sleep. The pain was like a cold chisel, hard and sharp. I screamed, but the blade just dug in edgewise. For ten, fifteen seconds, I shut my eyes, waiting. *Death,* I remember thinking, *hurts like hell.*

At some point—seconds, minutes, what-have-you—the knife between my ribs withdrew. Each breath was a bruise, but you'll live through those. I took in sips of air, weeping softly. I was crying for the reasons one does at such times: I was alive, not dead; young, not old; alone in the world at one a.m. But at bottom I was crying because I was lost again, marooned in my own thin skin. The "heart event," as an internist later tagged it, was an angry push-back from the blood, my systems saying *Stop! You're not fit to lead; we'll call the shots from here.* Each choice had been a false one, each instinct pie-eyed. I had no rudder except arrant failure, steering from crash to crash. It's a wretched thing, to be always wrong. You feel helpless and unmoored, a permanent child.

But even a lost boy knows he has no choice when crossed by the face of death. It is time to grow up, account for his blunders and resolve to take instruction from the facts. Fact number one: my body was not my muse and ought never to be consulted on major decisions or anything larger than lunch. Fact two: I was the son of erudite Jews, and what hopes I held for an engaged adulthood inhered in the values they'd pledged themselves to (if incompletely embodied): probity, seriousness, and faith in language to convey and receive the truth. Fact three: I wasn't a mixed-race hustler or a wannabe pimp-by-proxy and never again had a 'hood imprimatur to bully or lie to women. I was only, now and finally, what I was: a shy, scared man-boy with some leftover muscle and a closet full of masks that didn't fit.

Several hours later, I was having a tense chat with the resident on duty at St. Charles. (I'd managed, after a while, to climb the stairs and dial 911 from the gym. Alas, the school's medical center hadn't been built yet, and I'd been taken to the small Jesuit hospital four miles away in Port Jefferson.) The resident, a prematurely balding fellow maybe four or five years my senior, spent thirty seconds describing said *heart event* (something called paroxysmal superventricular tachycardia) and ten minutes grilling me about the drugs I'd taken that "undoubtedly" brought it on. "You may as well say what they are," he sniffed. "I saw tracks on your rear, some of them recent." I loathed him on sight and gave an abridged list, doggedly insisting that what had "brought it on" was a virus and overwork. Had he shown the least courtesy, I'd have told him all, but I'd be damned if some Country Day scion from Bronxville was going to tell me how to kill my liver. He released me that evening with a scrip for beta-blockers and hinted broadly that if this happened again, he'd tip the cops and have them cart me off.

But he was, of course, right. Two weeks before, I'd started back on a cycle of low-dose test, trying to brake the skid I was on with one last go at self-prescription. Whether it sparked the attack is unknowable now, given the array of other triggers—the heat, the stress, my advanced exhaustion, and the wee-hour training session. But trying to pin down cause is like asking Clyde Barrow whether it was the tenth or the twentieth bullet that did him in. I'd spent two and a half years playing Spin-the-Needle with a vicious conjunction of drugs, and if the street 'roids didn't get me, the ludes and speed would. I was a system rigged to fail. There are constitutions that can process poison and live to tell the tale, but I, for better or worse, am no Keith Richards. I'm around today only because an ugly scare stopped me in my tracks.

CURIOUSLY, THOUGH, FOR A COUPLE OF YEARS it looked like I'd gotten away cheap. I weaned myself off test and started in earnest with a psychiatrist in Smithtown, who pulled me through the worst of the withdrawal blues. He took my frantic midday calls, saw me on weekends, when my fear crescendoed, and convinced (or conned) me that I'd gain some grit from my brush with self-destruction. "A lot of smart guys have their heads handed to them and have to figure out what for," he said. "It toughens their hide but also makes them kinder, which is the only form of manhood I respect."

At the gym, where chronic soreness ruled out heavy lifting, I learned I could keep what mass remained by adopting Angel's mode of slow-and-low. (I was fortified by having read Ah-nuld's claim that he, too, had switched to light reps. It gave me gym-munity when someone walked by and said, "Hey, put some *plates* on that thing.") At my post-'roids weight of 175, I could still fake a body with tight-rolled sleeves and elbows pressed to ribs to pop my chest. That seemed to bring the dysmorphia down and got me back to work in the fourth-floor stacks. There, through repression and phased withdrawal, I hid out long enough to make Phi Beta Kappa and preposterously won admission to the Iowa Writers' Workshop on the promise (soon broken) of two short stories. And somewhere in the margins, I met a sweet girl, taking her down to live in my burrow, where we were as happy as moles with take-out menus.

But quietly, beneath my frazzled regard, my body kept falling apart. Every couple of months, I reacted to new foods and eventually found myself bloated or congested by milk, wheat, eggs, soy, booze, yeast, and chocolate, which ruled out anything that tasted like something. On a diet of baked chicken and cauliflower, it's hard not to pine for the Entenmann's aisle, and at night I'd slip from my girlfriend's bed to devour her crumb-cake singles, licking the wrappers clean. *What jury of my peers would convict?* I thought, but the sentence handed down was harsh: asthma, that misery, returned in force, backed up by frequent bouts of sinusitis. Mold made me wheeze, as did dogwood pollen and the burr of secondhand smoke. At that rate of ruin, I'd soon be living on kumquats and breathing through coffee filters.

And then came the big blow, in the spring of '79: a hell's-bells, three-in-the-morning panic attack that lasted for four choking hours. So ruinous was that night, and the thousands that followed, that I can barely muster the nerve to play it back; doing so always summons the dread of being trapped underwater on dry land. The runaway heartbeat and hamster-wheel thoughts; the mad gasp for air through a throat that clicked shut; the hands and feet crackling or numb as bricks, hose-washed with norepinephrine — if you have a bad case of it that goes untreated, it's all you can do not to run the streets naked, screaming *please!* at the top of your lungs. I did essentially that one night in San Francisco, two years after this started: tore down Fillmore in a bitter wind with my shirt and pants unbuttoned, dripping sweat. The young psychologist at the clinic the cops took me to held me by the hand till I stopped sobbing. "I can only imagine what that's like," she said when I told her, in gulps, about the fear. "No, you can't," I said. "I'm sorry, but you can't. I'm being held hostage. By myself."

That was after I'd gone to Iowa for a year, teetering on the edge of a full breakdown. For days at a stretch, I'd locked myself indoors, too scared to go to class or to shop for dinner, calmed only by the blather of TV. I got next to nothing written and quit the program rashly, fleeing to the coast to try a novel. I lasted for four years there and at least that many shrinks, going door to door in a frenzied search for someone who could mitigate the terror. But none of them succeeded in even *naming* the condition, let alone bringing aid, and I drifted east again to two more programs that I quit before earning a useless master's.

So went the eighties, a wash of exits and an enterprising list of symptoms: ringing in the ears; recurrent bronchitis; spasms in the neck and shoulders. I felt less and less viable by the month, locked in a Xanax spiral. The topping cruelty: I shrank to my old weight, 150 pounds of flaccid arms and jeans that wouldn't stay up. In photos from those days, I'm a bag of bones, a wraith in a porn mustache. If I hadn't been terrorized by fear itself (along with heights, guns, pills, pain, and, above all, suffocation), I'd likely have found a way to end it all, hopeless and self-blaming as I was. It's one thing when bad luck takes you down, another when you've cut your own legs out. Dabbling in gray-market anabolics, I'd made a right shambles of my nervous system, and at three a.m., watching infomercials for knives that sliced through metal, I gouged myself with metaphor, including the worst phrase in tennis, *unforced error.* In bitter hindsight, Mom had been right: you are who you are, or someone worse. For breaking that law, I'd gotten the max: a life just as shriveled as hers.

MEANWHILE, FROM THE REDOUBT of his fourth — and last — marriage, my father watched with a fluid mix of bafflement and worry. He knew about the panic and the years it quashed, but not about the drugs with which I'd fouled myself, and despaired of his oldest son's feckless drift from one false start to another. He flew each spring to see me in northern California, read my halting fiction with go-go cheer, and wrote the checks that kept me in treatment long after it seemed a lost cause. "I floundered till thirty-two," he'd say to remind me that life was long, not short, and that many a big career was built from the salvage of past debacles. When I pointed out that I was now *thirty-three* and serving Thai noodles in SoHo, he refused to brook my pessimism, saying the writers who made it refused to take *no* as an indictment of their work. "There is such a thing as adaptive deafness," he counseled. "Catch a case of it and don't let go."

Thus was I raised, and thus suspended: between the dueling forks of Mom's fatalism and Dad's bulldog faith. He'd survived a father who was bent on mayhem and the extirpation of hope, and he'd be damned if he'd watch me go down easy, beaten by young mistakes. So when a left-field chance came, in 1989, for a job at the *Village Voice,* he pushed (and prepped) me to apply, saying I was a natural editor. This was a blood insult to editors everywhere, but I nonetheless got the job—thanks to my brother. After his own follies in the 1980s (stomping grapes in Montfort; stringing for a Cypriot weekly), Ivan had made a connection at the *Voice* and in bottle-rocket fashion had written a series of features that instantly launched his star. A born journalist if there was one, he threw off epic prose about the crack years' demons and saints: Charlie Barnett, the great street comic who trashed his genius for drugs; Earl "the Goat" Manigault, the god of Rucker Park till freebase killed his jump shot and credit rating.

Those stories, collected in the first of Ivan's books, effectively got his editor promoted and opened a masthead slot. As a thank-you to Ivan, the *Voice* gave me the job editing its butched-up sports page. It didn't pay much, but I couldn't complain: it took me all of a day to polish the week's submission on lesbian pheasant hunts. With time on my hands, I went looking for stories to write and spotted a couple of corkers off the bat. By the time the *Voice* canned me for shirking my job to trawl the streets for leads, I'd gotten a head of steam up with two big clips and was soon casing the dark side for *GQ.*

THAT I WAS ABLE TO WORK the docks during the worst of a crime pandemic owed to my second stroke of fortune. On my seventh or eighth shrink (I seem to have lost count after a Reichian had me strip for her during a session), I found one who named my panic disorder ten minutes into the first session. Just a week through a course of an SSRI, I stopped waking up with a pounding heart and forebodings that dogged the day's movements. Soon he switched me to a new drug, Paxil, and my weight and former vigor came back. Tinnitus and bruxing, insomnia and heartburn—the symptoms sloughed off me like winter skin, the dry, dead crust of a tuned-down brain. He invited me into a group he was forming of the chronically terrified, and those Wednesday night sessions were symphonic marvels of truth and solicitude. I was so grateful to the man that I wrote a book about him; he parried the tribute by getting addicted to coke and losing his marriage and life savings.

Meanwhile, I'd gone back to the gym with a joy I'd lacked for a decade, and slowly, gratefully built a body of reconditioned parts. It took years of diligence and mindful eating to add back thirty pounds of muscle, and even on good days my retooled frame was no match for the one in '76. Shot were both shoulders from years of stopless benching, my lower back whinged after dead-lift reps, and anyone daft enough to time me running a mile would've needed to pack a lunch and a flashlight.

Still, at forty, I looked, at least in passing, like a man in salable shape, and the Pump, once a virulent, blood-borne drug, was now my midlife koan. It hurt but healed me, robbed but revved me, the brute dialectic of love. I had no kick coming, though; I was home again, at ease among the weights and plates. In the most elemental way, my life started in the gym; it's where, in Erikson's phrase, I got "twice-born." Handed a wheezy contraption of bones, I constructed a frame to hang my flag from, then tore it down and put it back up leaner. It creaked and groaned and dripped in winter, but the damn thing kept on standing, and now, at fifty-four, this stately ruin is inseparable from the self inside it. I've long lost touch with who I was before I started lifting; that kid is gone, dumped below cost, like the comic books I sold or gave away. I mourn him and wish I'd found a less crude way to exorcise his frailty, but at some point the old road had to come down so the new road could go in. I shudder to think who or where I'd be if I hadn't found my way to that field-house basement. I might *still* be in college in my middle fifties, surfing YouTube for clips of *Gilligan's Island* and a stop-frame shot of Ginger's breasts.

In the summer of 2007, after a series of hospitalizations for a fast-moving case of emphysema, my father sat me down in his kitchen in East Quogue and asked what sort of parent he had been. It was a delicate time in our loop-the-loop discourse: he'd come down hard on a feature I'd written about my autistic son, and things had been said in a volley of posts that stopped us speaking for months. Tiptoeing the burn pits of our past, I said he'd done his best work when I was in trouble, seeing me through a torrent of crises, more than I could count. Dad laughed, dislodging the tube in his nose. "That's a fancy way of saying I wasn't much good the other eighty percent of the time."

I matched his laugh, hedging my bets. "Well, early on, yeah, there were some...gaps. But you came on strong in the second quarter, which is when I really needed the help."

"Thanks, but what you're saying confirms the point. I left you two to fend for yourselves long before you were ready."

"Again...but with the proviso that—"

"No, no. I'll plead to it, fair and square."

"Erm—what?"

He tilted wearily in his seat, hands stuffed down in his sweatpants pockets and jaw slung onto his chest. His hair, that thatch of untamed wire, had turned the color of ash, and I noted, with a catch of help-less grief, that his skin was gray as well. The authority in his bearing, once a physical thing, a bulling presumption of power, had ebbed as his strength and shoulders sagged and was now at the vanishing point. With every hiss from the tank beside him, I heard the bell tolling, faint but sure.

"I *was* too involved in my own affairs to do the nuts and bolts of raising boys. You were entitled to more than a couple hours a week of throwing the football in Offense-Defense. What was missing was some steady show-up time, and I didn't give it to you and I regret that."

"I—but remember, Dad, there wasn't much to spare."

"No, in fact, there *was,* after I left your mother. I had whole weekends to devote. Instead I let my loneliness do the talking and jumped back in with another woman. Yes, it was the sixties and there was plenty of that happening, but you two needed me to cool it a while and give you time to breathe. I ignored the advice I always gave writers: Don't just *do* something, *sit* there."

He apologized then, a thing that cost him strain and a prolonged fit of coughing. I leaned across the table and said sorry back to him for having been a horrid mess half my life, as well as a petulant shit. We laughed to keep from breaking his no-tears rule, and he asked me, in the beer-aided spirit of disclosure, if there was anything I regretted and hadn't told him.

"Um, besides not begging you to sell your tech stocks before the bubble burst in 2000?"

He laughed, more a grimace than a grunt.

For thirty-odd years, I'd kept my own counsel about those crazed summers in the seventies, leaking bits and pieces to girlfriends and gym rats, but never (*No, God, no*) to Dad. The embarrassment and camp and beefcake squalor—his son shaking ass in a SWAT TEAM thong—were far too awful and cringe inducing to tell someone with his hard-shell pride. But a couple of things had happened in the interim to peel back the lid a bit. The year-and-a-half stretch in group therapy had stripped away some of my shame, the sense that I alone had defiled myself with dopey, juvenile stunts. The other thing, oddly, was the story about my son, in which I went public with the havoc and heart stab of raising a disabled child. There (and in a second piece four years later, about taking my sweet boy surfing), I poured out my sorrow and agonized love for a child locked inside his own skull. Both were published against Dad's wishes—"career suicide" was the phrase he tossed about, though from the pitch of his consternation, it was never entirely clear whose career he was talking about.

For once, though, *I* was proved right, not him, the first such case of man-bites-dog since I'd warned him, in vain, against low-rise briefs during his bachelor stint in the late seventies. The articles sounded a deep chord in readers and moved him, on reflection, to pass them around to many of his writer friends. This resolved for me that a truth worth telling outweighs the risks involved, and so I took a long pull of my third Corona and let the damn thing rip. Beginning in the middle, I told him about Angel and his power over women and white boys, then circled back to the day in Kenny's house and that first hot spike of Deca.

Out it came, in full Huck-a-Poo color — the bachelorette parties in Bensonhurst; the cave-dark fuckfests in the Flower district — though I left off telling about the night at Lou's, when the whole thing went to hell. Dad listened and asked questions and pressed for details on the makeup of the drugs I'd shot, astonished that anyone would wash his organs with compounds from basement sinks. He was aghast and furious that I'd kept this from him, and nearly as vexed to be told of it now, when he was "almost off the planet," he said. I reminded him of the day I'd fainted in his office all those years ago, but he shrugged and squinted and couldn't recall it and said it didn't matter. "We tell each other the truth, Paul: that's always been our contract, through all the ups and downs since Park West Village. It sometimes hurts to hear it and to say it, too, but what else do we have if not that?"

I thought about it a moment, looking back on our record. Despite the long hitches and parsed disclosures — the ten, twelve years I stopped speaking to him after his breakup with Mom; the stilted dinners during the steroid years, when we talked around the elephant at the table — I'd been, on balance, more frank with Dad than with anyone else I'd known, and I was flattered to think, because he told me so, that the same held true for him. Even when I wasn't being straight with him, I was conjuring his specter in my head: the voice and visage of sober fact; the firm hand on the tiller. Avoid or dissemble, half-truth or whole, one thing was clear at that table: I'd been having a conversation with him all my life and would keep my end going till I died.

"You're right," I said. "I had my reasons, but now I can't think what they were."

We sat there a while in sunk-eyed silence, listening to the machine that fed air to him hiss through its crenellated hose. At some point there was a scratch on the glass behind him. Bondit, the four-legged mental patient he'd saved from extinction at the pound, jumped and pawed at the patio door, yawping to be let back in. He half-stood to tug the balky slider; she entered, biting the remnants of her tail. "Come here, crazy dog," he said, patting his thighs. Instead she made straight for the pie à la mode he hadn't managed to finish. He tried to grab the plate, but she knocked it to the floor, where pie and ice cream parted for creative reasons. "Bad girl!" he yelled at her. "Bad, bad girl! Doesn't *anyone* in this family know how to act?"

No, we surely don't, but we write about it. I can't wait to read that dog's collection of stories.

About the Author

Paul Solotaroff is a contributing editor at *Men's Journal* and *Rolling Stone*. He has written features for *GQ, Vogue, Esquire,* and *Best Life,* and he was nominated for a National Magazine Award in 2004. His work has been included in *Best American Sports Writing of the Century* and other anthologies. The author of two books, *Group* and *The House of Purple Hearts,* he lives in New York City.